Fearless for Truth

A Personal Portrait of the Life of
George Raymond Beasley-Murray
10 October 1916–23 February 2000

Paul Beasley-Murray

D1091305

First published 2002 by Paternoster Press

Paternoster Press is an imprint of Paternoster Publishing
P.O. Box 300, Carlisle, Cumbria, CA3 0QS, U.K.
and P.O. Box 1047, Waynesboro, GA 30830–2047, U.S.A

08 07 06 05 04 03 02   7 6 5 4 3 2 1

British Library Cataloguing in Publication Data
A catalogue record for this book is available from the British Library

ISBN 1-84227-134-2

Typeset by A.R. Cross
Printed and bound in Great Britain
for Paternoster Publishing
by Bell & Bain Ltd., Glasgow

To my Mother
With love

Contents

Chapter 9
Southern Baptist Theological Seminary:
James Buchanan Professor of New Testament

Chapter 10

Chapter 11

Acknowledgements

There are a number of people to whom I wish to record my gratitude for the help they have given me in writing this book. In the first place, I must acknowledge the generosity of the deacons and the members of Central Baptist Church, Victoria Road South, Chelmsford, Essex, who every year grant me a period of 'study leave' and so made the writing of this book possible. Secondly, I am grateful for the help and advice given by Rev Dr Raymond Brown (who succeeded my father both as minister at Zion Baptist Church, Cambridge, and as Principal of Spurgeon's College, and is a church historian), Rev Dr Anthony Cross (who also at one time was minister of Zion Baptist Church, Cambridge, and who is an authority on Baptists and baptism in the twentieth century) and Rev Dr Roger Hayden (who was baptised by my father at Zion Baptist Church, Cambridge, and who is Secretary of the Baptist Historical Society), all of whom made detailed comments on an early draft of the book. Thirdly, I wish to thank my friends Alan and Ursula Franklin, in whose home much of this book was written. Above all, a special word of gratitude must go to my mother, who has given much help and encouragement at a time when she herself has been having to work through her own great sense of loss after the death of my father.

Finally, given my closeness to my father, there is the question of whether this has limited my ability to engage critically with all that was entailed in his life and work. Hopefully, however, in spite of this inevitable limitation I have been able to do justice to the life of one who meant so much to me.

Preface

Within a matter of a few weeks after my father's death three people quite independently suggested I might write his biography. Initially I was somewhat hesitant and could see a number of reasons why such a suggestion might not be right. No one could pretend my father dominated the twentieth-century Christian scene like Karl Barth or Billy Graham. Yet, as I reflected on this I realised that my father—through his leadership and his writings—made an important contribution not only to the life of Baptists but also to the wider Christian world too. At the very least for the sake of future church historians I felt that it would be good to tell my father's story and reflect upon some of the issues with which he sought to grapple.

A stronger objection to involving myself lay in the fact that no son can ever be truly objective about his father, and all the more so in my case where I have a sense of a great debt to my father for the way in which he helped me to develop my own understanding of Christian ministry. However, I dare to believe that, with the exception of my mother, I understood my father better than any other person—not just because I grew up in the family home, but because many of my own experiences of Christian ministry have not been dissimilar to his. In writing this biography I have become conscious of how close I still am to my father. Indeed, the writing of it has coincided with the period when I have been grieving for him. Inevitably, therefore, this portrait of my father cannot be truly objective. It is very much a personal appreciation.

I have been aware that I have been writing for a number of audiences, which in turn have shaped the book in a variety of ways. Those who knew and appreciated my father—family and friends, and no doubt a good number of former students—will probably be glad to read the story of their loved one and friend. Those who knew of my father, but never really knew him as a friend—Baptists and Christians of other traditions—may be less interested in the personal details than in the contribution my father made to the Baptist denomination and indeed to the wider world of New Testament scholarship. A younger generation who have never heard of my father, let alone met him—perhaps theological students preparing for Christian ministry—may be helped by the way in which he wrestled with some of the very theological issues which face them too. Future church historians may be grateful that somebody so close to him has gathered and preserved this material that later they in turn can make their judgement about his role in the developing history of the Baptist denomination. My prayer is that in one way or another there will be plenty to interest all these different groups.

I have struggled with the approach I should adopt. Some friends advised me simply to give a brief outline of my father's life and then follow it with a series of chapters in which I dealt with various theological themes which were of particular relevance to my father's life. Others advised me to adopt a more chronological approach and deal with the themes as they arise. It is this latter approach which I have adopted. Even so it will be noted that when dealing with these particular themes on a chronological basis I have sometimes included at that stage developments which took place a little later.

There was also the question as to whether I should adopt an impersonal or a personal approach. Did I, for instance, talk of 'George' or of 'my father'? Should I leave myself out of the story or occasionally bring myself into it? I have opted for the more personal approach, because it seems unnatural for me to refer to my father as 'George', and because some of the personal references give perhaps a little more colour to the story.

Introduction

Fearless for Truth

The title of this biography was my mother's idea. She it was who suggested the phrase 'Fearless for Truth'. I believe that she was absolutely right. No title better sums up my father's life than this. One of my father's essential characteristics was his passion for truth, wherever that may lead. Not surprisingly, therefore, more than one person has written to me and likened him to Bunyan's 'Valiant-for-Truth'. Throughout his life my father was concerned for gospel truth, however costly that search might be. An unashamed evangelical, he refused to be confined within any one particular evangelical mould, but rather sought to allow the scriptures to mould his thinking. It was this fearless passion for truth which caused him to make significant contributions in such diverse fields as Christian baptism, ecumenism, the doctrine of the person of Christ and the 'last things'.

To what extent my father would have recognised 'fearless for truth' as a description of himself, I do not know. In many ways he was not a self-conscious person. Indeed, it was precisely this lack of self-consciousness that enabled him to speak and act without worrying how this might affect his standing with others. If he believed something to be right, he would happily speak and act accordingly, even if those words and actions were to complicate life for him. His approach to life is well-summed up in a short prayer he wrote as he expounded Matthew 14.1-12 ('The death of the forerunner') in his popular commentary on that Gospel: 'Lord, help me to grow into your likeness, *to stand fearlessly for your truth,* to love the unlovely and to forgive those who treat us spitefully.'[1]

This fearlessness for truth was recognised by others. Bernard Green, for instance, a former General Secretary of the Baptist Union of Great Britain, commented:

> In whatever he said he was always unmistakably an evangelical. But he was not a rigid one... He was unashamedly true to his own deeply held convictions, and was not afraid to differ from other evangelicals within a fixed and closed dogmatic system. When he felt convinced that he must differ from views on the right or left he did so firmly but graciously. He was not the sort of person who looked over his shoulder to see who might hear what he said![2]

Needless to say, it often took considerable courage on the part of my father to pursue the truth as he perceived it. This courage is reflected in an incident recalled by one of his former students:

> Towards the end of my college course, I preached at a church and received a majority call—I was told there was quite serious problems within the fellowship. I met George in the college and explained the call and the problem. He looked at me and said: 'Now is my soul troubled, and what shall I say? "Father, save me from this hour?" But for this cause I came to this hour' (John 12.27). I accepted the call. Now looking back I realise that this particular verse in John's Gospel was a 'foundation stone' in his own thinking. For him, life meant 'accepting God's call' even if it meant facing serious problems. George had courage.[3]

The story of my father's life will reveal that there were indeed many occasions when he took courage into his

---

[1]   *Matthew* (Scripture Union, London, 1984).
[2]   Letter 31 July 2000.
[3]   Rev Norman Harris in a private letter dated 10 June 2000.

hands as in his own way he sought to stand for the truth of the gospel.

There was, of course, far more to my father than simply being a man who was 'fearless for truth'. Another very apt summing up of my father is contained in the words 'The mind of a scholar, the heart of an evangelist', a description coined by my father's friend, J.J. Brown, and used first at my father's induction to the church at Ashurst Drive, Ilford, and repeated in his tribute to my father following his death.[4] As this biography makes abundantly clear, from first to last my father had a passion for evangelism, a passion never dimmed by his increasing learning. For my father there was never a conflict between heart and mind. In a way that is true of very few others engaged in theological teaching, he held perfectly in tandem this mind of a scholar with the heart of an evangelist. In a way too that is true of very few evangelists, my father was able to use his mind in the service of the gospel. In words which Jack Brown used to sum up my father:

> He has never wavered from the conviction that Jesus Christ entrusted him with a Gospel of reconciliation. He has used his gifts of communication to urge listeners and readers to be at one with God and with each other. This, after all, is the purpose of Christian mission, and mission is the force which fills George Beasley-Murray's life. His preaching and caring, teaching and writing, befriending and counselling have a single-minded aim: to make Christ known as the way, the truth and the life.[5]

As a family, of course, we had a very different perspective on my father. It was not that we did not recognise his fearlessness for truth or his passion for evangelism. Rather, it was that first and foremost we

---

4   *Baptist Times*, 2 March 2002.
5   'A Personal Appreciation', in Paul Beasley-Murray (ed.), *Mission To The World* (Baptist Historical Society, Didcot 1991), 19.

knew him as a man who loved us all deeply, as a husband and as a father. Naturally, we were proud of his many achievements, but it was who he was rather than what he achieved which caused us in turn to love him.

Chapter 1

Beginnings

My father was born on 10 October 1916, the only child of George Alfred Beasley and Kathleen Letitia (née Brady) Beasley. Both his parents were of Irish extraction, although they were Londoners by birth. His parents had married early in the Great War. His mother at the time of her wedding was only nineteen, and his father was twenty-five. They married secretly in their local parish church because Kathleen's father refused to assent to the marriage. It was in that same Anglican church that my father was subsequently 'baptised' as a baby.

Sadly my father never knew his father, for in December 1917, when he was just over a year old, his father, who was serving with the army, was killed in a road accident on Shooters Hill, Plumstead, in South London.[1] His mother was distraught at her husband's death. For two weeks she did not utter a word, despite the pleas of her parents and friends. Two nuns, however, discovered her and befriended her, and helped her back to normality. She was ever after grateful to those nuns, and said that she would bring up her baby—and indeed any children she might have of a possible future marriage—in the Roman Catholic faith.

Fortunately she was not left on her own to care for her son. She was part of a large close-knit East-End family, which was very supportive of her. Her 'wild

---

[1] Unfortunately there is very little information about George Beasley or the family from which he came, apart from the fact that he and his sister were the only children of the marriage, and that his sister became a nun, living and eventually dying in Europe.

Irish Catholic father' (my father's description) was a bookmaker, who had won and lost fortunes on the horses and was known in Stratford as 'Honest Tom Brady'. If the truth be told, he could be cruel and was not the best of husbands. His wife, Annie, 'a gentle Protestant', spent her time looking after her nine children, of whom Kathleen (often called 'Kit') was the eldest. As a child my father spent a good deal of time playing on the Wanstead marshes with his nine uncles and aunts, some of whom were not much older than himself (his youngest aunt, Ann, was in fact only a few weeks older than him).

After the war Kathleen married again. Her second husband, George Murray, she had known from school days, when they had been in the same school. Like many young men of that time, he had given his age as eighteen, but had actually only been sixteen years old when he joined up. He returned from the war quite severely wounded. He had been through some of the worst battles in the First World War and suffered ever afterwards from the effect of having been gassed. He had also been involved in the fighting at Gallipoli— even as a child I can remember seeing tiny fragments of shrapnel which had entered his forehead in that battle and which for years kept on 'emerging'.

Although George Murray never formally adopted my father, he treated him as his son, and my father for his part was always happy to call him 'Dad'. Indeed, he was the only 'Dad' he ever knew. Of George Murray my father in a sermon once commented: 'My step-father was very kind to me... It wasn't until later that I realised that he never attempted to discipline me, nor indeed, advised me in any respects as I became older. I think that there was a genuine hesitation to do so.'

George Murray frequently had breathing problems as a result of his having been gassed in the war, and therefore found it very difficult to hold down any job, let alone any well-paid job. At the time of their marriage George Murray had a job in a glass manufacturing factory. He was a hardworking but mild man. Unfortunately he loved to gamble, a habit which later had dire consequences for the family. Kathleen was easily the strongest person in the marriage. Somewhat volatile and temperamental, she was a very lively character and was always the 'life and soul of the party' wherever she went. As a young girl she would have gone on the stage had her father allowed her. Always smartly dressed, often wearing hats with enormous feathers, she loved to go to tea-dances or to the races at Ascot. When she later visited my parents in Ilford and then in Cambridge she stood out from the church people, who in those days tended to be simply dressed. She was a clever woman, who would have gone far had she had the advantages of a good education. My father may have gained some of his courage from her, for she was also a fearless character. Alas, she died in her early fifties, toward the end of February 1950, as a result of careless surgery undertaken on her as a teenager. In spite of his earlier ill-health, however, George Murray lived until 1979, when he died at the age of eighty-one.

My father's step-sister, Joyce, was a child of this marriage. True to her promise, my mother had her daughter baptised in a Roman Catholic Church, the church of St Francis, Stratford. At the same time my father, then four and a half years old, was re-baptised by the priest. Years later my father still remembered the occasion. He wrote:

> Doubtless one reason for the clarity of the memory is the fear I had when the priest lifted me up, and I saw the font filled with water; I thought he was about to put me in it head first! I let out a howl, but after being set down with very little use of water I felt very silly. That was my introduction to the Roman Catholic Church, and the association lasted barely three years. It was sufficient, however, to stamp my mind

with an impression of religious awe that remained with me through the years of adolescence.[2]

Eighteen months after the birth of Joyce the family moved up to Leicester, to 3 Evington Road. There Kathleen and George Murray opened up a small news-agents shop, which also sold tobacco and sweets and ran a little library. Although my father never served in the shop, he did have to get up early in the morning to deliver the newspapers—the money earned paid for his piano lessons. In the evenings, when the shop was shut, my father used to take some of the shop's library books to read in bed—later in life he attributed his literary skills to the reading of these books. Although the shop proved to be a successful business, after a few years it had to be sold to pay off some debts of George Murray. George and Kathleen bought another shop in the centre of Leicester, but again this had to be sold because of gambling debts. The family then moved from the south side of Leicester to the north side of the city, where Kathleen began to take in lodgers in order to make ends meet.

My father's step-sister remembers him as being a real daredevil of a character when he was a young boy, who enjoyed leading other children in dangerous pursuits. One, for instance, was to climb on to a narrow outside ledge of a nearby railway bridge spanning the London to Leicester railway line. Together with his pals he would share cigarettes up in the tree tops—but he said he gave up smoking when he was ten! It was around this time when boys at school were sharing smutty and in-accurate stories about sex, he found his aunt Nora's manual on sex and marriage and took it to school to make known to his friends the true facts—he was ever 'fearless for truth'!

---

2   'My Call to the Ministry', in C.A. Joyce (ed.), *My Call to the Ministry* (Marshall, Morgan & Scott, London, 1968), 35-36.

At the age of eleven my father passed the scholarship exam for the City of Leicester Grammar School for Boys (known locally as 'the City Boys').[3] At that stage life for him became more serious, for homework and in particular music left little time for fooling around with friends. Furthermore, with a mother who was suffering from bouts of serious illness, he was often needed to help around the home. On one occasion in his first year at City Boys he had to miss school in order to clean the house and cook for the lodgers. Money was tight at the time. There was no money, for instance, for bus fares, so my father used to have to walk for just under an hour to get to his school in the centre of the city. As was common at the time, it was only by going without in other areas that his parents were able to pay for his school uniform. For much of my father's school days George Murray was out of work, partly for health reasons, and partly because it was the time of the Depression. Fortunately, after his conversion, there were friends who were prepared to help my father with his studies. One of the neighbours in Raymond Road was the chief city librarian who provided my father with a lot of books. After having passed the London General Schools Examination ('matric' as it was known), he left school on attaining his sixteenth birthday—his parents needed him to earn money for the family. He began work in the offices of the City of Leicester Gas Company, giving all his earnings to his parents.

One of his mother's younger sisters, Nora, went up to Leicester to live with my father's parents to help look after the children while his parents were in the shop. When my father began to learn to play the piano at the age of seven, it was she who encouraged him. Later in life my father used to recall how Nora made him prac-

---

3   Many years later, on the afternoon of 21 July 1960, my father had the pleasure of speaking at the prize-giving of the 'City Boys'.

tise, and at the beginning would often put his fingers onto the right notes. Being very self-disciplined, he got used to beginning his piano practice at 5 am. His sister Joyce remembers him at mealtimes sitting at the table near to the piano so that as he ate he could fiddle on the piano. Needless to say, whenever there was a family party my father was always called on to play songs old and new. On 25 March 1935, at the age of eighteen, he was awarded the Licentiate of the Royal Academy of Music (LRAM) for 'pianoforte', and was duly 'qualified to begin practising as a teacher'. His sister Joyce tells the story of the day when Paderewski, the great pianist and Prime Minister of Poland, heard my father at a piano competition and praised him on his performance—unfortunately I have been unable to corroborate this story. Certainly, music at this stage was my father's life. A career as a concert pianist beckoned. In 1933, for instance, posters picturing my father at the piano went up all over Leicester advertising an 'Invitation Recital' on 9 October at the Edward Wood Hall, London Road, at which 'Leicester's Brilliant Young Pianist, George Beasley-Murray' would be playing.

It was my father's mother who first joined Beasley with Murray, as the concert posters indicate. She wanted concert-goers to know that George Beasley was in fact Mrs Murray's son. Later in 1938, at the suggestion of Dr P.W. Evans, the Principal of Spurgeon's College, the matter was regularised when my father officially changed his name by Deed Poll, thus honouring his father and his step-father.

My mother originally questioned the need for this first chapter—or at least the need to go into so much detail. The truth is that from a psychological perspective our early years are of vital importance for our later growth and development. In some respects my father had a very unsettled childhood. The loss of a father, the regular unemployment of a step-father, financial insecurity and frequent moving of house, could all have been destabilising factors for my father. Fortunately, his mother's strong personality, marked as it was by warmth and generosity, seems to have outweighed many of the difficulties my father faced. It is also important to recognise that my father came from very ordinary beginnings. Unlike many of those whose names were found with his in later editions of *Who's Who*, he was certainly not born with a silver spoon in his mouth. Perhaps it was because of his own ordinary beginnings that in later years he was always able to relate to ordinary people. The fact was that in spite of his undoubted giftedness and ability, he had what a London Borough of Camden Labour Councillor once termed 'the common touch'.[4] As a pastor and as a preacher of the gospel—and indeed as a theological teacher and principal—this stood him in good stead.

---

4   Julian Fulbrook in a letter dated 28 June 2000.

Chapter 2

Conversion and Call to the Ministry
(1931–1935)

Conversion

After leaving London my father had no contact with any church. For a number of years he was a happy, healthy pagan! However, things changed in 1931, for when my father was fifteen years old his mother took in a lodger who had a son the same age as my father. This boy, who had moved to Leicester from Alnwick in Northumberland, was crazy on football. He discovered that a football team was connected with a nearby church in Gedding Road, called North Evington United Free Church. However, in order to play in the team one had to attend the church's Bible class. Not wanting to go to the Bible class by himself, he persuaded my father, much against his wishes—my father had no time for football, music was his great passion—to go with him to the class. The Young Men's Bible Class was not exactly lively—the leader, who was not a great speaker, used to read his talk while the men chatted amongst themselves. However, my father was greatly impressed by the face of the Bible class leader: 'Never had I seen a face that bore so clearly the marks of kindness and friendliness as that man's face.'[1] Shortly after he had begun to go to the Bible class, the young minister of the church, the Rev Warwick Bailey, looked into the Bible class and chatted with my father. My father was deeply impressed and made up his mind to attend the morning services

---

[1] 'My Call to the Ministry', 36. The Bible class leader was Horace Biggs, the father of Dr John Biggs, President of the Baptist Union of Great Britain in 1989.

of the church. He had never heard a sermon before and was spell-bound by his preaching. Later he wrote:

> Here the preacher was a dazzler. I did not understand all he said, but again I was attracted by his face—it was clear and honest and good. I had not met men like these before. Neither had I encountered this kind of religion.[2]

At the beginning of 1932 a week of mission was held at the church. Warwick Bailey, who had left Spurgeon's in July 1930 to help develop this new estate church,[3] had invited two students from Spurgeon's College, Ernest Brown and Tom Getley, to come and conduct the mission. In preparation for the mission a week of prayer was arranged. My father went along and was astonished at what he saw: 'I had never heard people talk to God so naturally. They seemed to know Him!' It was all so very different from school, where the headmaster used to read out formal prayers from a book. Then came the mission itself. My father, still fifteen at the time, was absolutely fascinated by the meetings.

> One evening the preacher took the theme of the meaning of Christ's death. For the first time in my life I, who had seen crucifixes since I was a child, learned that the cross was for my sake; that the love of Christ shown on it embraced me as truly as it did anyone, and that I personally could know forgiveness for ever and eternal life. When that dawned on me it was like the coming of day. I could not hold back from Christ. I went forward to express my desire to receive Him— and went home walking on air.[4]

---

2   'My Call to the Ministry', 36.
3   North Evington United Free Church was a daughter church of Melbourne Hall, Leicester, at that time a Baptist church, which had transferred seventy church members to the church in North Evington with a view to establishing a Christian witness on the new estate.
4   'My Call to the Ministry', 37.

Subsequently he was baptised and was received into the membership of the church on the first Sunday evening in April 1932.

It is interesting to reflect on that mission. At the time, the Spurgeon's students, as also the church, could have felt it was a failure. For there was only one convert—a young teenager. It would not have been surprising if some thought the whole effort was a waste of time and money. Not surprisingly his mother and step-father found it difficult to understand what was happening to their son. Reflecting on that period in a sermon on 'God as Father in the teaching of Jesus', my father commented:

> When I became a Christian in my teens an invisible barrier came between us. He [my step-father] could not understand the new motivation my life had received. My mother...too was perplexed at my enthusiasm for God and she strongly resisted any attempts of mine to persuade her to seek the salvation of God for herself.

There was a lack of understanding on the part of his family—there was also a good deal of mockery on their part too. It was a good number of years before their attitude began to change. In the meantime, as a result of joining the church at North Evington, my father began to experience

> a family life such as I had not known before. The words of Jesus to his disciples after the refusal of the rich young ruler to become a disciple struck me very forcibly: Mk 10.29-30 ['I tell you that anyone who leaves home or brothers or sisters or mother or father or children or fields for me and for the gospel, will receive much more in the present age. He will receive a hundred times more houses, brothers, sisters, mothers, children and fields—and persecutions as well...']. I learned, in fact, what Jesus meant in teaching us that God was our Father with the corollary that the church was our family.

It was in that particular expression of the family of God at North Evington that my father first began to serve his Lord. In those days the church had no organ, but instead a grand piano to accompany the congregational singing. Not surprisingly he was invited to play that piano for the Sunday services, as well as for mid-week meetings. He became a Sunday School teacher of a boys class in the 200 strong Senior Department of the Sunday School. Looking back on those days Deryck Smith, then one of the boys he taught, wrote:

> George was always a very good communicator and put the lesson and the claims of Jesus Christ over to us very well, and there was always a challenge for us. There was no time like the present with George—yesterday was past, we all had today, but none of us knew what tomorrow might bring. He often used to say to us, 'Behold, now is the accepted time, now is the day of salvation'.

It was with the encouragement of Deryck Smith's father, Albert, one of the deacons of North Evington, that my father began to take part in church services in some of the villages around Leicester.

> At that time, my father, Albert Smith, used to go to Crosshills Baptist Church (between Thornton and Bagworth) and to Newbold Verdun and Barlestone Baptist churches to conduct Sunday evening services, quite a number of times a year. After George's conversion, my father invited George to go with him, and for George to lead the service, and my father give the sermon. George enjoyed this new experience very much. The next time he went with my father, George gave his testimony, as well as conducting the services.[5]

---

5   In a private 'tribute' enclosed with a letter dated 30 June 2000.

Call to Ministry

The Spurgeon's mission not only led to my father's conversion. It also led directly to his call to ministry.

> The wonder of God's love for people like me, the marvel of Christ's victory over sin and death in his resurrection, the breathtaking hope of his coming in glory to share the power of his resurrection with me, all this made a deep impression upon me. When I grasped these things and saw their implications for life, I felt that everybody ought to know about them. More explicitly it seemed to me that since God had made them known to *me*, I ought to make them known to others. I believed therefore that God had called me to know Christ and to make Christ known. He had brought me to Himself that I might be a preacher![6]

For nearly two years my father wrestled with his sense of call. By the time he made application to Spurgeon's College he was preaching on two Sundays out of three. At the same time he was a leader in the junior section of the Boys Brigade, a Sunday School teacher, and involved in both Christian Endeavour and the Young Life Campaign. He was torn between making music his career or fulfilling the vision he had received of ministry.

Music was his life: 'I walked, cycled, worked, ate and drank to its accompaniment (often in time to it!) and it invaded my sleep.'[7] How could he give it all up? Needless to say, his parents were totally unsympathetic. However, at the age of eighteen he made the decision to turn from music. 'I felt broken in spirit. For six months I did not touch a piano—I was afraid lest I should be drawn back from my objective.'[8] To make matters worse he began to study the grammar of New Testament Greek and found that by comparison with Beethoven

---

[6] 'My Call to the Ministry', 37.

[7] 'My Call to the Ministry', 38.

[8] 'My Call to the Ministry', 38.

and Chopin and Liszt it bored him to tears. 'I had an awful fear that I had made a terrible mistake, and that I ought to turn back while there was time. Yet I knew in my heart I could not go back! I was beginning to learn that he who desires to preach the cross must learn to feel its weight.'[9]

Application to Spurgeon's College

On 9 June 1936 my father wrote to Rev Ernest Welton, the Spurgeon's College Secretary, with a view to making application for entrance to the college. Founded by the great Victorian 'prince of preachers', C.H. Spurgeon, it seemed the obvious place to train. As already mentioned, it was through a mission conducted by two Spurgeon's students that my father had been brought to Christ. It was also the college at which his pastor, Warwick Bailey, had been trained.

After a good deal of correspondence he filled in a formal application form on 23 March 1936, in which he stated:

> Two causes have impelled me to seek to enter the ministry: the first is a wholehearted desire to dedicate my life, with every talent and gift that it can possibly yield, to the glory of God. The second is the utter indifference of men concerning the things of God, and their ignorance of the consequences of unbelief have made me long to win them to Christ and be the means of their salvation.

Along with his application form he submitted a specimen sermon. The text was John 13.27. The title was 'Satanic Salesmanship'. The theme was the betrayal of Judas. It was an evangelistic sermon, which ended with this appeal:

---

[9]   'My Call to the Ministry', 38.

Jesus himself will hold out his wounded hands and plead for
their return, but they will harden their hearts and go out into
the night; blackness, when it might be glorious light. Gloom
when it ought to be wonderful joy. My brother, my sister,
when you leave this hall—will it be night or will it be light?

In those days, along with a formal interview held in a
room at the Metropolitan Tabernacle with the members
of the College Council sitting round a very large table,
there was also an entrance exam in Latin, Classical
Greek, English, and the scriptures. My father had done
some Latin at school. Greek, however, he had to learn
on his own.

Chapter 3

Spurgeon's College: Student (1936–1941)

It was on the first Monday in September 1936 that my father made his way from Leicester to Spurgeon's. 'I walked up the drive to the college buildings to begin my course...confident that God was calling me to be an evangelist and a pastor able to expound the Scriptures.'

Spurgeon's College is one of the seven Baptist colleges in membership with the Baptist Union of Great Britain. It moved to its present site in 1923 in South Norwood, a London suburb midway between the inner-city and the city fringe. When my father began his course, it was a residential community made up of some forty students and staff. The full-time faculty was limited to four men: Dr Percy Evans, the Principal, who taught New Testament, was regarded by many as a wise man and was much respected by the leadership of the Baptist Union; William ('Billy') Gaussen, a tutor in subjects such as Latin and Logic, and who by 1938 had given forty years of service to the College and was beginning to find it difficult to remember his students' names; Frederick Taverner, a tutor in Greek and Hebrew, a loveable eccentric who once left his book on the hallstand at home and arrived at the College with a clothes-brush under his arm; and Dr Frederick Cawley, the Old Testament tutor, who had seen service with the Baptist Missionary Society in India, a strong-minded and somewhat ascetic Scot, who became a prime mover in the college encouraging some of its brighter students to study for the external London BD. As befitted a college in the business of training preachers, in addition to the formal lectures, there was a sermon class. J.J. Brown, who was a contemporary of my father's, described the 'wit and wisdom' of the weekly exercise, attended by the whole college body, in these terms:

Critics pulled no punches. Said one: 'We missed our annual ramble this year, but the sermon this morning made up for it'! Another thought it was most appropriate that the preacher chose his closing hymn from the section of the hymnbook 'For those at sea'! A tutor commented: 'This sermon is like a rice pudding that's been dropped on the floor. It has taste but no shape!' But the final observations by the Principal, were always brilliant, tactful and telling.[1]

From the very outset of his time at Spurgeon's my father found himself in a position of leadership amongst his fellow students. Each intake of students was known as a 'Batch', and the member whose surname stood highest in the alphabetical list became leader of the 'Batch'. By dint of alphabetical chance, my father became the 'Batch leader', and as a result had the responsibility for calling and presiding over Batch meetings, arranging prayer times and representing the Batch at consultations between student officers and staff. Nor did Batch responsibilities end with college. For many years my father was responsible for arranging Batch reunions and generally keeping in touch with his former fellow-students. As an aside we may note that this particular Batch was composed of some very gifted men: for instance, not only my father, but also Godfrey Robinson and George Cumming were elected to the Presidency of the Baptist Union—sadly, Godfrey Robinson died before taking office, so another Batch member, Jack Brown, took his place instead. Now only two members of that Batch remain: Jack Brown and Ken Witting, who in September 2001 celebrated sixty years of Christian ministry.

My father proved to be an able student and was encouraged to study for the London BD alongside the normal college curriculum. It was not simply innate ability which made him a good student, he was also

---

[1]   From a private paper, 'Random reminiscences of life at Spurgeon's College half a century ago'.

disciplined in his approach to study. One of his fellow Batch members commented: 'I don't know whether there is such a thing as inborn genius. Certainly George would have denied it. The reason [for his mastering of such subjects as Greek, Latin, Hebrew, Ethics, Psychology and Logic] was simply hard work. I was in the habit of rising in the morning at what I thought a reasonable hour, but frequently when I woke I found George dressed and shaved and working at his desk. He had been there for two hours'.[2] My father would have agreed with Eddison that genius is made up of 1% inspiration and 99% perspiration. Later, as College Principal, if there was one thing he could not abide it was laziness on the part of a student. Laziness for him was akin to a mortal sin.

In the third year of his time at Spurgeon's my father became very involved with the theological students section of the Inter-Varsity Fellowship (IVF).[3] He was the college representative and in this capacity served on IVF committees. Because of his deep involvement in IVF things he almost jeopardised his BD. It was an important time for him. It was, for instance, through the IVF that my father came to know F.F. Bruce, then a classicist, with whom my father began to share theological interests. It was also through the IVF that he met Dr Douglas Johnson, the first General Secretary of the

---

2   Rev K.W. Witting in a private letter 6 June 2000.

3   The IVF, now the Universities and Colleges Christian Fellowship, traces its origins back to 1910 when the Cambridge Inter-Collegiate Christian Union split from the Student Christian Movement (SCM) on doctrinal issues. The IVF 'was endeavouring to preserve the historic Christian faith under the control of the plain statements of Holy Scripture', while the SCM 'aimed to embrace all possible views and to adapt the faith into terms which 'the modern mind could accept', Douglas Johnson, *Contending for the Faith: A History of the Evangelical Movement in the Universities and Colleges* (IVP, Leicester, 1979), 77-78.

IVF, who had a tremendous influence on my father's life.

There was, for instance, an occasion when he was in Douglas Johnson's house, that Johnson, who had been trained as a physician, said to him: 'I can't understand evangelical theological students. They all want to be missionaries or evangelists, but none of them seem to be willing to make the sacrifice to be backroom boys and to interpret the Scriptures and produce books that will influence theologians and people in the universities.'[4] Father pondered this at the back of his mind. However, he was convinced that God would have him be a pastor–evangelist.

Toward the end of his third year Ashurst Drive Baptist Church, Ilford, asked my father to preach 'with a view', which he did on 30 June 1940. After hearing him again, the church in October unanimously invited my father to become their pastor in a year's time when he had finished his theological course. Father initially hesitated because he really wondered whether he should be going on into further education, perhaps to read for a further degree. But that was not to be. It was a very difficult time for the war was on. The deacons at Ashurst Drive were very kind. They said: 'Come to us and you can have your mornings to study. We will be very happy to support you in this and you can serve us for the rest of the day'. So in November 1940 my father accepted the call.

It was in the summer of 1940 that he met my mother. My mother, Ruth Weston, was one of three children born to John and Daisy Mabel Weston (née Batley). The Weston family lived at that time in Lewisham. John

---

4   To appreciate the significance of this statement, one has to realise that at that time there was a real dearth of evangelical biblical scholars. When, for instance, in 1941 Douglas Johnson convened a group to plan for serious theological research at an academic level, not one of the group was teaching theology in a university. See Johnson, *Contending For the Faith*, 210-212.

Weston, who had been born in Dublin, worked as a clerk in St Pancras Town Hall. His job, however, was secondary to his preaching. Almost every Sunday evening he was to be found preaching at Wildfell Hall, Catford. He was also much in demand as a preacher both in this country and in Europe. John belonged to the 'Kelly Brethren', one of the more exclusive branches of the so-called 'Plymouth Brethren', although John himself, however, did not restrict himself to the Brethren and was happy to associate himself with other evangelical Christians.

In 1940, my mother, who was born on 3 June 1922, was only just eighteen years old. She had left the Prendergast School and started a course in business management at Pittman's College, although her real desire was to become a nurse. During the summer break she went on a two-week Christian Endeavour holiday in Ilfracombe. For one week of that holiday a student from Spurgeon's College, my father, was the leader. On the Wednesday of that week, my father, having spent all the previous night in prayer, told my mother that he felt that God would have him marry her. This came as a great shock to her, for up until that point my mother had had no real conversation with my father, apart from a day or so previously pointing out to him the need to care for one of the members of the houseparty! But as my father insisted right to the end of his life, he had never doubted the Lord's guidance at that time and time had proved him right. For him his conversion experience had been dramatic and so was his choice of a wife.

After this event, my father returned to Spurgeon's College and my mother to her home in Lewisham. But within a week or two the Battle of Britain started and for the next six months many of their evenings and weekends seem to have been spent sitting in the cellar of my mother's home in one of the worst bombed areas of London. But even then, sweet talk was rationed, for he spent most of his time struggling to prepare for his

London BD, while at his encouragement my mother read books such as Karl Barth's *Credo*.

As is still the custom, the college was required to commend its students to the Baptist Union in order that they might be enrolled on the its list of probationer ministers. Of my father the Principal wrote:

> G.R. Beasley-Murray is an unusually good man. He has the advantage of an attractive personality, but deeper qualities than the surface ones are his. He has a keen and studious mind, assimilates and knows how to employ knowledge, has depth and definiteness of conviction without becoming contentious or hide-bound, is a friendly man with powers of leadership. His preaching is excellent, and he will prove to be a good pastor...

Chapter 4

Ashurst Drive Baptist Church, Ilford: Minister (1941–1948)

The Church

Ashurst Drive Baptist Church, formed only a few years previously, was situated in a newer part of Ilford (in East London) and set in the middle of a large housing development to the north of Eastern Avenue, a main road leading to Gants Hill. The church's premises were not all that impressive. The church met in what was intended to be a hall—there was room on the plot of land for a 'sanctuary', but the church itself was never built. Today Ilford has a large Asian population, but in the 1940s Ilford was almost entirely white. The only significant ethnic group was the Jews.

My father was the church's second full-time minister. Indeed, the appointment of a full-time minister was an act of faith on the part of the church, because at the time the finances did not appear to allow it. The forecast presented by the then church treasurer to the church meeting in April 1940 suggested that if my father were called to the pastorate, the general account would show a deficit of £100 by the end of that financial year. Nonetheless, the church did not allow money to have the final say and on 12 October 1940 the church meeting issued a unanimous call to my father to become its pastor. The starting stipend was fixed at £236 per annum, the normal stipend for a young Baptist minister, and included the use of the Manse. Fortunately the church's faith was rewarded, for the congregation increased significantly so that finances were never a problem.

The beginning of his ministry was marked by a series of special meetings. There was a 'family welcome service' on Saturday 26 April 1941, for which an appeal had to be made for tea, milk and sugar—all things strictly rationed because of the war. On Sunday 27 July the services were conducted by Dr Fred Cawley, the Vice-Principal of Spurgeon's College, and took the form of an extended ordination service. In the morning Dr Cawley gave the 'charge to the minister' and in the evening the 'charge to the church'. The evening service included the act of ordination itself. My mother vividly remembers the day of ordination for two reasons. Firstly, because my father had forgotten to collect his one and only suit from the dry cleaners and so had to wear a borrowed suit which was far too large. Secondly, because in response to Dr Cawley's comment that 'You must be very happy that your son is in the Lord's service', his mother, with the typical outlook of any other non-churchgoing person, replied: 'Yes, it's a safe job'!

The following Thursday there were two further services of 'recognition' with a public tea in-between at which greetings were received from 'local ministers and friends'. The service at 4.30 pm was conducted by Rev Theo Bamber, the minister of Rye Lane, Peckham, then one of the largest Baptist churches. As we shall see, Theo Bamber and my father maintained a deep affection for one another, even though their views subsequently diverged. The later service at 7 pm included what Baptists today would call the 'induction' of a minister to the church and was presided over by the Area Superintendent, Rev Henry Cook. The guest preacher for that evening was Dr Martyn Lloyd-Jones, the celebrated physician turned preacher and minister of London's Westminster Chapel. As a young minister my father greatly appreciated the ministry of Martyn Lloyd-Jones and was an active member of the Westminster Fellowship, a fraternal for ministers of an evangelical frame of mind run by the 'doctor'. The meetings of this large fraternal, which numbered well over 200 mainly Free Church ministers, were occasions 'when sloppy thinking, poor exposition and poor theology were mercilessly demolished'.[1] In later years my father was greatly saddened to see Martyn Lloyd-Jones lose his earlier vision of working with other Christians.[2]

From the outset it was a very exciting and dynamic ministry. People flocked to hear this 'new voice in Ilford'. Attendances at the morning services that August averaged 139, and evening services averaged 170. Compared to some of the larger churches in the United States these numbers may seem small—but for a relatively undistinguished estate church in an ordinary London suburb, such numbers were good. Furthermore, a war was on, with the result that some people had moved out of London for safety, while others were away with the armed forces. After the first month of his ministry ten people had applied for membership, although as my father noted in the 'Newsletter' that 'nine are being transferred from other churches', which he felt 'does not do us any credit'. My father longed to see people come to Christ. By the end of the first year of his ministry the church secretary reported that there had been '27 known conversions—27 baptisms (and more to follow soon)'. Baptisms and applications for membership became so frequent that extra church meetings had to be held to cope with the numbers. Members learned to come early to services if they wanted to sit with their friends.

---

[1]   Oliver Barclay, *Evangelicalism in Britain 1935-1995: A Personal Sketch* (IVP, Leicester, 1997), 50.

[2]   In October 1966 Lloyd Jones made a plea to all evangelicals to put their fellowship with other evangelicals above other church loyalties and 'come out' of their denominations. See Barclay, *Evangelicalism*, 82-87.

Evangelism

It was first and foremost an evangelistic ministry. My
father had a passion for winning men and women to
Christ and his church. The church minutes record one
evangelistic effort after another. In the words of my
father, 'If the people will not come to us, we will go to
them'. There were house-to-house visits and monthly
tract distributions in the area. An Easter 'campaign'
with the title of 'History Crisis Week' was conducted by
students from Spurgeon's College. During the summer,
open-air meetings were held in the nearby park, outside
the cinema and also outside a local factory. In October
1941 my father proposed that the church take over the
local Savoy Cinema for Sunday evening services
throughout the following month. This proposal 'met
with enthusiastic and unanimous approval' of the
church meeting. Unfortunately the owners of the
cinema refused the church's request. A series of so-
called 'cottage' meetings, what today we would call
evangelistic home groups, was organised, which involved members opening their homes and inviting
neighbours to hear the gospel from specially recruited
speakers from the district. Airraids interrupted some of
the meetings, but non-believers came.

There were special services taken by Christians in
various professions: one Sunday evening, for instance,
it was Christian policemen, another Sunday evening
Christian nurses. There were also guest evening services where no presuppositions of faith were made as
he discussed topics of general interest like 'Is there life
after death?' and 'Can we believe the Bible?' For one
particular Saturday evening guest service my father put
an advertisement in the local paper for an atheist
prepared to debate the Christian faith with a Cambridge
scientist, Dr R.E.D. Clark. The editor of a local newspaper, a declared atheist, volunteered to come. It proved
to be a learning experience for my father, since the
atheist editor had essentially only one query: 'If there is

a God, then why is there so much suffering?' Not surprisingly my father's deacons were somewhat alarmed by the placing of the advertisement. My father, however, never doubted that the Christian faith could face any opposition or criticism. And so it proved to be.

Rex Mason, who later became a Baptist minister and subsequently an Old Testament scholar, was a teenager in the church at the time.

George completely revolutionised my conception of Christianity and the ministry. The previous minister had been a kind elderly man [actually at the time he had only been in his 40s!] whose pulpit style and content, however, bored my brother and me stiff. George had a lively and most effective presentation in manner, and the content was of the highest intellectual quality, already showing the interest and ability of the scholar which were to follow later... I suppose the time of intellectual discovery in the sixth form is the period of greatest arrogance and superiority in one's life when one thinks one 'knows it all' and is intellectually above Christianity. George's preaching and scholarship, and his readiness to discuss questions in personal conversation, alike all made the profoundest impression on me... He always remained my 'model' for ministry, as he did for many others, although, inevitably, most of us fell far short of the target he presented.[3]

Long before church leaders in this country and elsewhere were talking of the need for 'seeker-friendly' services, my father was actively putting on 'meetings' which had the needs of non-Christians in view. 'Why must our services always be services of worship?', he asked. 'Why not sometimes propaganda meetings (in the best sense of the term), with community singing if one must have hymns, but with the non-Christian solely in mind? Rather let us fail in our experiments than die in our ruts. One finds it hard to understand

---

3   Private letter of 23 May 2000.

why we always assume that an outsider can sincerely join in the worship of a Being in whom he does not believe.'[4]

Commitment

It was a very challenging ministry in the sense that my father was always challenging the church to be more evangelistically committed. His pastor's letters in the church's newsletter constantly touched on this theme. In September 1941 he wrote:

> The burden of the lost is not upon us. The horror of the fact that the vast majority of the men and women about us in this borough are living their lives without God, without Christ, without hope in the world, and they are *hell-bound*, has never gripped our imagination. We are not convinced of the 100% truth of the Gospel. We are dull in faith toward God and in vision respecting man. Until this burden becomes so intolerable to you that you find no way of easing it but to *toil* with me to bring the people about us to Christ, I shall give you no messages on Sundays except those calculated to stir up your souls to activity for the Lord.

Three months later in December 1941 he wrote:

> Our whole Church must exist for one purpose alone, viz. the propagation of that Evangel; when it ceases to stand for any less worthy cause than that our usefulness to God will also cease.

Again in February 1942:

> Oh for such a spirit at Ashurst Drive that folk around us would begin to talk of the 'Ashurst spirit' that marches on when others mark time, that interprets difficulties as the

---

4 'Vulnerable Points in the Christian Armoury', *Spurgeon's College Students Magazine*, Summer Issue 1950, 3.

clarion call to advance, that thus makes trying days triumph days!

In May 1942:

> If men and women are passing into eternity with less opportunity of hearing the Word of Life than formerly, then we must *intensify* our efforts to enable them to hear it, not slacken off.

At one stage my father provided everyone in the church with a copy of a little booklet by Howard Guinness with a single word title: *Sacrifice*. The theme of the booklet was how much were church members prepared to sacrifice for the furtherance of the kingdom. At a later stage in his ministry, when the baptistery had not been opened for nearly six months, he rebuked the church for its slackness!

Looking back over this period, how wise was it for my father to have 'flogged' the church in such a manner, particularly during the period when the war was on and when for many people the emphasis was on survival? The evidence would appear to be that he judged it correctly. The most striking thing about the church and deacons' minutes of that time is the joy and enthusiasm of the members.

The Lord's Supper

It was a ministry which underlined the importance of the sacraments of believers' baptism and the Lord's Supper. The former might be expected of a Baptist minister, but not the latter. In almost all Baptist churches then, the Lord's Supper was celebrated just twice a month and the communion service was separated from the main service. In the autumn of 1945 my father proposed first to the deacons and then to the church that the Lord's Supper be celebrated every Sunday morning with the exception of the first Sunday in the

month, when the Lord's Supper would be celebrated at
the evening service. He felt very strongly that the Lord's
Supper should be central to Christian worship. The
minutes of the October church meeting read: 'Mr
Beasley-Murray went on to explain that the only interpretation that could be intelligently gathered from
Scripture that the basic reason why the early Christians
met together first thing on the Lord's Day was for the
"breaking of bread"... If we see a principle which appears
to be true, we ought to carry it out'. After a good deal of
discussion the church, at my father's suggestion, agreed
to a six-month trial. The trial then turned into a
permanent arrangement.

Difficulties of War

It was a very difficult time, for the war was on. When
my father first came to Ashurst Drive, the evening
services in the winter were held at 4 pm because of the
'black-out'. At that time black-out was total. There were
no lights in the street and of course no lights from
people's windows. Walking in the darkness was quite
dangerous, not least when it came to crossing roads.
Nonetheless my father believed it right to return to the
old time of 6.30 pm:

> We are continuing our evening services at 6.30. By this means
> we hope to reach numbers of local people who are not
> sufficiently scared by the 'black-out' to be prevented from
> attending. When I realise how many millions in this land go
> nightly to see and hear Clark Gable, Spencer Tracey, Jeanette
> MacDonald, and the rest of their kind; how many workers of
> all ages leave their homes in darkness to toil for their country
> and return while it is yet dark; then how few Christians are
> prepared to endure a little inconvenience for Christ's sake, I
> am ashamed.[5]

---

5   Ashurst Drive *Newsletter*, October 1941.

The war affected the church in all sorts of ways. One Sunday there would be a good congregation, but the next, after heavy bombing during the week, the mothers and their children would have been evacuated and gone away, and then a week or two later they would slowly come back, thinking they would be safe. Then, after another lot of bombing, the people would scatter again. This made running a Sunday school exceedingly difficult, for there were times when the children disappeared literally overnight.

The bombing raids caused tremendous destruction and loss of life, even in Ilford. By the end of the war most of the houses that were still standing had been damaged and needed a total overhaul, with hardly a house left intact.

As soon as a raid was over, my father would set off on his bicycle to offer help. Inevitably this involved many a hard experience. One Saturday, for instance, there was a day-time raid and father helped to search through the rubble for bodies. He found one man who was still alive but had had his face blown off. That night he found it difficult to concentrate on the sermon he was due to preach the next day. Then the words of Isaiah flashed through his mind, words that were later seen to be descriptive of Jesus: 'His face was marred more than any man'.[6] This made such a profound impression on him that he changed his sermon.

Not surprisingly my mother found the bombing very stressful, but not so my father. Many a time in the midst of a bombing raid she would express her doubts as to whether they would come out alive, but his reply was always, 'There is sure to be someone alive at the end, and it might be us.' In part his lack of fear reflected his natural optimism. In part, too, it reflected his faith. Even at that relatively early stage in his life he was not

---

[6] Isaiah 52.14 AV: 'his visage was so marred more than any other man'.

afraid of death—in that respect he truly lived out his faith.

The difficulties of the war produced a tremendous bond between pastor and people, but they also affected the life of the church, not least in the immediate years after the war. People's energies were understandably sapped. Everyone had been buoyed up through the war, during which they had given of their best, but afterwards the strain began to show, with the result that in most of the churches an inevitable inertia set in. Ashurst Drive was not exempt from this, even though numerically the church continued to grow.

Marriage

It was while my father was at Ashurst Drive that he married my mother. For the first eight months of his ministry he lived alone in the Manse at 262 Perth Road, looking after himself for the most part, although one of the members did come in to clean while others often invited him into their homes for evening meals. Prior to their marriage my father had asked my mother's parents if they would be willing for her to go to what was then the Bible Training Institute in Glasgow (today it is the International Christian College, Glasgow). My mother was still a teenager at that time and my father felt that it would be helpful to her in her role as a future minister's wife to undertake some theological study. Perhaps surprisingly my mother's parents, who—as we have already noted—belonged to the Plymouth Brethren, agreed. So in the autumn of 1941 my mother went up to Glasgow.

The original plan had been to get married in the summer of 1942. My parents felt that it would be better for my mother to wait until she was twenty before she got married. However, in March 1942 it was suddenly announced on the radio that people of my mother's age were being called up to work in the armed forces, on the buses or in factories. My father impulsively decided that they should get married quickly—he was later to quip 'we had to get married'—and within two weeks he had arranged the wedding. Had he not done so, it is likely that the marriage would have had to have been postponed to the end of the war. My parents were married by Dr Evans, the Principal of Spurgeon's College, on 4 April 1942 at Ashurst Drive. The newsletter recorded: 'The bride was charming and Dr Evans conducted the marriage ceremony with obvious particular interest.'[7] While they were on honeymoon my mother registered as a married woman, and to her delight she was told that 'as a vicar's wife' she was 'certainly needed in the church'.

While my parents were in Ilford three children were born. I was born on 14 March 1944 during what was evidently one of the worst air-raids during the war, with a plane being shot down at the end of the road. Twice my mother had to whisk me off to Leicester for safety because this was the period of the 'doodle-bugs' and the rockets. On one of those occasions my mother received a letter from Miss Clara Rogers, the lady who had previously helped to clean the house while my father was a bachelor, to say that one problem with my father was that he kept piles of his books in his Morrison air-raid shelter, while he slept upstairs in the bed. My father felt he had his priorities right, for he said that he could always slip down if a bomb came.

My sister Elizabeth was born on 12 October 1945, just after the war was over. My brother Stephen was born on 18 December 1947 in the middle of one of the coldest and bleakest winters of the century.

The Piano and Peer Gynt

During his Ilford days and long after, my father loved to play the piano at home as a form of relaxation. I have many happy memories as a child listening to him

---

7   Ashurst Drive *Newsletter*, May 1942.

playing some of his favourite pieces. In Ilford he gave public performances too, playing concertos with a local symphony orchestra, and throughout his life he continued to give semi-private performances in churches and elsewhere.

There was, however, one piece of music which he found it useful to play at evangelistic meetings.[8] This was the Peer Gynt Suite by the Norwegian composer Edvard Grieg, which contains such favourites as 'Morning Mood', 'In the Hall of the Mountain King' (otherwise known as the 'Dance of the Gnomes') and 'Solvejg's Song'. Originally the music was for piano and orchestra, but it was also set for two pianos—or, if need be, my father would play it on a church piano accompanied by the church organist. The music itself is beautiful, but this was not the reason for my father playing it. Rather he played the music in order to tell the story of Peer Gynt by Henrik Ibsen, a drama for which Grieg had written the incidental music.

The story is complex and needs time to tell—indeed, the whole drama lasts some four hours. However, as my father would draw the story to a conclusion, he would point out that Peer Gynt is the perfect illustration of a greater than Ibsen: 'What does it profit a man to gain the whole world and forfeit his life?' (Mk 8.36). Or to put it another way, Peer Gynt is a modern 'Prodigal', who returns home at last having utterly wasted his life. But there is an immense difference between Peer Gynt and the prodigal, because when the prodigal realised what a fool he was, he returned to his father—and as a result a broken relationship was restored and life was renewed for him, and he became a wiser and happier man. At this point my father would go on to make a gospel appeal: 'Does Jesus wait to bring you to the Father and so to the life of God's Kingdom? If

---

8   One of the last times my father ever played this piece was at a Harvest Guest Service—'Music and the Harvest of Life'—at Chelmsford in September 1995.

so, open your life to him, God's own representative and begin to live.'

Resurrection

From the very beginning of his ministry, the resurrection of Jesus was a key theme in my father's preaching. It became a key theme in his writings too. While at Ashurst Drive he wrote a tract with the provocative headline, *Man Alive after Death and Burial* pictured on the front of a newspaper entitled 'Eternal News', a tract which proved to be very popular and remained in print for many years.[9]

Another popular piece, written in 1946, was a little tract entitled *Jesus Is Alive!*[10] The opening couple of paragraphs give the flavour of what was a lively exercise in evangelism:

> 'Blue pencil nonsense!' said an irate heckler to a Gospel preacher in Hyde Park. Maybe that is your reaction to the above title. How can Jesus Christ be alive? Everybody knows that he died on a cross two thousand years ago. Yet Good Friday is followed by Easter Sunday, and they say that he was seen alive on that day. That's the basis of Christianity. If it is true, so is Christianity. If it is false, then Christians are wrong and the Church lives by fostering a pathetic mistake. Is there any way of dinging out the trust? Yes, and a pretty compelling business it is too to anyone who takes the trouble to follow it through.

After a whirlwind tour of the evidence for the resurrection, the tract ends: 'If these things be true, men and women, wake up and find him!'

---

9   It was published by the Victory Tract Club, date unknown.

10   Unfortunately I cannot ascertain when or where it was published. The piece illustrates a feature of my father's writing—the frequent use of exclamation marks—which for good or ill has been emulated by his eldest son!

My father returned to this theme in the very first book he wrote: *Christ is Alive!*[11] which was given a foreword by F.F. Bruce, his friend from IVF days. Although my father carefully reviewed the evidence for the historicity of the resurrection, his book was not aimed so much at non-Christians as at Christians, who he believed had yet to face up to the implications of the resurrection. This emphasis came out very forcibly in his introduction:

> Some years ago the late Dr W.Y. Fullerton described a visit he paid to the mimic Calvary in the village of Domo d'Ossala, in Italian Switzerland. A series of chapels had been erected, with pictures of effigies depicting the scenes of our Lord's Passion. The first showed Christ before Herod; the second, Christ grasping the cross; the third, Christ shouldering its weight; the fourth, Christ carrying it along, and so on. The climax of the scenes was in the church itself where there was a great picture of the cross, raised, with Christ upon it, and in the skies astonished angels gazing down at the tragedy of human sin and divine love. Up to this point the path was well worn by the feet of the devout pilgrims. For years they had come to witness anew the sufferings of their Saviour, and doubtless had mourned and wept at the sight of His agonies. But there they had stopped. Their Christ was dead. 'Beyond the church there was another shrine', wrote Fullerton; 'but the singular thing was that the path, well worn up to this point, now became grass-covered. Evidently nobody went any further. Though it was a wet day, and the grass was long, I went to the summit, and there, behold! was found the Chapel of the Resurrection! The builders of the Calvary (let that, at least, be said to their credit) did not stay with the dead Christ, but the people, the worshippers, never got any further... The grass-grown path, untrodden by human feet was a witness that could not be disputed'.

---

[11]   *Christ is Alive!* (Lutterworth, London, 1947).

A more perfect reflection of the mind of the Church of the ages would be difficult to find. That which had been the central affirmation of the first disciples is now of no importance to the average Christian. It is not talked about, it is not preached on, it is not even wondered at; it is simply ignored.

The effect on Christian thought of this neglect of the Resurrection of our Lord can scarcely be exaggerated. It has affected the whole gamut of theology. For the largest section of Christendom, the fitting symbol of Christianity is a crucifix; the impression is given to the world that the Saviour is someone over whom we should weep. Even Protestants, in their constructions of the doctrine of the cross, have left Christ on it and presumed that His saving work finishes with His death. The atonement is consequently explained in terms of a sacrifice on our behalf, a satisfaction of God's justice, a payment of our debt, a revelation of God's love, *and that is all*. It somehow seems to have been overlooked that the resurrection is an integral part of our Lord's work for us, so that salvation is essentially a deliverance from a living death in sin to a new life of righteousness in God.[12]

Sixteen years later my father returned again to the theme of the resurrection when he was asked to give four talks on the BBC during the Lenten season of 1963. 'I enquired whether anyone in former years had spoken on the Resurrection of Jesus Christ. No, came the reply, none had done this'. My father thereupon decided to look at the resurrection and its meaning for us. The talks were well-received. A reviewer in *The Guardian* wrote: 'Dr Beasley-Murray in the first of the traditional Lenten talks moved right away from the customary pious fog and talked factually about the evolution of Christianity as an historian rather than as a preacher.'[13] Such was the response of listeners that these lectures were subsequently reproduced in printed form the fol-

---

12   *Christ is Alive!*, 11-12.
13   Ian Rodger, *The Guardian*, Saturday 16 March 1963.

lowing year under the simple title of *The Resurrection of Jesus Christ*.

Unlike *Christ is Alive!*, the talks published in this book had a non-Christian audience in mind. Although my father spoke of the talks as being 'aimed at people who were prepared to do serious thinking late in the evening',[14] there is a light touch to the talks. What's more, the talks are full of illustrations and quotable quotes—still a rich source for any preacher having to prepare sermons for Easter Day. The following two excerpts are examples of the way in which my father knew how to grip his audience:

His first talk, entitled 'Christ's Resurrection: A Spotlight on Existence', began with the story of an incident that occurred at a mass meeting of workers in Moscow shortly after the Russian revolution:

A little priest mounted the platform... He addressed the crowd: 'You have heard all the arguments which have been brought forward to prove the new world view. But my friends Christ is risen!' One might have expected a howl of laughter to greet the cry, but it did not come. Those workers had heard the cry many times. It occurs at the climax of the Russian Easter night service, when the mourning and fasting is ended, and the presiding priest proclaims the good news, 'Christ is risen'; the people embrace and kiss one another and call out in reply, 'He is risen indeed'. On this occasion, as the priest sent forth the ancient cry it was as though a sleeping volcano erupted: from thousands of throats there burst forth the response, 'He is risen indeed'.

My father went on to ask:

Now was that priest simply playing cleverly on the emotions of the crowd? Or had he better reasons for his action?[15]

---

14   *The Resurrection of Jesus Christ* (Oliphants, London, 1964), vii.
15   *Resurrection of Jesus Christ*, 11.

My father began his fourth talk on 'The Christian Outlook on the future' in this way:

> It is reported of a German bishop, about to be executed by a firing squad, that when he was placed against the wall and the command fire was given he cried out, 'Goodbye you that are dead; I'm going into life'. That was a heroic affirmation of faith; but was he right, or was he wrong?[16]

Throughout my father's ministry the resurrection was a major theme. As President of the Baptist Union in 1968–69, he urged the churches to mark the week leading up to Easter by going out to tell others the good news of Jesus and in particular to use Easter Day for evangelistic purposes. In this respect he quoted the conclusion of a *Daily Telegraph* article, published at Easter 1968: 'The churches have an immense fund of goodwill and interest on which to call, particularly at Easter. Every year nearly half of the 27% who intended to go to church were not expected to do so. A manufacturer, faced with such a vast market potential, would do better than the churches are doing in marketing and advertising his product.'[17]

Although he wrote of Easter as offering a good opportunity for faith-sharing, his emphasis on Easter had not only strategic and theological roots, but also personal roots. In one of his later sermons, entitled 'What it means to me to be a Christian', my father wrote: 'As a teenager I feared death—deeply, and was tormented by it. But as I learned the implications of the death and resurrection of Jesus, death lost all terrors; for he who loved me to the death of the cross carried his love for me to the throne of the universe, and it is almighty love which holds me in his hand. Why don't Christians believe Christ—truly—and let their view of death be controlled by their understanding of him?'

---

16   *Resurrection of Jesus Christ*, 40.
17   See 'Easter 1969', *The Fraternal* 127 (January 1963), 4-7.

Life Between Death and Resurrection?

In an article written for *Young Life*, the official organ of
the National Young Life Campaign, my father sought to
tackle the problem of the 'Intermediate State'.

> Such references as we have to the condition of the departed
> do not favour the idea that they are in a state of un-
> consciousness. The latter conception is largely due to taking
> literally the metaphor of sleep as a figure of death... An
> example of intense and joyous activity in the world of spirits
> this side of the Second Coming is the preaching of our Lord
> to 'the spirits in prison', which, I am persuaded, has to be
> taken as it stands and not made to refer to the preaching of
> Noah to people once living but now dead. And this preach-
> ing was done by our Lord before His spirit was clothed in
> resurrection![18]

My father repeated these views in an evening lecture
course he was giving during the summer of 1947 for the
newly formed London Bible College. Unfortunately his
view did not find favour with the Council of the China
Inland Mission (CIM).[19] It would appear that, in a
particular lecture my father, on the basis of Peter's
reference to the preaching of Jesus to 'the spirits in
prison' (1 Pet 3.19), speculated on the possibility of a
second chance of repentance after death. Present at the
lecture were some candidates of the CIM, who on their
return to the CIM hostel reported my father's comments to some influential laymen who just happened
to be there for a meeting of the CIM council. Although
none of them had any theological training, they were
alarmed by this 'heresy' and immediately got in touch
with the Rev Ernest Kevan, the Principal of the London

---

[18] 'After Death—What', *Young Life* Vol. XXI. No 27 (July
1946), 74.
[19] Founded in 1865 by the great missionary pioneer, J.
Hudson Taylor, it became the Overseas Missionary Fellowship.

Bible College, to tell him so. Ernest Kevan, conscious of his dependence on these men, for several were on the council of the new college, pleaded with my father to withdraw what he had said. My father was astonished and said that these views were ones which he felt were true to scripture and were therefore not ones to be discarded lightly. In the end he assured Ernest Kevan that he would quietly withdraw from lecturing at the end of the session, so that the members of the CIM could be assured that they would have no need for further disquiet. This was a good example of my father's fearlessness for truth, even if, as in this case, it brought to an end an activity which he loved. Fortunately it did not end his friendship with Ernest Kevan himself.

Not surprisingly my father expanded on this preaching of Christ to 'the spirits in prison' in his popular commentary on *The General Epistles*:

> In the eyes of the Jews, the generation of Noah was the most wicked of all history: 'The generation of the Flood has no part in the world to come and will not rise in judgement', runs a Rabbinic saying. Peter declares: 'It's not true! The death of Christ avails for all men of all time, even for the wickedest of all! Moreover, it was none other than the Lord Himself who proclaimed redemption to them! His pity extends to such!'
>
> From this we may learn the universal scope of Christ's saving work. Possibly Peter also wanted his readers to draw the conclusion that on this account there was hope for their own generation, even though it had sinned more greatly than the Flood generation through its refusing the proclamation of a greater than Noah, and was facing the last judgement (4.7)... In such a spirit Niemöller, despite his passionate opposition to Hitler, could yet declare: 'If Jesus Christ did

not die for the sins of Adolf Hitler, neither did He die for the sins of Martin Niemöller!'[20]

Academic Developments

During his time at Ashurst Drive my Father gained a MTh degree in New Testament studies through King's College, London. Prof R.V.G. Tasker, who held the Chair in New Testament Exegesis, was very helpful to him and my father often used to visit him in his home for tutorials. Significantly, Tasker was a recent convert to evangelicalism—prior to a mission to King's College in 1941 at which Martyn Lloyd-Jones was the speaker, he had been a 'moderate liberal'.[21]

My father also wrote articles and reviews for the *Evangelical Quarterly*, and prepared papers for the summer school of the Tyndale Fellowship. One paper he submitted to the *Evangelical Quarterly* was, however, turned down, not because it was not good enough, but because it dared to propose a later date for the Book of Daniel. F.F. Bruce, who edited the journal, wrote:

There are some hawk-eyed friends who keep their eyes open for the least deviation from the strait-and-narrow path of orthodoxy; and while we want to be as comprehensive as possible, we can't take too many risks. About two years or so ago an article appeared on 'The Westminster Confession of Faith' which led to a block cancellation of subscriptions in Northern Ireland! We are not yet financially solvent... It is deplorable that we still have to entertain such materialistic considerations in dealing with contributions to Biblical scholarship, but as things are at present, we must... You know that the Evangelical world has been so indoctrinated with 'Daniel in the Critic's Den' and so forth that in the eyes

---

[20]   G.R. Beasley-Murray, *The General Epistles: James, 1 Peter, Jude, 2 Peter* (Lutterworth Press, London & Abingdon Press, New York & Nashville, 1965), 59.

[21]   See Barclay, *Evangelicalism in Britain*, 72-73.

of many one might as well turn Unitarian right away as maintain a Maccabean date for Daniel.[22]

Instead my father had to turn to the *Baptist Quarterly* for publication.[23] Reflecting on the impact that article made on him, Dr David Russell, who later became an authority on inter-testamental literature and who himself produced a commentary on Daniel, wrote:

> In hindsight, there may not have been anything in it to ruffle many feathers, but at the time it demonstrated clearly to me his willingness to 'stick his neck out' in his commitment to honest scholarship and in his pursuit of truth, not least as this affected his understanding and interpretation of scripture. It signalled a quality that was to characterise his whole scholarly life—his profound respect for scripture and his openness to new understandings of it, even though this might appear to break the mould in which he and his colleagues had received it.[24]

Probably his most significant article appeared in the very first issue of the *Journal of Theological Studies* in 1947 on 'The two Messiahs in the Testaments of the Twelve Patriarchs'.[25] In it he maintained that the original author of the Testaments distinguished two Messiahs—one from Levi and one from Judah. At the time many were not convinced by the thrust of my father's argument. However, when in due course the texts found in the Qumran caves were published and studied, they vindicated my father's viewpoint for they supplied further evidence of the distinction between those two Messiahs in certain Jewish circles toward the end of the pre-Christian era.

---

22   Letter dated 22 March 1947.
23   'A Conservative Thinks Again About Daniel', *Baptist Quarterly* 12 (1948), 341-346, 366-371.
24   Some private 'Recollections and Reflections' on my father's life written in June 2000.
25   *Journal of Theological Studies* 48 (1947), 1-12.

After gaining his MTh, in which he had specialised in New Testament studies, my father wondered whether he should start doing a PhD. He went to Spurgeon's College to see Dr Percy Evans and Dr Fred Cawley to gain their advice. They were askance at his suggestion and said a man still in his 30s was far too young to be doing doctoral studies.

Looking Further Afield

It was through going to a Baptist ministers' fraternal while he was in Ilford that father heard of Zion Baptist Church, Cambridge, which had been experiencing a long ministerial interregnum. Some weeks later he contacted Mr Tebbit, the London Area Superintendent, to see if the church was still vacant. He wondered whether it might be possible to go to Cambridge and do a PhD while pastoring a church. He told the Area Superintendent that he did not want to preach 'with a view' until he had had an opportunity to talk to the deacons and see if they would be willing for him to engage in studies at the university. In those days this was an unusual way of proceeding. However, my father felt he did not want to preach 'with a view' under false pretences. He wanted to be open about his intentions. The deacons were more than willing, with the result that my father preached with a view which in turn led to a call from the church, a call accepted by my father.

Not surprisingly the Ashurst Drive church were deeply disappointed to hear the news. Nonetheless they assured him of their 'continued love and interest in his work for the Lord Jesus Christ' and thanked God for this man 'whose grace, forthrightness and selflessness has been a glowing example to the whole church and an encouragement to each one of us to know the Lord more perfectly'. The deacons' meeting minutes for 14 January 1948 records: 'Our membership as at 31st December 1947 stood at 228. The net increase in membership during the six and a half years of Mr

Beasley-Murray's ministry was 133. There had been 91 baptisms during that period.'

Chapter 5

Zion Baptist Church, Cambridge: Minister (1948–1950)

The Church

Toward the end of February 1948 we moved to Cambridge. Zion Baptist Church is situated on East Road. It was and is an unfashionable town-centre Baptist church. At the time it was in a distinctly poor neighbourhood, with, as my father noted, 'ten pubs on this short road of half a mile long!' On the other side of Parker's Piece was—and is—the more fashionable St Andrew's Street Baptist Church. Before my father's time the 'tradition' was that if a Zion church member moved up in the world, then they transferred their membership to St Andrew's Street.

Zion Baptist Church is a barn of a place. Although the 'sanctuary' could hold up to 1000 people, at the beginning of 1948 the morning service only numbered some forty people, with some 100 present at the evening service. The church, largely made up of working-class people, was in poor heart. Morale was low. My father once described it as a 'backward-looking church' in the sense that there was a wistful looking back to a remarkable period of the church's history, when there had been full congregations on a Sunday and a huge Sunday School.[1] But the two world wars had changed all that. The congregation was now relatively small, and—to my mother still in her 20s—appeared at the time to be elderly.[2]

---

[1]   Address given at Zion Baptist Church's 'Roots' Day on 16 September 1995.

[2]   In fact the congregation was not quite as elderly as it appeared. Roger Hayden, in a private communication, mentions

For my father all this was a new experience. In Leicester he had been converted in a new church on a new estate which had not long ago received its first pastor. At Ashurst Drive he had been the second minister of a young church which was brimming with life. But here at Zion the church was more than 100 years old and the life had gone out of it for the most part. The much-loved previous minister, Vellam Pitts, who as a result of almost losing his faith at one stage had left the pastorate of Zion to run a private prep school (The Shrubbery!), was still a very vocal member of the church. The minutes of that time reveal that there was scarcely a church meeting when he did not make his thoughts known.

The church was spiritually run-down. One indication of this was that its life was devoted to preparing for their annual Christmas market, which at that time was responsible for financing the ministry. The first planning committee would meet in January and then at monthly intervals throughout the year. My father made it clear to the deacons that he favoured direct giving instead. Nonetheless he did not oppose the custom in his first year of ministry. Instead he sought to turn it into an evangelistic opportunity. In the customary introductory message of welcome from the pastor for the Christmas Market programme he wrote:

> In welcoming you to this event, we would also give you a hearty welcome into the circle of this church's friendship. We are a group of very ordinary people, drawn together chiefly because we have first been drawn to God. In our mutual friendship we seek to cultivate His friendship. What makes God want the company of men and women like us is beyond our telling, but we know he wants *your* company quite as much as ours. And the gifts He offers are far greater than anything we have for sale. To have his forgiveness, and

---

the names of five couples in either their 40s or 50s, whose children numbered ten early teenagers.

belong to his family, to know his presence and that there's a place with him hereafter, most of all to have His Son Jesus Christ as one's Saviour and Lord—these are far more priceless than anything we can put on our stalls. We hope you'll take them!

In the event that was the last Christmas Market. The next year the members decided to have a Gift Day instead of the Christmas Market, and the giving increased markedly.

An Evangelistic Ministry Begins

The induction service took place on Sunday 29 February 1948, when Dr Cawley of Spurgeon's College was the preacher. This was followed by a 'public welcome meeting' on Saturday 6 March at which the Rev Theo Bamber was the speaker. The *Cambridge Evening News* that week went on to say: 'During his college course and since, Mr Beasley-Murray has been closely connected with Christian work amongst students, being particularly interested in the Inter-Varsity Fellowship, on whose committees he has served both as student and as a graduate.'

As at Ashurst Drive, so at Zion my father quickly developed an evangelistic ministry. At his first deacons' meeting in March 1948 he asked for 'large notice boards at the front and side of the church' and proposed that plans be made for special monthly evangelistic services in the following winter, with guest preachers and a large London choir. At the church meeting in July 1948 he suggested that the galleries in the church might 'be opened for these special services as he thought people unaccustomed to coming to church might prefer to slip unobtrusively into the galleries rather than sit in the body of the church'. He further proposed that these services together with systematic monthly visitation of the roads in the area would then lead up to a campaign during Easter week to be led by students from

Spurgeon's College. In that connection one of those students still remembers the occasion when they were going around in a car with a broadcasting system advertising the mission.

> The usual patter was: 'Have you got anything on tonight? We have a special service (event) at Zion Baptist Church'. Suddenly the microphone was pushed in front of me; and at that moment we passed the public house 'Adam and Eve'— and I said, 'Calling Adam and Eve, have you anything on tonight?'. There was such an explosion of laughter from the back seat of the car, and George was in danger of 'dying with laughter'.[3]

My father was quite happy to experiment with the Sunday evening service, seeing no reason as to why it should be a repeat of the morning service. On some evenings he showed 'Fact and Faith' films. At a time when few people had a television, these high-quality American films were extremely popular and would be attended by over 500 people. On another Sunday evening there was a religious brains trust with a local scientific editor, a Cambridge theologian, a local GP and a university administrator: 'Questions are invited on any aspect of religion—they may be submitted to the pastor in writing up to 6.20 pm.' On another Sunday evening four London policeman came to give their testimony under the title 'These men want to arrest you!'. At one stage over a series of Sunday evenings my father read out to the church the whole of the Book of Ezekiel! He also ran the equivalent of 'Songs of Praise' with people requesting their favourite hymns.

On some summer Sunday evenings the service was held outside on Petersfield (the green alongside the church). Unfortunately that event proved a disaster, in the sense that the church people did not know how to

---

3   Letter from Rev Norman Harris to Dr Raymond Brown dated 10 May 2000.

behave in a natural 'non-churchy' manner. Most of the women, for instance, turned up with hats and gloves, and when it came to finding a seat, everybody sat in the same places as though they were still in church. My parents did not know whether to laugh or cry.

Gradually the congregations increased in size. The giving increased correspondingly. In January 1949 the church treasurer reported to the church meeting that there had been a 50% increase in the weekly offerings. A number of students were attracted to the church as a result of my father's ministry, of whom many were very supportive of his ministry. When, for instance, my mother started a Girls 'Covenanter' Bible class, Alan Charles, an Australian postgraduate student, started a Boys 'Covenanter' Bible class.

The Care of the Flock

As at Ashurst Drive, so too at Zion, my father proposed that 'a communion service be held every Sunday morning as an integral part of the service, except on the third Sunday when it would be held in the evening as at present.'[4] The church warmed to that suggestion.

All this was while he was doing a full-time course at the university. One might well have imagined that the pastoral work of the church was neglected, yet the evidence is that this was not so. One former member looking back recalled that 'George was much appreciated for his pastoral care and visiting—he was never too busy to respond to needs and...had a regular visit to church members'. He was determined not to lay himself open to the charge that he pursued his studies at the expense of his pastoral responsibilities—he confined

---

4 He raised this at his first deacons meeting in March 1948, but it was not discussed 'owing to the lateness of the hour'. He raised it again in April, when it was agreed to support the pastor's suggestion and to take the matter to the May church meeting.

much of his studying to late at night and into the small hours of the morning. True, he also knew the importance of sharing the load. At the deacons meeting in October 1947, when the church was in the process of calling him, it was reported that my father 'would demand a great sacrifice of time and effort from the deacons and all workers in Zion' and asked the deacons 'to take notice of this point before deciding on sending an invitation' to him.

Difficulties

The two years spent at Cambridge were very formative and enjoyable years in which my parents made some strong friendships both among the members of Zion as also among students who attended the church, friendships which lasted over many years.

However, the two years were also difficult years. To begin with there was no Manse available. The church secretary had promised that there would be a house for us by the time of the induction, but in spite of repeated telephone calls from my father, when we as a family arrived in Cambridge there was no house for us to go to. The church Manse had been let to a tenant who could not be persuaded to leave. The upshot was that for the first six months we had to live in dilapidated church rooms above the early nineteenth-century Sunday School hall. There was no bathroom, and at that stage my mother had three children under the age of four. Almost as soon as we arrived, all three children fell ill. True, they only had normal children's complaints like whooping cough and measles, but nonetheless it did not help. Then to cap it all, my father discovered that he had been misled by the University of Cambridge. Prior to the move he had written to Prof. C.H. Dodd to make sure he could be accepted as one of his doctoral students. He had also written to Canon C.E. Raven, then the Regius Professor of Divinity and Vice-Chancellor of the University, and to other academics, to ensure that everything was in order. However, several weeks after arriving in Cambridge my father went to confirm the arrangements he had made, he was told that there had been a dreadful mistake—everyone had overlooked a new rule that debarred anybody in pastoral charge from doing a PhD in Cambridge. This came as a terrible shock to my father. With a heavy heart he registered instead for the two year Part III of the Theological Tripos, which would lead to a Cambridge MA—it was really the last thing he wanted to do. After all, he already had a London MTh. It was only later that he realised how beneficial this further grounding in the New Testament was to be, enabling him eventually to do a doctorate from a very broad basis.

The Part III of the Cambridge Theological Tripos was the equivalent of an MTh degree elsewhere. My father chose the option to specialise in New Testament studies which meant that in his examination papers he had to be able to translate and comment on any passage from the Greek New Testament and write essays on any New Testament theme. My father became a member of Jesus College, a College well-known for producing theologians. The Dean of Jesus at that time was the celebrated Gospel scholar P. Gardner-Smith, who in his supervisions made my father work through a major commentary on each book of the New Testament. In addition to learning Aramaic and Syriac, he also took courses from C.H. Dodd on John's Gospel and on the Christology of the New Testament, and attended the postgraduate New Testament seminar chaired by Dodd.

These Cambridge years had an enormous influence on my father's theological development. There he met theological 'giants', who in turn introduced him to the writings of other theological 'giants'. The influence of these men and their writings is illustrated in a later interview with Alan Culpepper, one of his Louisville colleagues:

What books and teachers were the major influences on Beasley-Murray, and what did they contribute to the shaping of his mind?

(1) C.H. Dodd's influence on Beasley-Murray focused both the subjects to which he devoted his attention and the perspective and method with which he approached the New Testament. Beasley-Murray appreciated especially Dodd's work on the nature of the gospel and its relation to history, his teaching on the Kingdom of God as the present power of God, his Christology, and his work on John. Dodd struggled with the text, writing on the text itself, not quoting other's opinions.

(2) B.F. Westcott, *The Gospel of the Risen Lord*, which related the resurrection of Jesus to the life of man in the cosmos, and his two commentaries.

(3) E.C. Hoskyns, *The Riddle of the New Testament*, which is an example of how the tools of criticism can be used in the service of New Testament theology. His commentary on John showed how a commentary should be theological as well as philological.

(4) Adolf Schlatter, whose influence is evident in the introduction to Beasley-Murray's commentary on John. Schlatter opened his eyes to the importance of the theological implications of the New Testament and the Jewishness of Jesus.

(5) Strack-Billerbeck. Awakening to the Jewishness of Jesus led Beasley-Murray to the use of Strack-Billerbeck's *Kommentar zum Neuen Testament aus Talmud und Midrasch*.

(6) R. Newton Flew influenced Beasley-Murray while Beasley-Murray was at Cambridge. *Jesus and His Church* shows the importance of the church to Jesus. Flew asked him to represent Baptists at a Faith and Order conference. Beasley-Murray declined, however, because he did not think he knew Baptists well enough at that point. Flew, a Methodist, gave George an overview of the Baptist heritage.[5]

---

5   R. Alan Culpepper, 'George R. Beasley-Murray', in Timothy George and David S. Dockery (eds.), *Baptist Theologians* (Broadman Press, Nashville, 1990), 571.

It is interesting to note that of these six influential theologians, four were Cambridge men.

It was a tough time financially. There were times when my parents had to scrape the pennies together to buy even a loaf of bread. The stipend from Zion was more or less the same as that received at Ashurst Drive. However, there was one signal difference: the family was growing! Mercifully in the October of 1948 my father gained the prestigious Dr Williams' scholarship for a period of two years. One church member remembers how 'his very worn shoes sadly showed the state of their finances'. But my father was confident that the Lord who had provided for his needs so far would continue to help him.

If ever my parents doubted God's guidance, it was in those days. They had moved to Cambridge convinced that this was what God wanted them to do. The way in which things had worked out prior to the move all seemed to be an indication that they were going God's way. But now everything seemed to be black. They had no proper home, the children were ill, and the way to do a PhD was blocked. My father was bewildered, he just could not understand why things seemed to have gone so dreadfully wrong. Nevertheless my parents pressed on. At this time the church people were very kind and considerate to them.

Invitation to Spurgeon's College

Then there came a bolt out of the blue. My father had just registered to do a Cambridge MA, when a letter came from Dr Cawley of Spurgeon's College to say that Dr Evans would be retiring in two years time and that he, as the new Principal-elect, hoped that my father would be willing to accept the position of New Testament tutor when it was eventually offered to him.[6] To say that the invitation was a surprise is an understatement. For only a few years previously Dr Cawley had told my father that by engaging in part-time lecturing at the London Bible College he had ruled himself out for doing any future post at Spurgeon's College.

The vision Dr Cawley put before him was ambitious:

As soon as we feel we have the buildings in fit condition, the Library brought up to University and Research standards, application will go forward for University affiliation. That being granted you will become a Professor of the University of London. By that time, of course, other openings in the academic world may have opened up, but I do not think you would be as happy on another staff as in your old College. More than that, by being with us at this time, moving ahead with the plans that are being now hammered into shape, you, in later life, will be able to look back upon such creative work as will have put Spurgeon's College in a position of academic eminence second to no other College in the Baptist Union, while at the same time preserving our distinctive theological witness. I can see that only in vision, for by that time my work will be over, but when that hour comes I shall be grateful to such young men as yourself who will have given reality to such dream. We have the ball at our feet. No other College has such grounds as we have. We are at the centre of London, and therefore the empire... In a word, I envy you in your youth and ardour and forward stretching spirit.[7]

At that point my parents began to see light in the darkness. Had my father registered for a doctorate, that would have occupied him for at least three years. But the MA course was only two years in length and could therefore be finished by the summer of 1950. As my

---

6   It was not, however, until 17 February 1949 that a sub-committee of the council agreed to invite my father to become a New Testament tutor.

7   Letter dated 29 September 1948.

father was later to say, at this point he was taught a tremendous lesson of guidance: 'that God knows our path better than we, and it is wise to reserve judgement on life's twists and turns'.

Nonetheless my father hesitated in accepting Dr Cawley's invitation. Indeed, he kept him waiting a month before he replied to his letter. My father felt it was too soon to go into theological teaching. He had assured his deacons that he hadn't just come to Cambridge to gain a degree and then jump ship in order to do some other work. He enjoyed church work and not least the challenge of helping the village churches of Cambridgeshire. My father felt that whoever was minister of Zion had a particular responsibility for helping these small village churches and he looked forward to getting involved in this particular work after he had completed his studies. But it was not to be. So on 18 September 1949 my father gave notice that he would be resigning from the pastorate in twelve months in order to take up an appointment at Spurgeon's College. The deacons at Zion were very gracious. They saw the hand of God in the college's invitation and so believed it right for him to go.

Chapter 6

Spurgeon's College, London: Tutor (1950–1956)

In the autumn of 1950 my father took up the post of New Testament tutor. However, there was much more attached to this post than simply teaching the New Testament. Because money was so tight in those years after the war, the college faculty at that time was limited in numbers (when my father began there were only two others, Dr Cawley and Eric Worstead), with the result that jobs had to be shared around. The college, for instance, was without a church history tutor, so my father had to teach church history. He was also college librarian at a time when the college library had to undergo radical change.[1] He was secretary of the college 'Conference' of former students, and in this role had the responsibility for organising the annual two-day June conference. These and other jobs too were his, which he gladly fulfilled.

Those first students to whom my father lectured were for the most part mature men—many of them had seen war service and were very strong in their sense of call.

Preaching

To supplement his salary, which in those days was less than the so-called 'minimum' stipend received by ministers in small churches who were on the Home

---

1 'The poverty of the library in theological books and those required for Degree work' was considered so poor by my father that he suggested to a meeting of the College Executive and Finance Committee on 22 February 1952 that the College might 'meet immediate costs by taking two students less'.

Mission Fund, almost every Sunday my father went out preaching, and this normally involved wearing a black jacket and black striped trousers. Although like almost all Baptist ministers at the time my father had worn a clerical collar at Ashurst Drive and Zion, from now on he wore a simple collar and tie (at that time still quite a rare thing for a minister to do).

With all the other demands on his time, it was understandable that my father did not preach new sermons every Sunday. Instead he was happy to preach the same sermon again and again. Needless to say, not to the same congregation. As a college tutor and later as college principal he was an itinerant preacher, sometimes preaching just to 'fill a pulpit', but often preaching at special occasions and in particular at church anniversaries. In preaching the same sermon, he believed that he was being a good steward of the resources God had given him. Like many Spurgeon's men of his time, he filed his sermons in A5 brown-paper envelopes, with the text written on the outside, together with the dates and places of where the sermon had been preached. Some envelopes had but one date and place—but others had many dates and many places. In view of his later writings on the kingdom of God it is perhaps not surprising that one of his most-preached sermons was on Matthew 6.33: 'Seek first the Kingdom'. First prepared for Ashurst Drive in July 1944, it was preached all over England and indeed all over the world some 112 times. Needless to say, it was not always exactly the same sermon. Within the one envelope I found eight different versions!

Along with the envelopes with his sermon notes, there were also envelopes containing outlines of prayers he prayed. Like most Baptist ministers, my father when leading a congregation in prayer did not read prayers from a book. But this did not mean he did not prepare his prayers. Although well able to lead extempore prayers, my father favoured thinking through the direction of his prayers before he prayed. He practised what Puritan divines of an earlier age termed 'conceived' prayers.

It was not until we lived in Switzerland that we had a car, so all my father's travelling was done by public transport. When he was travelling by bus and train he used to take with him *Teach Yourself* books with a view to learning one European language after another. In this way he developed a working knowledge not just of French and German, but also of Danish, Dutch, Italian, Norwegian, Russian and Swedish. All this in turn helped him with his theological studies.[2]

Because we did not have a car, this meant that even if my father was preaching in one of the London churches, unless it was nearby, he was never at home for Sunday lunch and tea. Family life adjusted accordingly: we had our 'Sunday roast' on a Saturday, while on Sunday we had a casserole or some cold meat.

Not infrequently I accompanied my father to his Sunday preaching engagements. As a result I heard him preach much more than my siblings. No doubt like most other children of the Manse at that stage I enjoyed listening to him. Having said that, I do remember one occasion when I felt desperately embarrassed—it was a Sunday evening at Erith and my father grew so passionate in his preaching that I felt that he was shouting away at the congregation. But to be fair, that was the only occasion when I felt embarrassed—apart from many years later when I heard him preaching at a Baptist association rally in Stockport, Cheshire, where he talked of his delight of being in Lancashire! It was through my father's preaching that I committed my life to Christ. I was eight years old at the time. It was on a

---

2   Not all his language work was done on a bus. As a family we were amused when, with a new-found enthusiasm for Danish, he wrote to a Danish Baptist friend to see if he could spend a few days with a family where there were children. They replied to say, 'We can do better than that—we have booked you in for a week at a children's camp!'

Sunday evening, but where we were I do not know. All I can remember was that my father was preaching on the opening words of the Lukan form of the Lord's Prayer, 'Father'. It was not a specifically evangelistic sermon. Nonetheless I sensed that I did not have that intimate relationship with God which Jesus had and that I needed to make some kind of response if I were to know God that way. So when we got home later that evening I knelt down and in a simple childlike way accepted Jesus as my Lord and Saviour. Inevitably, therefore, I owe so very much to my father's preaching.

My brother, Stephen, claims that my father was more of a teacher than a preacher.

> From my point of view, and I think this would be shared by those who admired him most, father's greatest strength was not his preaching..., but his Bible studies... However, when one realises that father's sermons came out of his own Bible studies and work as a textual critic, he really was a master of a style in a class of his own. The trouble was that most of us are not used to hearing such a mind think out loud. Our expectations are low and geared not to the skills of a biblical expert but to showman skills.

On reading my brother's comments my immediate reaction was to ask: 'But what is preaching?' Certainly in the context of a pastorate, where the flock have to be fed Sunday by Sunday, preaching, if it is to survive, must expound the scriptures and in this respect my father, I believe, was an able preacher. This is certainly the memory of those who heard him preach as a pastor. Dr Don Mason, for instance, a long-standing member of Ashurst Drive, Ilford, gave this tribute: 'Although carefully tailored to a lay congregation, his sermons never avoided difficult areas, and were always an inspiration. Walking home one night my wife summarised it so well: 'I do not know how anyone can listen to George and not become a Christian.'[3] Dr Alan Charles, who was an Australian postgraduate member of Zion Baptist Church, wrote: 'George was the most consistently interesting and challenging pastor under whom I have sat. He had the capacity to combine erudition (though it did not obtrude) with clarity of conviction even when dealing with abstruse passages.'[4]

Similar judgements of his preaching have been made by those who heard him preach at the Baptist Assembly and on other special occasions. One of his sermons, on John 1.1-18, entitled 'The Word comes among us', was entered into the North American Fourth Annual 'Best Sermons Competition' and was published as one of the best six evangelistic sermons![5] Inevitably in the letters I have received since his death, accolades have poured in which have highlighted his preaching: 'His preaching was passionate, thoughtful, stimulating and thoroughly Biblical', was how Bernard Green summed it up.

An annual 'Missionary Sermon' was given at the Baptist assembly meetings. Many still remember the sermon he preached at the 1965 Baptist Assembly on 'The Servant of God'. It was an exposition of Isaiah 42.4: 'He will not fail nor be discouraged till he has established true religion in the earth, and the shores and islands wait for his teaching.'[6] This sermon was essentially an exposition of the first so-called 'Servant Song' of Isaiah in which my father reinforced each of the main points of his exposition by using a well-chosen illustration, which will bear repeating.

The first point of the sermon related to the identity of the servant. In drawing attention to the inseparability of

---

3   Don Mason in a tribute in the March 2000 issue of the *Ashurst Drive Church Magazine*.
4   Letter of 23 July 2000.
5   James W. Cox (ed.), *Best Sermons* 4 (Harper, San Francisco, 1991), 3-9.
6   Subsequently published by the Carey Kingsgate Press, London, under the title of *The Servant of God* (1965).

the Servant–Christ and the Servant–People, my father emphasised the need for the whole church to be organised for mission. He commended the practice of Bishop Azariah, the first Indian bishop of the Church of South India, who 'when people in his diocese were confirmed ...made them place their hands on their head and say, 'Woe is me if I do not preach the gospel'.[7]

The second point related to the task of the servant— mission to the world. In this connection my father spoke of the city of Petra in south-east Jordan:

> It is set within an enclave of towering rocks and it looks very much like a bit of scenery for a Walt Disney film. Its buildings were literally carved out of the rock, which is soft and multi-coloured, like the many-hued cliffs of the Isle of Wight. The approach to it is through a long and narrow gorge, and therefore the place was virtually impregnable. The Nabataeans of ancient times settled here. They made an easy living by attacking caravans from their rocky hide-out. Eventually they adopted the easier method of taxing the caravans as they passed by, leaving them unmolested as long as they paid up. There was no reason why this shouldn't have carried on for ever, had it not been for a simple event: the caravans changed their route. Petra was not ruined by an invader. It died because the world passed it by. It stands as a marvel of nature and the ingenuity of man—beautiful, but dead. Let the churches of Christ take warning. Let the Baptists take warning. The risen Lord commanded, *Go* and make disciples. If we coddle ourselves in our hide-outs we shall simply *petrify*, and the Lord will have to look elsewhere for his evangelists.[8]

The third point related to the way of the servant:

> How are the Servant–People to carry out their mission at home and abroad? Not as the loud-mouthed propagandists of this world but by the unspectacular and more costly way

---

7 *Servant of God*, 6.
8 *Servant of God*, 9.

of suffering. Allow me to illustrate. Visitors to the Kremlin in Moscow, after viewing its many churches, are commonly shown two exhibits. One is an enormous bell, the greatest I have ever seen. It was intended to be placed in the bell tower of a church, but it could not be lifted. It transpired that a fire broke out in the building in which the bell was housed and the heat cracked it. So now it stands in the open air, a useless curiosity, the bell that has never been tolled. Nearby stands a cannon, immense and magnificent in appearance. Its cannon balls are so huge, they cannot fire them. An ordinary explosive charge would make them merely plop out of the cannon's mouth. A charge big enough to fire them properly would probably blow the gun to pieces. So there it stands, polished and brassy, the cannon that has never fired a shot, next to the bell that has never rung.

My father went on: 'Contrast these examples of the mania for size and impressiveness, so typical of our age, with the description of the Servant's way...'.[9]

In 1954 my father gave a series of lectures to joint meetings of the London Baptist Preachers' Association and the London Congregational Union Lay Preachers' Association on *Preaching the Gospel from the Gospels*. These lectures were subsequently expanded into a book of the same name, which was published two years later in 1956. The point my father was seeking to make in these lectures was that the life, miracles, teaching and parables of Jesus were all illustrations of the Good News. For example, the group of stories in Mark 1.21-32 are illustrations of the ongoing power of Jesus to save:

One needs little imagination to see how narratives of this kind were used to show what Jesus does for men, and what an impression they must have made when recounted by the eye-witnesses in the first person. 'There he stood in the synagogue, in the grip of an unclean power!', we can imagine Peter saying. 'He shrieked in terror before the holiness of the

---

9   *Servant of God*, 9,10.

Lord. We were breathless as Jesus faced him. He used no magic. He performed no tricks. He gave a command, and the demoniac was free. You should have seen his face and heard his shout when he realised what had happened! He was more than healed, he was a new creature! The crowd was filled with astonishment to witness such an act of power. But our Christ has done that to multitudes, and is doing it still!'[10]

To appreciate the original significance of these lectures it is important to realise that at the time they were given most so-called 'gospel' (or evangelistic) preaching—in evangelical churches at least—was based on the letters of Paul rather than on Jesus. Many of them would have agreed with a preacher of a former generation who had declared: 'While he [Jesus] came to preach the gospel, this chief object in his coming was that there might be a Gospel to preach.'[11] For many the Gospels depicted the model life which one had to live (the *didache*) once one had accepted the Pauline version of the Gospel (the *kerygma*). In such a context *Preaching the Gospel from the Gospels* was a highly significant book which came as an eye-opener to many. What was noticeable too, was the way in which his lightly-carried scholarship was marked by evangelistic passion. Thus after telling of an encounter he had with a Danish traveller who did not share his faith, the book concludes with these words:

God has spoken. The Son has risen. The doors of the Kingdom stand open. The hour of opportunity is present. By parable, by entreaty, by every means of driving home the message, let us persuade people that they enter whilst they may.

---

10 *Preaching the Gospel from the Gospels* (Lutterworth Press, London, 1956), 18-19.

11 R.W. Dale, *The Atonement* (Hodder and Stoughton, London, 1875), 46.

My father's prime contribution to the training of preachers was within the college itself. First as tutor and then later as principal it was his task to comment on sermons preached by students in the weekly sermon class. In this respect one of his former colleagues commented:

> George always felt that the Gospel was such an exciting message, but one morning in sermon class we had listened to a very long and tedious sermon from Mr X. As we walked across to the lecture room where it would be assessed, Stanley Dewhurst [one of the College tutors] in a typical aside to me said 'Old Mrs X, she doesn't half crack on'. But George was much more to the point. Off came the spectacles and he said, 'You've done an absolutely unforgivable thing. You've made the Gospel dull.[12]

Lecturing

There is no doubt that my father was an unusually gifted lecturer. In this respect some reminiscences from Ronald E. Clements, who entered Spurgeon's as a student in September 1951 and later became an eminent Old Testament Professor at King's College, London, are of interest:

> First, came the excellence of the teaching George gave. I came to believe (and still do) that we, at Spurgeon's, had the very best teacher of New Testament who was available anywhere in London at that time... His enthusiasm knew no bounds and his willingness to talk about his own work (without the slightest hint of self-congratulation) and the current topics of interest in New Testament research and publications were immensely valuable... I recall George coming to the classroom with Dodd's *Studies in the Fourth Gospel*, which he had just received, and telling us a little about its contents. There was

---

12   Frank Fitzsimmonds in a tribute given at Spurgeon's College 15 June 2000.

more than a touch of irony that for the next three-years I was in College I needed to read very little of the major New Testament textbooks for the very demanding New Testament syllabus, since everything was all there in George's excellent lectures. I could follow the course of scholarly discussion about the Kingdom of God in the New Testament teaching perfectly well, and with real understanding, since the issues were so well-presented...

The second feature that made George's teaching so helpful to me lay in his ability to combine evangelical fervour with a love of scholarship. The prevalent distrust of scholarship in the Church circles that I had moved into, the frequent, and often acrimonious, criticisms of those who were deemed to be 'unsound', the usually ill-informed attacks on scholars who were believed to have strayed from the path of 'God's truth' had all left a mark on me of uncertainty and anxiety. For all such George was a splendid example of fighting hard for what did matter and rejecting as nonsense the suspicious, and all too often very carping criticisms over issues that did not matter or which could never be resolved. He displayed a balance and integrity which established a real standard of intellectual honesty which I could respect and which I have tried to adhere to ever since.[13]

My father had the gift of relating biblical exegesis to every-day living. This comes out in an anecdote from another former student, but of a later era, who wrote to me:

During my final year at Spurgeon's (1967–68) your father was due to become President of the Baptist Union of Great Britain. He developed some problem with his throat which meant it was difficult for him to speak. This might have threatened his Presidential address on 'Mission'—which, by the way, I consider to have been the real turning-point in denominational life, although it seems to have been obscured by subsequent events. But it was of greater significance to us,

13 R.E. Clements in a private letter dated 3 August 2000.

as students, that we were preparing for finals with his lectures on 'Romans' far from complete. He tried tape-recording them, and we crouched around the machine listening to the hoarsely-whispered exegeses... I remember in particular a lecture given thus on Romans 8 which covered verse 28. He supported the RSV text: 'In everything God works for good...' rather than 'All things work together for good...' I remember the emphasis with which he affirmed, 'Things don't work, God works'. As you know, the textual criticism is debated, and the NRSV returns to the alternative, but I think the theology is beyond dispute. I treasure it all the more because...it was in the afternoon following that lecture that he went for a biopsy and was in due course found to be free from cancer.[14]

My brother Stephen, who gained a PhD in the philosophy of religion and became an academic in his own right, had an opportunity of taking a course with my father many years later in Louisville. Of that experience he writes:

His lecturing was in many respects [a series of] Bible studies. It is awesome to liberal and conservative alike to listen to someone not just lead a Bible study from a Greek text, but to be aware of all the different translations and possibilities of translation; and then on top of that to give almost every conceivable interpretation regardless of how zany one might think them to be. Father did not just list them but gave reasons for their cogency, and of course he let his listeners know why he preferred one interpretation to another. He did this with an enthusiasm and animation and at times with humour that kept one's attention. His meticulousness, up-to-dateness, and fairness to both opinions and questioners, meant that he made his audience feel educated just by listening to him. In other words, Father was a true professional. Put in evangelical terms, he could 'out-Bible' anyone. No

---

14   Rev Patrick Baker in a private letter dated 30 March 2001.

fundamentalist had anywhere as good a grasp of the text of the entire Bible. No liberal knew as many alternative interpretations or be as competent as he was in intellectual skills relating to Biblical interpretation. For the ordinary person it was a 'wow' experience, a pleasure just to hear a master of the art, a person who had both integrity and personal skills.

Eschatology

My father had long been interested in the Christian doctrine of the 'last things'. From student days he had on his desk a framed text bearing the words, 'His coming is as certain as the dawn'. His interest had first been stimulated as a student at Spurgeon's College by my mother's father, John Weston, who was often to be found on the platforms of meetings sponsored by the 'Advent Testimony and Preparation Movement'.[15] My father's own study of the scriptures quickly led him away from the kind of biblical interpretation which identified the 'signs of the times' with current events. Needless to say, this divergence of views brought about many an interesting conversation on the message of Daniel, Ezekiel and Revelation—let alone the teachings of Jesus!

It was as a result of my father's interest in apocalyptic literature that he was invited to contribute an article on 'The Apocryphal and Apocalyptic Literature' together with short commentaries on Ezekiel and Revelation for *The New Bible Commentary*.[16] Two things are worthy

---

[15]   The 'Advent Testimony and Preparation Movement' promoted the dispensationalism of J.N. Darby. Founded in 1917 it came into being at the time of the Balfour declaration announcing British support for the return of the Jews to Palestine. See D.W. Bebbington, *Evangelicalism in Modern Britain: A History from the 1730s to the 1980s* (Unwin Hyman, London, 1989), 191-194.

[16]   F. Davidson (ed.), *The New Bible Commentary* (Inter-Varsity Fellowship, London, 1953).

of note. Firstly, apart from Leon Morris who wrote on 'The Letters of John', my father was the only contributor whose work survived not only the second but also the third edition of this *New Bible Commentary*, though it was thoroughly revised. The work of other evangelical scholars had come and gone, but my father's commentary on the Book of Revelation in particular was deemed to stand the test of time. The second matter is that as a combined result of my father and all his fellow contributors giving their services without remuneration, all the profits derived from sales the *New Bible Commentary* were used to give financial viability to what eventually became the Inter-Varsity Press (IVP).

My father's area of research for his London doctorate was 'The eschatological discourse of Mark 13: Its origin and significance'. His supervisor was Professor R.V.G. Tasker of King's College, London, who had earlier supervised his MTh. The same day my brother Andrew was born (24 July 1952) he heard that his thesis had been accepted. It was a quite amazing feat, since although officially a part-time student he had managed to gain his doctorate within two years.[17] It was a day of double rejoicing.

In 1954 his thesis was published under the title of *Jesus and the Future*.[18] In this book he surveyed the interpretation of Mark 13 from Colani's promulgation of the 'little apocalypse' theory in 1864 right up until 1950, and then followed it with his own interpretation of the chapter in the light of its relation to other writings within and outside the New Testament. In his introduction my father set out the embarrassment it caused to scholars and preachers alike.

---

[17] The degree was officially conferred on him on 22 September 1952.

[18] *Jesus and the Future: An Examination of the Criticism of the Eschatological Discourse, Mark 13, with Special Reference to the Little Apocalypse Theory* (Macmillan, London, 1954, reprinted 1956).

'Mark 13 is the biggest problem in the Gospel'. So begins A.M. Hunter's discussion of this chapter. Anyone who has wrestled with its difficulties will agree with that verdict; it is borne out by the multitudinous solutions of the problems and the prevailing confusion in its exegesis. Embarrassment is experienced in all schools of thought in using it. Modern theologians largely feel compelled to ignore the discourse in their reconstructions of the teaching of Jesus. Preachers are aware of the predicament of the scholars; feeling incapable of solving the problems themselves, they neglect the material in their preaching. I cannot recall ever hearing a sermon preached on any verse of Mark 13. For practical purposes, the Synoptic Gospels are read without Mark 13, Matthew 24 and Luke 21; their omission from the New Testament would make little difference to the teacher and the preacher.[19]

Strangely enough, as a child I suffered similar embarrassment. I well remember hearing so much about Mark 13 that I looked the passage up in a Bible— and was so appalled by the chapter my father had chosen to study and to write about, that I never dared breathe a word of it to my friends!

Mark 13, then, was a challenge to any budding scholar—and not least to a budding scholar from the evangelical wing of the church. One of the most difficult of verses in that chapter is Mark 13.30: 'Truly I tell you, this generation will not pass away until all these things have taken place.' Of this verse my father wrote: 'In no section of our study is courageous thinking more required than in this.'[20] After weighing all the options he took courage in his hands and argued that Jesus was referring to 'a speedy coming of the End'. He went on: 'Undoubtedly the immediate sense of the saying defines the limits of Jesus' knowledge of the time of the end: it does not say that he knows nothing at all as to its coming; it affirms that it does not lie in his

---

19   *Jesus and the Future*, ix.
20   *Jesus and the Future*, 186.

power to define it more closely.'[21] 'We believe...that his conviction of the nearness of the victory was due to the clarity of that vision in his soul.'[22] Not surprisingly such exegesis caused consternation amongst many evangelicals.

Some years later F.F. Bruce, then the Rylands Professor of Biblical Criticism and Exegesis at the University of Manchester, reflected on the impact it made on evangelicals at that time:

> His claiming of the discourse as a whole for Jesus constituted a challenge to much prevalent opinion. Readers of more conservative outlook naturally welcomed this part of his thesis, but when they realised what this involved (in his judgement) for the exegesis of the reference to 'this generation' in Mark 13.30 some found themselves wishing that he had *not* claimed the discourse so cogently for Jesus. He dealt trenchantly with those expositors who, realising that the words of Jesus bore the natural meaning that the Parousia would take place within a generation, shrank back from the implications of that meaning for Jesus' power of foresight and explained the words as meaning something less than that. This, he said, amounted to trying to eat one's cake and have it. The Christological problems would be eased, he pointed out, if they were viewed in the light (a) of our Lord's plain statement that even the Son did not know of that day and hour (Mark 13.32) and (b) of the undoubted fact that the expectation of the final triumph of God within a relatively short period characterise the whole course of biblical prophecy.[23]

At the time my father did, indeed, come under a good deal of attack from fellow evangelicals for pointing out that Jesus was mistaken with regard to the exact timing of the Parousia. Alan Stibbs, the Vice-

---

21   *Jesus and the Future*, 189.
22   *Jesus and the Future*, 190.
23   F.F. Bruce, 'Biblical Scholar', *Spurgeon's College Record* 53 (December 1997), 8.

Principal of Oak Hill College, an evangelical Anglican theological college in North London, wrote:

> In the judgement of this reviewer, Dr Beasley-Murray would have been a wiser man to recognise that his own enthusiasm as a research student, to arrive here and now in this publication at some definite critical findings, may have unduly limited his own perspective. Instead of questioning our Lord's omniscience he might rather have himself disowned such an attribute (even on this subject on which he knows so much) and have frankly admitted that this is a problem the full answer to which he does not know. He says he has capitulated to facts. That is not true; he has rather been compelled by the evidence as he thinks it must be interpreted; and his preferences here may themselves be mistaken...
>
> Such a study makes the Christian believer conscious that unless we can believe simply and unquestionably in the infallibility of both our Lord's utterances and of the divinely inspired written word of revelation, the only alternative is to be launched into a stormy sea of restless uncertainty, where Dr Beasley-Murray's preference is only one voice among a welter of conflicting opinions.[24]

Three years later my father published his related *Commentary on Mark XIII*.[25] This time he set out not to please university examiners but rather to help preachers. Writing to thank his old friend Jack Brown for doing the indices, he said, 'There's a whacking great crown waiting for you in heaven. You'd better buy a bowler and get used to wearing it!'. He went on: 'A production like this will probably be considered by them [i.e. the theological faculty and students at Rüschlikon] the last word in obscurantism, while the IVF will swear to make the angels blush. What I would like to know would be whether a thoughtful preacher will find this

24 *The English Churchman*, 30 April 1954.
25 *A Commentary on Mark XIII* (Macmillan, London, 1957).

commentary a help to use the chapter in preaching or whether it will make him feel he can't use it any more!'[26] The *Commentary on Mark XIII* was certainly much more accessible to ordinary ministers. By contrast *Jesus and the Future* was hard-going, and not surprisingly so, because it was essentially a doctoral thesis.

My father was partially right with regard to the IVF. A.F. Walls, for instance, in his influential *A Guide to Christian Reading* published by IVP, judged my father's *Commentary on Mark XIII* in these terms: 'Close and learned criticism, with conservative conclusions, of a crucial passage: less satisfactory Christologically.' [27] On the other hand, F.F. Bruce, writing from a scholarly evangelical perspective, was very positive. Writing in the evangelical weekly, *Life of Faith*, he ended his review in this way: 'This is a work of scholarship, but it is also a work of truly *evangelical* scholarship; this appears pre-eminently on the last page in the pointed and practical application of Mark 13.37: "And I say unto you, I say unto all: Watch!"'.[28] More 'liberal' scholars were equally positive. The Methodist Vincent Taylor, although disagreeing on a number of points, ends his review with the words: 'We are only too grateful to Dr Beasley-Murray who bids us on many points to think again.'[29]

But my father was not awed by what others might think. He was concerned for what he deemed to be the truth. F.F. Bruce commented that it was because 'young men like George Beasley-Murray were willing to risk their reputation for conventional orthodoxy by saying what they believed' that there has become increasing openness within the world of evangelical scholarship.[30]

---

[26] Letter dated 26 February 1957.

[27] A.F. Walls, *A Guide To Christian Reading* (IVP, London, revised 2nd edition, 1961), 65.

[28] *Life of Faith*, 21 November 1957.

[29] *Expository Times* 69 (November 1957), 38-39.

[30] 'Biblical Scholar', 8.

Similar thoughts were expressed by Tom Houston, a former Director of the Bible Society and a leading figure in the Lausanne Movement: 'Your father's stand on that issue helped me to see that the stand of an Evangelical with regard to Scripture does have to be open to differing hermeneutics of the Scripture Text.'[31]

Evangelism and Billy Graham

My father, with his passion for evangelism, was a strong supporter of Billy Graham. He heard the American evangelist on his first visit to London in 1947 with Youth for Christ, and from then on was always ready to identify himself with Billy Graham's crusades. In 1966, for instance, night after night he was on the platform at Earls Court—he felt very strongly that it was incumbent upon him as a Baptist leader to show support for Billy Graham. I vividly remember him taking me to London's Harringay Arena in 1954—as a child I was puzzled by Beverly Shea, the American soloist at every Billy Graham meeting, who seemed to me to sing 'I would rather have "cheese" than silver or gold'! As a teenager in 1966 I was puzzled again—this time not by Shea's singing, but by my father's support for a preacher whose approach to preaching was very different from his own. My father, however, was convinced that Billy Graham was a very special servant of the Lord and was not prepared to put the mass conversions down to manipulation or to hysteria. This was God at work. As proof of this he would cite the large number of Spurgeon's students who were either converted through Billy Graham or received their call to ministry through attending one of the Billy Graham meetings. I shall never forget one occasion going with my father to Wembley stadium for an afternoon Billy Graham rally and seeing my father silently weeping as hundreds of people flocked forward in response to the

---

31   Private letter of 6 July 2000.

appeal. In response to my asking what was wrong, my father said he just felt overwhelmed seeing God at work in the lives of so many—and felt that by comparison all his evangelistic efforts in the past had been as nothing.

If there is one hymn associated with Billy Graham's crusades it is surely 'Blessed assurance, Jesus is mine'. Toward the end of my father's period as college tutor, he was a member of the 'Words' committee of a new hymn book to take the place of the *Baptist Church Hymnal* (revised in 1933). Some members of the editorial committee were far from enamoured with Billy Graham with the result that when considering the hymn 'Blessed assurance' they argued that it should be kept out of the new hymn book on the ground that its words were pure doggerel. My father accepted that the poetry of Frances van Alstyne was not the greatest, but maintained that in view of its associations with the Billy Graham crusades, the hymn just had to be included. His argument won the day. As a result 'Blessed Assurance' was included not only in the *Baptist Hymn Book* (1962), but also in its successor, *Baptist Praise and Worship* (1991).

The Principalship

The same day my father was inducted to the position of college tutor, Dr Cawley was installed as college principal.[32] He was then sixty-five years old and so in the natural order of things due to retire. Dr Cawley's tenure as Principal was inevitably short. Speculation began to emerge as to who his successor might be. Eric Worstead, a capable man with an attractive personality, had joined the college faculty at the end of the war and was senior to the other members of staff. On the other hand, my father was better qualified academically. To dispel doubts and rumours the college council made an an-

---

[32] The service took place at Bloomsbury Central Baptist Church, London, on Wednesday 27 September 1950.

nouncement on Friday 19 March 1954 that Eric Worstead would take over in September 1955. My father felt very strongly at the time that his and Eric's sympathies were so different that he would look for another opening.

My father would not have been human if he had not felt a tinge of disappointment at the council's decision. It was at this time that Fred King, then one of the last students alive to have been accepted into the college by Spurgeon himself, painted for my father a beautifully illuminated text, which read: 'God has a greater task for you than you have yet undertaken'. For many years this text hung in my father's study as a constant reminder that there was always yet more for him to do in the service of the kingdom. It was only toward the end of his life in June 1991, when those tasks were completed, that he passed the text on to me.

New Openings

In 1955 the Baptist World Alliance (BWA) marked their Golden Jubilee by holding a congress in London's Royal Albert Hall. This was a major event—not least for Spurgeon's, which, as London's Baptist college, was visited by many of the overseas delegates. The Russian delegation, for instance, stayed at the college. One of the major headaches in planning the congress proved to be the music. Many choirs were due to come from overseas, not least from the USA, and many of their choir leaders expressed the wish to direct the singing of the congress as a whole. The organising committee were uncertain what to do. In the end they invited my father to conduct the singing. The decisive factor was perhaps the fact that my father had only a few months previously conducted very successfully the singing at the annual Swanwick conference of the Baptist Men's Movement. Although my father's duties at the congress were time-consuming—he had to be present at every major meeting—he nonetheless loved it. He used to remember with amusement the occasion when the heat was such that he did the 'unthinkable' and removed his jacket to conduct. This proved to be an act of faith—for like everybody else at that time he used braces to support his trousers, he had no belt to keep his trousers up—fortunately his prayers were answered and his trousers held up.

My father had already been involved in BWA circles before 1955. He had represented the Baptist Union of Great Britain at the BWA Council meetings in Copenhagen in July 1952, when, amongst others, he had met Dr Duke McCall, who was eventually to become President of the Southern Baptist Theological Seminary in Louisville. At the Golden Jubilee my father renewed friendships made in Copenhagen and became known more generally to the wider Baptist family. As a result he was taken to one side by Dr Arnold Ohrn, the General Secretary of the BWA, and asked if he would be willing to be nominated as the next Associate Secretary of the BWA with special responsibility for Europe. My father was quite bewildered and uncertain, not least because he realised that such a position could be the end of his academic work. However, before anything was settled Dr Joseph Nordenhaug, the President of the Baptist Theological Seminary in Rüschlikon, Zurich, Switzerland, wrote on 16 February 1956 to see if there would be 'any possibility of us getting together one day for a chat' in London the following week. The upshot was that my father was offered a teaching position in Rüschlikon, which in due course he accepted.

It was only later that my father learnt that Dr Nordenhaug knew that the BWA officers were intending to have their invitation to my father ratified at the next meeting of the BWA Executive in the USA and for that reason got in quickly before a formal offer was made by the BWA. Dr Ohrn was very cross with Nordenhaug. My father, however, was in ignorance of all this. As he later made clear, had he appreciated the seriousness of the BWA approach, he might have declined the offer from Rüschlikon and accepted the BWA invitation.[33] Indeed, Dr Ohrn came back to my father again in April 1957 to ask him to allow him to be nominated for the BWA post, but by that time he had been at Rüschlikon for twelve months and he had no desire to leave.

Ironically, just before my father had accepted the Rüschlikon post, relationships dramatically improved with the Worsteads. Thanks to the generosity of some friends, Eric and Joy were given the opportunity to take a break at Caux, the Swiss centre of the Moral Re-Armament Movement (MRA).[34] At the time when they accepted the offer, they thought they were simply going for a holiday, but it proved to be more than that. In the words of Joy Worstead, 'it was a sort of rebirth, an empowerment of the Holy Spirit'. On their return to Britain their first thought was to try and restore relationships. They invited my parents to their flat to tell them what had transpired at Caux and to apologise

---

[33]   All this is recorded in a letter to Dr Cawley dated 1 April 1963.

[34]   The MRA began as an evangelical renewal movement in the early 1920s under the leadership of Frank Buchman, an American Lutheran minister whose life had been revolutionised as a result of attending the Keswick Convention in 1908. Initially entitled the 'First Century Christian Fellowship', the movement became known as the 'Oxford Group' as a result of its impact on hundreds of Oxford undergraduates, before being renamed in 1938 as 'Moral Re-Armament'. MRA sought to promote 'life change' in individuals through 'surrender' to God. It emphasised four ethical absolutes: honesty, purity, unselfishness and love. Adherents were expected to spend 'quiet times' in which divine 'guidance' was to be expected in the form of 'luminous thoughts'. Although over the years it lost its specifically evangelical roots, nonetheless it attracted many Christians: in the 1960s one notable episcopal supporter of MRA was Cuthbert Bardsley, Bishop of Coventry. For an evangelical critique see Bebbington, *Evangelicalism in Modern Britain*, 235-240.

for the past. It was then that my father told them that he had decided not to work under Eric and had made plans to leave at the end of the academic year to take up a post at Rüschlikon. He went on to say that in the light of their conversation he now regretted that decision and would willingly have stayed on had it been possible. The upshot was that my father was able to leave for Switzerland with relationships restored and confident that the college was in good hands under Eric's leadership. In a subsequent letter written to Eric from Switzerland my father wrote: 'It is a matter for deep thankfulness to me, as I know it is to you, that we have come to a better understanding of each other than we ever had before and a better appreciation of each other.'

Chapter 7

Rüschlikon: Professor of Greek and New Testament Interpretation (1956–1958)

Rüschlikon

Rüschlikon is a beautiful little Swiss village nestling between hills on one side and Lake Zurich on the other. The village is so insignificant that it does not feature on most maps of Switzerland. It is sandwiched between the town of Thalwil, an important railway junction and the larger village of Kilchberg, where the world-famous Lindt chocolate is made. When the wind is in the right direction one can often smell the chocolate in Rüschlikon! At the time we lived in Rüschlikon it was said to be the wealthiest village in the whole of Switzerland, since it was there that the multi-millionaire Herr Tuttweiler, the founder of the Migros supermarket chain, had his residence. But the wealth of the village did not stop one of the local farmers having his dung-heap almost in the centre of the village. Today a good number of significant businesses have moved out to Rüschlikon, but in the 1950s people normally travelled in to the nearby city of Zurich for work—either by bus or by train or even by boat.

The Seminary

Rüschlikon was the place chosen in 1948 as the site for a new International Baptist Theological Seminary. The seminary was essentially a gift of the Southern Baptist Convention to post-war European Baptists. Situated in 'neutral' Switzerland, the hope was that students could come to it from all over Europe, from East and West, as also from North and South. And come they did. There

were students from the Scandinavian countries of
Denmark, Norway and Sweden; students from the
Latin countries of France and Italy, Portugal and Spain;
students from the German-speaking countries of
Austria, Switzerland and Germany itself; and students
from the East from countries such as Czechoslovakia
and Hungary, Poland and Romania. In the early days
there were no students from the USSR, with only an
occasional student from Britain. At the time of my
father's appointment, the faculty was mainly composed
of Southern Baptists: 'Jo' Nordenhaug, the founding
president, who was of Norwegian origin; J.D. Hughey
from South Carolina, who later became seminary
President and then the Director of the Foreign Mission
Board itself; John Allen Moore from Texas, who had an
unparalleled knowledge of Baptist life in Eastern
Europe; John D. Watts who later became the third
seminary president and developed into an Old Testament scholar of some standing. The only Europeans at
that time were Claus Meister, a Swiss classicist, Arthur
Crabtree, an English theologian who later moved to
Eastern Baptist Theological Seminary in Philadelphia,
and my father.

My father entered wholeheartedly into the life of the
Rüschlikon community and was soon at home in this
international setting. To him it was a great privilege to
teach students from so many countries. Precisely
because the seminary was a veritable melting-pot of
nations, it was not surprising that from time to time it
became a place of considerable cultural tension. Partly
because he was English (and so able to be a bridge
between North America and continental Europe) and
partly because of the kind of man he was, my father
often helped defuse situations. It is no exaggeration to
say that his presence on the staff was much appreciated.
In the words of his former colleague, John Watts: 'He
had such a unique blend of excellent scholarship, deep

evangelical piety, and Baptist commitment, that he was a great role model for all the students and faculty.'[1]

The main seminary building had originally been a family home on the hill overlooking the village of Rüschlikon. It was a beautiful place. The facilities of the seminary were outstanding. In addition to all the usual facilities, there were purpose-built married quarters and comfortable accommodation for single students. As for the seminary library, it was quite easily the best Baptist theological library in Europe: the Southern Baptists ensured that money was no object when it came to buying books. In many ways it was an idyllic place to study—and to teach.

The 'lingua franca' at the seminary was English. All the lectures given were in English. It was an English-speaking island in the middle of a German-speaking canton. Unlike many of the students in the seminary, my father moved beyond the bounds of this English-speaking community, not least because we lived in an apartment in the village and so inevitably mixed with Swiss people. My father already knew 'theological German', but Rüschlikon gave him an opportunity to improve his German. Not surprisingly he was also keen to preach in German. Because in Switzerland itself there were few Baptist churches, he often went to preach in Baptist churches in Southern Germany, sometimes with the family, sometimes with students.

The two years spent in Switzerland proved very profitable to my father. He was able to hear such theological giants as Karl Barth, Emil Brunner and Oscar Cullmann lecture. It was at this time that he first met Eduard Schweizer, another outstanding Swiss New Testament scholar, and there developed a friendship which was to last many years. Indeed, of all the Christmas letters my parents used to receive, probably the one to which they most looked forward was that from Eduard Schweizer and his wife Elisabeth—for in

---

[1]　Letter dated 8 June 2000.

contrast to most other such letters, their reflective letter was always marked by spiritual insight. More than twenty years later, reflecting on their friendship at that time, Eduard Schweizer wrote:

> I think back to the time when we met over in Zurich. I came from R. Bultmann, E. Brunner and K. Barth; you came out of a very different tradition. We certainly did not, and do not, agree in everything. And yet, I always felt—and do so even more today—how much we are basically one. We are—and I think this includes also our respective spouses—very seriously concerned about the meaning of all our research and teaching for the real life of the church...
>
> How grateful should we be for that gift of God that he let us do our work in a period in which New Testament scholarship could—and who even expected to—focus on the very centre of faith. What we achieved, and what we shall achieve, was, is and will be fragmentary, but it is, with you as well as—I hope—with me, done somewhere in the centre of the message that the New Testament wants to convey to us. Therefore, shall we not praise our Lord, full of joy and gratitude?[2]

It was during these Rüschlikon years that my father was able to develop a relationship with some of the leaders of the Southern Baptist Convention. Long-lasting friendships too were formed with his American colleagues, friendships which were renewed at a later stage when my father was at Louisville, and again when my father was teaching alongside John Watts and John Kiwiet in Prague. And, of course, it was during these two years that my father was able to begin to make contacts with Baptists from all over the continent of Europe.

---

2   Letter dated 18 April 1980.

Life in Switzerland

As a family we thoroughly enjoyed our experience of living in Switzerland. True, there was the challenge of learning 'High German' as also of understanding the local Swiss-German dialect. All of us children were placed immediately in German-speaking schools and not surprisingly took a little while to adjust. But adjust we did, and loved it.

We also had the challenge of sitting through the Sunday morning services at Salemskapelle, the main Baptist church in Zurich, just a stone's throw away from the River Limmat, where in the sixteenth century Ulrich Zwingli, the great Swiss reformer, had drowned hundreds of Anabaptists. It was there in Salemskapelle that I was baptised at the age of thirteen—with my father being responsible for my baptismal instruction (I confess at the time I did not completely follow his exegesis of Romans 6!).

As far as I was concerned, family life changed for the better. Not only did my father seem to have much more time for us children, it was also at this time that he bought his first car. As a result we were able to make the most of the new opportunities that were ours. Every Saturday we went out as a family—in the winter we used to ski and in the summer we used to swim and walk. What is more, as a result of living on the continent some of the 'shibboleths' of British evangelical life were put to one side. Instead of attending church morning, noon and night on a Sunday, Sunday became a day to be enjoyed by us as a family. I shall never forget our surprise as children when we discovered one Sunday afternoon that we were not going for our usual Sunday afternoon drive to the deer park, but rather were en route for a family holiday in Italy. On a Sunday? Up until then it had been unthinkable. Why, in previous family holidays in Britain, Sunday had been treated as a day when one had to be dressed up in one's Sunday best—even if the sun was beating down, we were not allowed to go down to the beach, and certainly not allowed to swim. Switzerland, however, brought to us all a new freedom and a new happiness.

Baptism

Rüschlikon, with its more leisured lifestyle and its wonderful library, offered my father opportunities for further study.

He began to do more work in preparation for his projected book on the kingdom of God. But then a letter arrived from the Baptist Union asking him if he would write a book on baptism. The letter said that all the other denominations were writing and producing work on baptism, but not the Baptists. Father, however, felt this was not his field and therefore declined the invitation. He wanted to push on with his own work on the kingdom of God. But a week or two later another letter arrived asking him to reconsider their request to write on baptism in the light of the desperate dearth of material from a Baptist perspective. So he put away his notes in order to begin the work.

To be fair, my father was not a total stranger to the baptismal debate. Toward the beginning of his ministry at Zion, he had written an article on the 'sacraments' in which he had opposed an earlier article by L.A. Read on the 'ordinances'. The very use of the term 'sacraments' proved to be significant and was in fact a foretaste of things to come. Without denying the confessional nature of baptism, he argued that this was a secondary, not primary, aspect of baptism, for 'In every explicit mention of Baptism it is regarded as the supreme moment of our union with Christ in the redemptive acts for us and our consequent reception of the life of the Spirit.'[3]

---

3   'The Sacraments', *The Fraternal* 70 (1948), 3. See L.A. Read, 'The Ordinances', *The Fraternal* 67 (1948), 8-10.

Later as a tutor at Spurgeon's my father had returned to the baptismal debate with another article in which he challenged every one of the arguments put forward by the Church of Scotland in its first interim report on baptism. He concluded: 'Our denomination has much to learn of the theology of Baptism from our Scottish brethren. It is to our shame that they have so little to learn from us. Yet that little is crucial: *To die and rise with Christ, and therefore to be baptised, is the prerogative of him who confesses, 'Jesus is Lord' — of him and of no other; for the Baptism wherein God acts is the Baptism wherein man confesses.'* [4]

Furthermore, before he had left England he had already agreed to write on 'Baptism in the Letters of Paul' for the collection of essays to be edited by Alec Gilmore, entitled *Christian Baptism*.[5] This in itself entailed a good deal of scholarly research. But so much more was demanded if my father was to do justice to the request to write a significant work on baptism. It was with a real sense of reluctance that my father devoted himself to the task. God's timing, however, was right. Had the invitation from the Baptist Union come a year or so later, it is doubtful whether my father would ever been able to find the necessary time for the research required. As it was, at that stage my father was relatively unencumbered with administrative and denomination-al responsibilities and so was more free to rise to the challenge. Even so, considerable dedication was re-quired on his part. It was only by dint of long hours of studying that the spade-work was done. The work on baptism would never have been completed if he had worked 'normal' hours. One of my abiding memories is that after having come home for an early

---

[4]   'The Church of Scotland and Baptism', *The Fraternal* 99 (1956), 10.

[5]   *Christian Baptism: A Fresh Attempt to Understand the Rite in Terms of Scripture, History, and Theology* (Lutterworth Press, London, 1959).

evening meal, my father would then regularly return to his study in the seminary, where he would then burn the midnight oil as he laboured over his books.

Trouble at Spurgeon's

At about this time difficulties arose at Spurgeon's College. The principal, Eric Worstead, who had been so profoundly helped by the MRA, was anxious that others should know of this work and somewhat unwisely lent his support to a full-page advertisement in the *Baptist Times* of 6 June 1957 commending the MRA. At the time neither Eric Worstead nor his wife Joy realised the effect Eric's public support of the MRA would have on the college council. Some of the ministers on the college council immediately demanded his resignation.[6] They believed that the MRA was not gospel-centred and that the principal's endorsement of the movement represented—or could appear to represent—a departure from the historic Christian faith. The Rev W.H. Tebbitt, the council chairman, accused him of heresy. A number of emergency meetings were held to resolve the matter. The MRA ideals of 'absolute love', 'absolute honesty' and 'absolute purity' were greatly lacking among some of the more 'orthodox' brethren. In the words of Stanley Dewhurst, a tutor at the college, it was all 'an unholy mess'.[7] Matters came to a head at the beginning of the September term 1957, when Eric Worstead found himself in an untenable position and on 2 September he resigned immediately. The college was thrown into turmoil. The future for the college looked dire.

It was in these circumstances that the college council chairman, Charles Johnson, and college treasurer, William Booth, flew over to Zurich on an 'exploratory'

---

6   Rev Geoffrey King raised the matter at the April meeting of the council and was supported by Rev Theo Bamber.
7   In a letter to my father dated 13 July 1957.

visit to see if my father would be willing to return to England and take over the principalship. Subsequently the college council on 13 December 1957 passed a resolution unanimously inviting my father to become principal of the college 'to commence duty on a day convenient to all parties'.

Father's first thoughts were to say 'No way. I can't start a new job at Spurgeon's and write a major book on baptism. It is out of the question.' Furthermore, my father was very happy in Rüschlikon. As far as he was concerned, he was there for the long-term and he would gladly have stayed there for the rest of his life. However, gradually he changed his mind. The chief factor in causing him to do so were the letters he received from ministers—a number of 'round robins' signed by pastors were sent to him asking him to come back. My father was moved by these letters which came from men, many of whom were going through a tough time. He felt uneasy enjoying the relative ease of life in Switzerland compared to the situations which ministers as a whole faced in Britain. My father almost became ill as he wrestled with the invitation.[8] In the end he felt that he must go back—it was his duty—and so he agreed to return.

Significantly, before he accepted my father got in touch with Eric Worstead, who by then had become the part-time minister of a small Baptist church near Sevenoaks, to say that he would only accept the invitation if Eric approved. Furthermore, should he do so, he would like to think that he would be around if he needed to consult him. Eric replied that he could think of no one else in the denomination who could take over the reins and gave him his blessing.

The faculty at Rüschlikon, as also the Southern Baptist Convention, were very gracious to him. Strictly

---

8   In a letter to Frank Fitzsimmonds dated 2 December 1957 he spoke of his predominating mood being 'one of gloom rather than of joy'.

speaking he was breaking his contract. However, they realised the extraordinary nature of the situation and released him from his promise to stay a minimum of five years.

Among the many messages of congratulation which poured in, there was a letter from Douglas Johnson, the General Secretary of the Inter-Varsity Fellowship, who in earlier days had encouraged my father to think of becoming a scholar:

> I do hope that it will be your honour to install into the evangelical elements of the Baptist denomination a combination of true evangelicalism at the basic points with a scholarly approach at the right and proper time. Unfortunately, for too long, there has been a divorce between the Evangelicals whose hearts are all too good, but their heads not quite so strong; and whose heads are all too strong and do not seem to have a heart! Let us hope that you can recapture something of the great tradition of Spurgeon along with the true scholarship in these changed times.[9]

---

9   Letter dated 17 January 1958.

Chapter 8

Spurgeon's College: Principal
(1958–1973)

Difficulties

So at the end of April 1958 back to England we returned. Although my mother was delighted to be near to her parents and the wider family, the move back was not easy. It was certainly difficult for us children. We had already suffered the disruption of being taken out of English schools and being put into Swiss schools, where not only was the language different, but the curriculum was also very different. Now we had to suffer the further disruption of returning to English schools. In my own case, for instance, this involved going back to my old school, but having to be put down a year because from my school's point of view I had done very little in the intervening two years. The result was that school from thereon was a struggle for me.

Our domestic arrangements were not the easiest. Instead of living in the large house we had previously lived when my father was a tutor, we now lived in the principal's first-floor flat within the main college building itself. The flat was fairly small and had to be extended to accommodate the family. There was little privacy. To gain entrance we had to walk up the main college stairs in full sight of everybody. None of us liked that—not least my sister, who at the age of twelve understandably hated having to walk through a college full of men. The flat had no kitchen. Previous principals had always had their meals sent up on trays from the college kitchen. Because there were six of us, we found ourselves having to have all our meals with the students—which was a far from ideal situation. But after a year college turned what had been a broom cupboard into a small kitchen. My father's study had a beautiful view of the college grounds, but it was not at all soundproof—its door opened immediately into the main hall of the college. Fortunately my father had the gift of being able to work in spite of student laughter and music coming from the Junior Common Room downstairs.

Relationships in the college were not the easiest. Division, anger and guilt abounded as a result of Eric Worstead's departure. Not all the members of the faculty were happy with my father's appointment, neither was the college matron happy either—it is clear that some had hoped for an internal appointment and had made plans accordingly. It did not help that on my father's return the college council gave no recognition to the faculty for their role in keeping the college going at a time of particular stress. Furthermore, some of the students were also hostile to my father and to the college council—in part because there were those who felt that Eric Worstead had been treated unfairly. Sadly, Eric Worstead, who died in 1998, could never rid himself of the repeated nightmares of the situation he went through in 1957. Years later, Dr Raymond Brown, when Principal of Spurgeon's College, invited Eric Worstead back to the college to show a belated appreciation for all he had done for the college as tutor and then in his short time as principal.

Life back at Spurgeon's was all so very different from Rüschlikon. Certainly from my point of view, it was a much more constricting life. Rüschlikon had opened up a new and much freer way of living. By comparison Spurgeon's had little to offer us. With hindsight perhaps, I felt that not only had my father sacrificed a more comfortable way of living for Spurgeon's; so too had we as a family.

An Invitation to Manchester

It was in the midst of all these difficulties that my father received a letter from Professor Mansfield Cooper, the Vice Chancellor of Manchester University, to meet with the committee responsible for finding a successor to the John Rylands Chair in Biblical Criticism and Exegesis left vacant as a result of the death of T.W. Manson. The John Rylands Chair at that time was probably the most prestigious position outside the universities of Oxford and Cambridge. What's more, unlike the Oxbridge chairs, it was open to a Nonconformist. Unlike almost any other theological chair, it called for someone equally at home in the Old Testament as in the New Testament.

For a number of days my father wrestled with the invitation, but finally on 20 February 1959 wrote to decline the invitation:

> From my personal view point, there is no position in the academic world which I could more wish to occupy than the chair of the late Doctor Manson, with its unique tradition of Biblical scholarship. As it is, I feel that I have been set in a place in which I must evidently continue for some time to come.

But my father felt he just could not leave the college at this crucial period when stability was needed. That same day he also wrote a letter to Dr Ernest Payne, the General Secretary of the Baptist Union, in which he conveyed something of the 'agony' he had experienced in coming to that decision:

> I confess that it is not wholly without some degree of uneasiness that I take this step, for inner convictions are not always satisfactorily analysable, but I should feel that I was going against such as I could perceive of the will of God for me and for Spurgeon's if I even expressed a serious willingness to leave in the immediate future. In some sense I feel the

cross has been made heavier by virtue of this decision, but neither do I feel that I can cast it away.

When he reported to the college council chairman, Charles Johnson, that he had turned down such an offer, there was no understanding at all of the sacrifice my father had made. As far as Charles Johnson was concerned, there was no more prestigious a position than that of the Principal of Spurgeon's College!

The distinguished Baptist Old Testament scholar, H.H. Rowley, who had himself a professorial chair at Manchester and who had been responsible for bringing my father's name to the committee as 'the best man' for the Rylands chair, did understand what was involved. His response to my father proved to be highly significant:

> Do not bury your talent beneath the load of administration. There are many men with a gift for administration. Scholars are few, and by your scholarship you can serve Spurgeon's. The more widely your work is recognised in the world of scholarship, the more you will lift up the status of Spurgeon's College, and give your men reason to hold high their heads and to look to you with confidence.[1]

As we shall see, this in effect was precisely what happened. As a result of his writings, the academic standing of the college rose to new heights. What would have happened had my father accepted the Manchester invitation is a subject for speculation. Undoubtedly had he gone to Manchester he would have had a greater influence on the world of scholarship. On the other hand, as college principal he touched more lives—through the ministers and so their churches. This influence upon (future) ministers was all the greater in that the college at that stage was a residential community and as such had a far greater

---

[1] Letter dated 21 February 1959.

impact on the lives of its students than today, when so many students are church-based rather than college-based, and even the college-based students tend to live out.

Having made the decision not to proceed with the John Rylands Chair, it gave my father much pleasure to see his old friend, F.F. Bruce, moving from Sheffield to Manchester to take up the position. Strange as it may seem, only some seven years or so later I myself went to Manchester, where along with my vocational studies at the Northern Baptist College I began my doctoral studies at the university, with F.F. Bruce as my supervisor. Indeed, much of my time was spent in the John Rylands Library on Deansgate, then and still separate from the University Library on Oxford Road.

The Scholar

My father did not need the encouragement of Rowley to continue to work at his studies. The pressures upon him were enormous. There were not only lectures to prepare and to give and a college to run and to represent, there were also denominational responsibilities to fulfil and to shoulder. Yet in spite of all these pressures upon him as college principal, articles and books continued to issue from his typewriter (there were no word processors around at that time). It was in this period too that my father was awarded the earned (as distinct from honorary) degree of Doctor of Divinity from the University of London for his book *Baptism in the New Testament*.

The habit of studying seemed to be in his blood. From childhood my father had eagerly devoured library books and in his college days was the keenest of students. This devotion to study continued into the pastorate and into his life as a New Testament teacher. Some of my earliest childhood memories are of my father working in his study. His trousers used to wear out at the knees, not because of kneeling at prayer, but because of sitting at his study table—although he often said that a commentary should in fact be written on one's knees! As an aside I may mention that my father never worked at a normal-sized desk, rather he needed the largest of surfaces on which to put all his papers. As a college tutor he used to work at home on a large extended dining room table. Later as a college principal he worked at a very large desk, the breadth and width of which were vastly beyond the norm.

Needless to say, my father worked in his study not just during the day, but almost every evening too. He regularly burned the midnight oil in his study. In the summer, when he was too tired to do any creative work late at night, he would mark London University examination papers. My mother's role was to look after us children and guard him from unnecessary interruptions. As children we happily accepted the fact that father spent his evenings in the study. It was not that the study was out-of-bounds to us children. Far from it. We were always welcome for a chat. But at the end of the chat he would return to his work.

It is important to state that my father did have time for us children. For instance, we often gathered around the piano for a sing. We played tennis together. We were not infrequently taken out to the theatre (ironically, it was often to the Westminster Theatre, whose performances were sponsored by the MRA!)—and in particular enjoyed attending performances of Gilbert and Sullivan. Although most Sundays he was away preaching, he always kept one Sunday a month free for the family. We had days away together as a family— often going to Tankerton on the Kent coast or to Brighton on the Sussex coast. And, of course, the annual family holiday was always a highlight of our life together. I never remember my father taking away any kind of work on holiday. But time was not wasted. As a family we never sat down to watch television together—indeed, we were amongst the very last families ever to own a television. Life could be fun, and often

was, but there was also an earnestness attached to life.
Even in the school holidays we children always had to
do a certain amount of school work each day

Some have described my father as a fanatical student,
others as a workaholic. When others were relaxing, he
was working. There is no doubt that his work-rate put
others to shame. But if my father was a driven man, he
was not driven by the so-called 'Protestant work-ethic'.
Rather, he was driven by his love for his Lord, to whom
he wanted to give his all. He was very conscious that,
unlike many of his contemporaries, he had been spared
to survive the war—if God had spared him, he
reasoned, then he had spared him to enable him to
serve him.

Not surprisingly, the standards my father set for
himself he expected from others. One of his former
colleagues remembers an occasion when one of the
students was called in:

> He was behind with his work and an explanation was
> required. He couldn't claim that he had a wife and had
> children. That wasn't allowed in those days. For all that he
> didn't lack excuses which went on and on until at last he
> finished by saying, 'Consequently when the evening comes
> I'm tired'. It was too much for George. He whipped off his
> spectacles, an infallible sign that he was about to explode
> and he said, 'Who gave you to understand that you can stop
> working when you're tired?' George could understand the
> Book of Revelation, but student indolence was something he
> never managed to comprehend.[2]

In the draft of the final address my father gave to
Spurgeon's students in July 1999 he wrote at length of
'the call to discipline':

> If we are to engage with seriousness in the task which
> confronts us in the service of the gospel we shall require to

---

2   Frank Fitzsimmonds in a tribute given at Spurgeon's
College on 15 June 2000.

exercise discipline in our use of time, and in our application to study in the time which we have at our disposal. I cannot tell you how many men in the ministry I know who have expressed regret that they did not exercise a more rigorous discipline when they were students, and more fully exploit the golden years of their theological education. There is a perversity in our nature which allows us to anticipate with great expectations opportunities that are before us, and then to undervalue them when they are given... We have all been stirred by the records of martyrs for Christ, by accounts of the heroic achievements of pioneer missionaries, by stories of ministers who have identified themselves with the poor and embodied the gospel of love in their living as well as in their preaching. When is the time to start serving Christ like that? Is it not here, in the place where we are seeking more fully to learn Christ.[3]

Relationships with Students

In earlier times there was a fairly rigid distinction between staff and students. Staff—and the principal in particular—were very much authority figures. My father began to change that. For instance, as an attempt at fostering closer relations between the teaching staff and students, my father did away with the 'top table'. Instead he encouraged the members of the staff to sit with the students for the midday meal and students to occupy his table! Students began to be addressed by first names—but the change to calling the principal by his first name had yet to come.

By comparison with today, student life at the college seems to have been fairly regimented. But this was in fact the order of the day for all Baptist theological colleges. (And not just Baptist colleges: when I was at Jesus College, Cambridge, in the 1960s gates were locked at 10 pm.) At Spurgeon's there were, for instance, set hours for study. Strange as it may seem today, students

---

[3]   This section of the address was in fact never given.

(who were, of course, grown men) had to gain the principal's permission to go out for the evening.[4] Indeed, they had even to get the principal's permission to get engaged! Those, of course, were the days when the college was a residential community primarily for single men. But in April 1959 the college council made the daring decision that men in their final year of a three or four year course might apply to the principal for permission to marry (up until that time only those who had stayed on for a fifth year were permitted to marry).

In a very real sense my father as principal held the lives of the students in his hands. One of his key responsibilities, together with his staff, was commending leaving students to the Baptist Union for accredited Baptist ministry. Such commendation could not always be taken for granted. There were times when that commendation was withheld. It is not, therefore, surprising if at that stage many of the students considered my father a somewhat intimidating figure.

However, I believe that the gulf between my father and his students must not be over-emphasised. He did not live life in some splendid academic ivory tower. He took opportunities to get alongside his students. Whenever there was a football match between Spurgeon's and some other theological college, he tried to be there on the touch line. On the night of 5 November he was there leading the singing around the bonfire ('The King of Caractacus' was one of his favourites'). And, of course, there were the college missions to the Elephant and Castle in 1960 (based on Spurgeon's old church in central London, known today as the Metropolitan Tabernacle) and to the London Borough of Dagenham

---

4   Robert Amess, now Chairman of the Evangelical Alliance, commented in a private letter of 6 July 2000: 'Signing the pad outside his study with "permission to have an evening out please sir" speaks of a bygone age, but also of an authority both readily acknowledged and exercised.'

in 1963 (based on the four small Dagenham Baptist churches) when the whole college—the principal and his staff along with the students—went out together on mission

As the over 500 letters and cards which my mother received after my father's death testify time and again, he was essentially a humble man. He did not stand on ceremony. He did not give himself 'airs and graces'. If at times he seemed awesome to his students, it was not his position, but rather his utter dedication to the Lord expressed through his person. Certainly, when students were in trouble, they discovered that the principal was not just a scholar, he was also a pastor; he was always there for them when they had problems.

After my father's death, a former student wrote to say that he had been able to finish his college course and remain in Baptist ministry because of my father's pastoral care: 'I want to do justice to the very real pastoral side of his character. He could not have been kinder or more helpful to me, right through my College career.' For some of the time 'I went through an extreme form of...neurotic illness... He did not "write me off", but secured expert psychiatric help for me... At certain points in my College course I went through periods of doubt. Your father was a marvellous listener...he became a spiritual 'father figure' to me'. In the words of another former student: 'I shall remember him as a "son of encouragement".'

My father, however, recognised that there were limitations to the pastoral care which he and his staff could offer, limitations imposed not so much by time as by position. For some students it was difficult to be truly open with someone who was perceived as being able to put an end to their ministerial 'career'. For this reason in the autumn of 1972 my father got the backing of the college council to appoint the Rev Frank Cooke as a part-time college chaplain.

His pastoral care for students continued even when they had left college. He arranged post-collegiate resi-

dential conferences for former students who had been
in the ministry for eighteen months. They, together
with their wives, were encouraged to come back and
talk about their experience in their first pastorate, to
voice their problems, their disappointments and their
hopes for the future. He also began the custom of
praying for past students at the Friday morning act of
worship in the chapel.

This care for past students extended to those who for
one reason or another had left Baptist ministry. There
was, for instance, a former Spurgeon's student who left
the ministry after his marriage ended and he entered
into a homosexual relationship. Even though my father
disapproved of his actions, he never allowed this to
spoil their friendship, but instead kept in touch with
him by having occasional meals with him in central
London. After the first such encounter the former
student wrote: 'You were very gentle with me considering the present circumstance of my life, but I was
grateful for the friendship shown... Thank you again for
your thoughtfulness.' Not surprisingly he was there at
my father's funeral.

Student Issues

An immediate problem facing my father as principal
was what to do with the 'Venturers', a group of students
led by Bryan Gilbert (himself a trained musician) who
were engaging in what was then termed 'skiffle evangelism'. The minutes of the college council meeting at
the beginning of April 1958 (i.e. while my father was
still in Switzerland) record that 'In discussion with the
group of students involved, the Faculty had expressed
its strong distaste for the use of this kind of music with
Gospel songs.' The council were divided on the issue,
but 'finally agreed not to impose a ban but at the same
time it was to be made clear to the students that they
must not identify the name of the college with this
venture and must not seek press publicity'. For my

father the issue was not so much the style of music, as rather the way in which the time being devoted to the music was having a deleterious impact on the students' studies. However, he proved to be extremely supportive of what the Venturers were trying to do and bought all their records to boot! However, the very fact that this was an issue showed how the college (as no doubt the churches) was finding it difficult to come to terms with popular culture.

Another issue which surfaced in the late 1960s was that of charismatic renewal, which had arrived from California and was being actively promoted by such figures as Michael Harper, then on the staff at All Soul's, Langham Place, in central London.[5] The minutes of the college council meeting held on 9-10 April 1968 speak of the principal reporting that 'A number of students (fourteen in all) have been influenced by the new Pentecostal teaching... On the whole the students are earnest, sincere and restrained.' Four years later there is a minute of a college executive meeting held on 22 September 1972 to the effect that in response to the principal's report members urged 'special care to be taken to ascertain whether candidates had any Pentecostalist leanings'. There is no doubt that the enthusiasm of some of his more charismatic students tried my father's patience—while their theology at times stretched his understanding. Nonetheless, while he had real reservations about charismatic renewal, he was sympathetic to its emphasis on life in the power of the Spirit. All this is made very clear in a sermon he preached around this time on the Holy Spirit:

The specifically Pentecostalist doctrine of the baptism of the Holy Spirit, as an operation of the Spirit separate from the

---

5   For an account of how charismatic renewal spread among British Baptists, see Douglas McBain, *Fire over the Waters: Renewal among Baptist and Others from the 1960s to the 1990s* (Darton, Longman and Todd, London, 1997).

incorporation into Christ which marks regeneration, is a grave mistake... But I would wish immediately to qualify the assertion by admitting that the mistake of the Pente-costalists—new and old!—in their doctrine is not so grave as the failure of the Churches to recognise their urgent need of the Holy Spirit's aid, and to beseech the Lord the Spirit to work through them in the might that is His. For too long we have held the doctrine of the Holy Spirit as a lifeless dogma—just as for many of us, the anticipation of the Last Judgement and the victorious Kingdom of God is a dogma without power to cause either dread or joy. I view the witness of the Pentecostalists as a call from the Lord to the Churches to know in truth and in life the power of the Holy Spirit to enable them to play their part in the world today. For unless the Churches know the quickening grace of the Spirit, there is no hope for them, and no prospect for the world except the death knell.[6]

A similar approach to the charismatic movement is found in a wide-ranging course on the Holy Spirit my father later wrote for the Christian Training Pro-gramme of the Baptist Union. Although disagreeing with the expression 'baptism in the Spirit' to denote the experience of the Spirit in the lives of believers, he argued that 'the important issue is neither the vocab-ulary used, nor the mode of receiving, but the reality of the experience of the Spirit'.[7] It is unfortunate that this course material never received wide circulation—indeed, in form it was only duplicated as distinct from printed. For in spite of its accessible style, it was a detailed and careful study combining New Testament scholarship and theological insight, and certainly had—

---

6   'The Holy Spirit and the Church', in A.H. Chapple (ed.), *Sermons For Today* (Marshall, Morgan & Scott, London, 1968), 103.

7   *The Holy Spirit* (Baptist Union, London, n.d.—probably mid-1980s), 52.

and still has—far more to offer than the run-of-the-mill paperback on the Holy Spirit.

Then there was the issue of women. Although there have been women Baptist ministers since the 1930s, Spurgeon's was not at the forefront of admitting women into college. The college's slowness reflected the evangelical constituency it served—the churches themselves were none too keen to commend women for ministry, nor indeed receive ministry from them. Not surprisingly, many of the Spurgeon's students reflected the attitude of the churches and were themselves opposed to women in ministry. My father, however, did not share these attitudes and perceived 'men in the church' rather than 'women in the church' to be the problem. For this very reason, when asked to write a study conference guide to the New Testament understanding of women in the church, he entitled it *Man and Woman in the Church*. The final paragraph of what is largely an exegetical study reads:

> The Church has much to do to work out the implications of these insights. For centuries it has been under the bondage of a clouded understanding of the Scriptures, wherein the glory of the gospel has been restricted through a Judaism framed apart from the revelation and redemption wrought by Christ; and Church order as interpreted by male clergy has taken precedence over the kingdom of God and salvation for the world. Man and woman, created for partnership, have been redeemed for partnership in service. It is high time to make that partnership truly effective in the service of God in His Church and in his world.[8]

My father's only reservation about admitting women to Spurgeon's rested in his feeling that it would not be helpful for the women students themselves to be overwhelmed by the number of men training for

---

8   *Man and Woman in the Church* (Baptist Union, Department of Ministry, London, 1983), 13.

ministry. His preference would have been to admit all potential women ministers to just one of the Baptist colleges, whether it be Spurgeon's or indeed any other one. But this was not to be. In 1961 my father admitted the first woman to the college: Margaret Jarman, a former Baptist deaconess, who eventually, in 1987, became the President of the Baptist Union, the first woman minister to hold this office. Then in the autumn of 1962 Gladys Seymour was allowed to attend lectures in the college for two years. She too, in turn became a Baptist minister. The first woman to 'live in' was Sue Melville, who later became a Methodist minister. With all these women my father had a good relationship. As one student wife, later herself to become a Baptist minister, remembered with gratitude: 'his respect for women and his ability to address them in a genuine and non patronising way, recognising their worth as people and in the work of Christ's Kingdom'.[9]

Ordination and Beyond

In contrast to most other denominations, Baptists in the United Kingdom have tended to entrust to their college principals the task of ordaining candidates for ministry. Furthermore, whereas in other denominations candidates for ministry are often ordained together, amongst British Baptists the custom has normally been for ordinands to be ordained in the church that commended them for training for the ministry. The result of these twin practices was that every summer my father was engaged in a frantic round of ordinations all over the country. What's more, these ordinations involved my father not only taking the actual rite of ordination but also preaching to the ordinand concerned. No bishop ever had such a full and varied range of ordination charges as did my father. Needless to say,

---

[9]   Rev Frances Godden 18 July 2000.

for the ordinands concerned, these personalised services were very special.

As I went through my father's papers I came across many ordination sermons, among them the sermon my father preached at my own ordination[10] (my father did not actually ordain me—he did, however, preach the sermon). Although special to me, the exegetical approach was in fact very typical of the kind of ordination sermon he preached. As was his custom, the sermon did not consist of a full text—but rather of a series of notes. It also contained a number of references to a series of illustrations, but the terseness of these references has caused me to omit them.

Disciple and Teacher, Servant and Master: 'A disciple is not above his teacher, nor a servant above his master. It is enough for the disciple to be like his teacher, and the servant like his master' (Mt. 10.24).

Observe the terms: The disciple is sent out to be a teacher. But he always remains a disciple—a learner. The servant is sent in the name of his master—and he always remains a servant. This is how Jesus went—always learning from his Father, always obedient to his Father.

(1) *The disciple shares the reproach of his teacher, the servant shares the rejection of his master.* See Mt. 10.32: 'If they have called the master of the house Beelzebub, how much more will they malign those of his household'.

That Jesus should ever have been called Beelzebub was the most shocking instance of the total rejection he suffered at the hands of the religious leaders of his time. Jesus was a tool of the devil! The spirit in him was the power of evil. Therefore everything for which he stood was to be rejected as abhorrent. This led him to the grave words about blasphemy against the Holy Spirit.

If Jesus should suffer such rejection, how much more will his disciples know it? See John 15.20. Basic to the message

---

[10] 10 October 1970, South Norwood Baptist Church, Holmesdale Road.

of Jesus and integral to the experience of the early disciples is the inevitability of the disciple sharing his master's fate: see Matt 5.11,12; Lk 9.57ff; Mark 8.34; Mark 13.10. The sermons of the Book of Acts are chiefly delivered in hostile surroundings. The missionary progress of the Church through the ages is marked by the blood stains of its heralds. Recognise the inevitability of hardship as a minister of Christ. It is in this that his partnership is learned and experienced.

(2) *The disciple shares the attitude of his teacher, the servant shares that of his master: and that is a love which stoops to the lowliest and costliest service.* See John 13.16: 'I have given you an example that you should do as I have done for you. A servant is not greater than his master, nor is he who is sent greater than he who sent him. If you know these things, happy are you if you do them'.

The first implication of this statement: preparedness for menial service. Footwashing was the slave's job! The humility of Christ is to be expressed in readiness for work that only a 'Christly' man would do. The second implication: preparedness for sacrificial self-giving for the salvation of the world. See Phil 2.6-8—and v5.

No doubt this is for the whole Church and not for the minister alone (Phil 2.5 addressed to the church). But the minister must lead his people in this kind of ministry, and set them an example. It is unthinkable to tell people to walk in the steps of Jesus, and stand back. The servant church requires the servant leaders to show them the mind of the servant of the Lord.

(3) *The disciple shares his teacher's success, the servant shares his master's glory.* See John 15.20: 'If they kept my word, they will keep yours also'. Light in the darkness! The power and blessing of God that was with Jesus is with the disciples of Jesus. See also Luke 6.40: 'A disciple is not above his teacher, but everyone when he is fully taught will be like his teacher'. This is in contrast to the terrible results of the blind leading the blind: he who knows the truth of Jesus will be able to lead them into the power of that truth just as Jesus did.

This is the joyful, reverse side of the principle enunciated by Jesus. If men rejected him, men also listened to him. Even on the cross. And especially through the cross. See John 12.31,32. When was Jesus to draw all men to him? When his servants made him known through the preaching and living of the gospel. If Mark 13.10 puts the mission in a context of suffering, Matt 28.18 puts it in the context of victory and power. If it be true that the march of the church has been marked with blood stains, it has also known joy and life. So today. Against all the pessimists, let that never be forgotten. And go, expecting to see response to your ministry. Your Lord's power is limitless. Let your trust match that power— and so will your joy.

Ordination did not mark the end of a college principal's link with his students. The Baptist Union delegated to the college principals responsibility for 'probationary studies' during the first three years of their ministry. However, my father extended that sense of responsibility to include a concern for the general well-being of his former students.

Theological Education

As college principal he was constantly advocating the cause of theological education for those called by God to ministry. Many in the evangelical constituency to which the college appealed were suspicious of the theological training Spurgeon's had to offer—indeed, they were suspicious of all theological training. So time and again in the *College Record* he had to reiterate the aim of the college. In December 1967 he wrote:

We seek to combine pastoral efficiency with evangelistic power, and a preaching that can face the untruth of our age with the truth of God in all its length and breadth and height and depth... Spurgeon's College has never set out to produce slick salesmen of religion or purveyors of semi-religious panaceas for the ills of our time. Rather our students are expected to wrestle to an understanding of 'the depth of the riches and wisdom and knowledge of God', and that they may be equipped to help their congregations to enter it too.

He continued:

> The heavenly wisdom involves a great deal of very earthly labour... But then, who said a theological college was created for amusement?

He went on to defend the College for preparing students to take the London BD examinations:

> It is undeniable that a degree of itself is no guarantee that a man can build up the saints in their most holy faith and win estranged men and women to Christ; but no one has ever made such a foolish claim. It is undeniable, however, that a consecrated student who knows his calling and his Master has become a more fit instrument in God's hand through the discipline he underwent in gaining a degree, and the knowledge he acquired on the way.[11]

In December 1969 he returned to the theme:

> Recently I participated in a discussion of the relevance of theological teaching to the work of the ministry... I am sure that when the last trumpet is sounded it will interrupt someone in the midst of a statement about the proper balance of a theological education, but not till after the trumpet is sounded are we likely to get the final word on some of our problems.

He went on to speak of the need for students to acquire 'the tools for the job', and in particular 'the ability to

---

[11] 'The Heavenly Wisdom Involves a Great Deal of Earthly Labour', *Spurgeon's College Record* 45 (December 1967), 2-4.

handle the great commentaries on the Bible and the aids to its interpretation'.[12]

My father was convinced that serious study of the Bible went hand in hand with those who would serve in the churches as pastor–evangelists. The last address my father ever gave was to graduating students at Spurgeon's College in June 1999. There he reflected on his own final college year:

> The blitz of London had already started. We could see from the roof of the College bombs exploding all over London. Nightly the death toll was mounting. We were horrified to think of the sufferings of people, the more so in that we could not do anything about it, for our course was not finished and we had a commitment to fulfil. At times our studies seemed irrelevant, and academic qualifications appeared meaningless. As I look back on my life I can see that from that point on two strands of tension claimed me: evangelism and study of the Bible, and they are still with me. You who are graduates of this College have known the tremendous privilege of time and opportunity to dig deep into the scriptures and theology. It has given you the tools and basis for your ministry, whatever service for the Lord and wherever in the world he may send you. Be sure, however, that you do not accept the notion that having graduated you have 'arrived' and do not need to pursue further study. On the contrary, there is an urgent need freshly to think through the Christian faith and to find new ways of proclaiming it. God has gifted you for ministry *today*; seek his guidance that it may always be relevant to *today*'s people.
>
> My plea therefore to you this morning is that you hold together the two strands of the tension that is inherent in our vocation. Some evangelists, alas, have little knowledge of the New Testament, and consequently their teaching is often superficial. You, as I, may have listened to evangelistic

---

12 'From the Principal's Study', *Spurgeon's College Record* 49 (December 1969), 6-10.

sermons that have consisted of a string of illustrations followed by a prolonged appeal to come to Christ. On the other hand, some scholars have so consistently adhered to one line of research in theology they hardly know how to communicate the gospel. Believe me, I have known more than one professor of missions who was incapable of leading anyone to the Lord.

For my father the key to effective ministry was the holding of the two together. 'It is my conviction', he concluded, 'that nothing is so urgently required by the Church of God and the world at large as informed evangelical leadership worthy of the gospel. We have a message from God, resources for grasping it, opportunity to use them, and grace available for the task committed to us, plus the power of the Holy Spirit'.

The Learning of Greek

As a biblical scholar my father was a great advocate for the learning of Hebrew and Greek, as also of Aramaic and Syriac. In particular, as a teacher of the New Testament, he was passionately committed to the learning of Greek. This is made abundantly clear in an address he prepared for Spurgeon's students at the graduation ceremony in July 1999:

> Let me make it clear that I have no desire to see honest preachers of the gospel transformed into second-rate scholars of ancient languages, and so ruined for any useful calling in life. The issue, however, which every ministerial student should face is whether he is willing to enter on a life's ministry of the Word of God in a condition of being incapable of using the basic tools of authentic Biblical and theological scholarship. Kittel's ten volume *Theological Dictionary of the New Testament*, for example, is the most valuable single contribution to the New Testament which modern scholarship has produced, and it is locked against the person who knows no Biblical languages. The com-

mentaries of the giants of exposition like Westcott, Lightfoot, H.B. Swete and R.H. Charles are sealed with seven seals against the minister without Greek; and well might he weep, like the prophet of old, because he cannot even look upon them! Many of these writings were the products of the toil and reflection of men of God who devoted the best part of their lives to the elucidation of a single book of Scripture, like Westcott on the Gospel of John, de Witt Burton on Galatians, and Charles on Revelation. Only they will despise these works who have never read them. For this reason the attitude of the student who intends to throw away his Greek New Testament as soon as he has gained his degree in New Testament studies is as foolish as the decision of an instrumentalist who, after having painfully acquired the mastery of an instrument, determined never to play it again.

For the record it is worth noting that my father practised what he preached. He was so much at home in his New Testament that he used to take it into the pulpit and translate from the Greek then and there as he read from the scriptures prior to preaching his sermon. In this respect he was like some of the early Baptist leaders who preferred to translate directly from the Greek and Hebrew, rather than allow an English translation to block the work of the Holy Spirit.

Theological Training by Degrees

Throughout his time at Spurgeon's one of my father's key objectives was to gain academic recognition for the courses offered by the college. As far as he was concerned, Spurgeon's was a theological college, and not just a Bible college.

In June 1959 my father reported to the college council that he had explored the possibility of Spurgeon's students becoming internal students of King's College, London. But this was not to be. So for the remaining years of his principalship Spurgeon's students took the external degrees of London University through King's. But this arrangement meant that by comparison with the internal students, Spurgeon's students were not playing 'on a level field'. The former were taught by those who were setting the exam papers, while the latter were taught by those whose first sight of the exam papers were on the day of the examination itself. The results of this could prove to be quite disadvantageous for Spurgeon's students. For this reason from 1964 onwards my father reluctantly (for it involved so much extra work) acted as an examiner in the Diploma of Theology, and in New Testament studies in the BA, BD pass, and BD honours papers—as the minutes of the college executive meeting on 9 December 1964 report: 'This affords a valuable contact with the university.'

Clearly such a relationship with King's, beneficial though it was, was not ideal. So my father explored other options. At one point, for instance, he looked into the possibility of moving the college down to Canterbury with a view to becoming part of the new University of Kent there. This idea, however, was shot down by the then Trustees of the Falklands Park Estate, which owns the college property.[13]

During the academic year of 1970–71 my father began to engage in cautious explorations with the Council for National Academic Awards (CNAA), the degree-awarding body for polytechnics and other colleges of higher education. The aim of these negotiations was to see whether the college might be able to construct a three year theological degree course of its own which might be validated by the CNAA. To this three year course would be added a 'pastoral' year, not overseen by

---

[13] According to a former colleague, Dr Rex Mason, this was the only occasion he saw my father over-ridden. 'In every other respect his leadership was so respected by all that he seemed to get his way without effort and certainly without any kind of brow-beating. Everyone knew that he had only the best interests of the college at heart and trusted him because of it.'

the CNAA, which would lead to the college's own Diploma in Pastoral Studies. Progress in these explorations with the CNAA was slow, but finally a CNAA visiting party to the college on 18 May 1973 recommended at the end of its investigations that the college's scheme be accepted and that it be introduced in the academic year 1974–75. By that time my father was not around for the implementation of the CNAA degree. However, without his initiative and without his academic standing, there would have been no CNAA degrees at Spurgeon's College.

Evangelism

It is important to realise that my father was not just concerned for academic standards in theological education. He was also concerned to see his students develop their evangelistic gifts. He had only been principal a couple of years when, in 1960, he committed the college and its students to an evangelistic campaign based at the Metropolitan Tabernacle as part of their reopening celebrations. In that time the students along with my father and his staff visited 7,000 homes, as well as clubs, dance halls, works canteens and pubs. Three years later a similar mission took place in Dagenham.

My father had a passion for the lost—and was determined that his students shared that passion. In this respect Rev David Coffey, General Secretary of the Baptist Union of Great Britain, when preaching at my father's funeral, recalled his report to the student body when he had just returned from the Berlin Congress on Evangelism in 1966, which had been sponsored by the Billy Graham Evangelistic Association:

> George told us how Billy Graham had called for a return to the dynamic zeal for world evangelization which had characterised the Edinburgh Conference of 1910. He told us of the thirty-foot high clock in the Kongresshalle's foyers; second by second it recorded the net gain in the world's

population. During the days of the Congress the population of the world had increased by 1,764,216 people for whom Christ had died and who needed to hear the message of Christ before they themselves died. George told us how he had walked the streets of Berlin at the end of the Congress asking himself how faithful he had been to the Great Commission of the Lord to evangelise the world. He told us he was making a fresh commitment to do the work of an evangelist and invited us to make a similar commitment.

Up until that time it was customary for the principal to be responsible for instruction in evangelism and pastoral care. Although my father had involved working ministers in helping him teach these courses, from the outset of his principalship he was keen to have a member of faculty whose work would be dedicated to the more practical areas of preparation for ministry. A major obstacle in achieving such a goal was finance. In the autumn of 1965 my father was in touch with a former student of the college, Dr Ralph Mitchell, who had become a member of the Billy Graham evangelistic organisation, to see if Billy Graham would be willing to sponsor a 'Billy Graham Chair of Evangelism and Pastoral Instruction' at Spurgeon's College. In a personal letter written on Christmas Eve 1965 Billy Graham expressed his interest and happiness in such a possibility. Unfortunately by September 1966 it became clear that the Board of the Billy Graham evangelistic organisation felt there was too much of a drain on their finances for that to become possible. Nonetheless, the seeds of American help had been sown. In the autumn of 1967 and with the help of other American friends,[14] my father was able to appoint for a three-year period Dr Lewis Drummond as the first lecturer in Evangelism and Pastoral Instruction at Spurgeon's College—indeed,

---

[14] The First Baptist Church in Memphis provided the first year's salary. The Foreign Mission Board of the Southern Baptist Convention provided further money.

this was the first such appointment in any British Baptist theological college. Lewis Drummond took up his appointment on 23 September 1968. At the time my father wrote:

> Evangelism and the care of souls have been as the life blood of Spurgeon's College from the days of its founding. Everybody knows that Spurgeon was the pastor–evangelist par excellence. His College was established for men who were mastered by the apostolic conviction, 'Woe is me if I preach not the Gospel', and such men were received in order to help them become effective pastors. Spurgeon's only published lectures, the famous *Lectures to my Students*, were devoted precisely to the dual theme of evangelism and pastoral instruction.[15]

In 1968 my father became President of the Baptist Union. The office of President is a one-year appointment, which involves addressing meetings up and down the country and generally giving a lead to the denomination in that year. My father chose evangelism as his theme. On 29 April, the Monday evening of the 1968 assembly, he preached in a crowded Westminster Chapel on the theme of 'Renewed for Mission', which came from the slogan used at the 1964 Nottingham Faith and Order conference, 'One Church renewed for mission'. In his sermon my father made many significant statements:

> As a denomination we have sought to give intensive consideration of the One Church. It is time that we gave equally intensive consideration to renewal by the Spirit and Mission for Christ.
>
> If indifference to Christ is the sin of contemporary western paganism, unbelief is the sin of the contemporary Church. Ultimately our failure is a failure of faith. It is

---

15   *Spurgeon's College Record* 47 (December 1946), 4.

strangling the life of our congregations, and it is killing the mission given to us.

Congregational worship, in most of its forms today, is only remotely connected with the worship of the New Testament Church. In the apostolic era its centre was the Lord's Supper and the entire congregation was drawn into participation in the word and worship.

Why cannot we present witness to the Gospel of Christ without being trammelled by hymns and prayers that are meaningless and unrelated to unbelievers. Why cannot we be free on Sundays to say nothing of other days of the week, to express the Gospel in ways intelligible to pagans?

We require a willingness for the work of the Church to be not simply a gathered congregation, but a gathered ministry.[16]

After giving a clarion call to mission—mission with a particular focus on Easter Day—he ended his sermon by providing an opportunity for the congregation to stand as an indication that they were committing themselves to Christ.

As a follow-up to his presidential sermon my father encouraged the Baptist Union to publish an *Evangelism Year Book 1968–1969* which featured the call for evangelistic action in Holy Week 1969. He got the Bible Society to offer to Baptist churches a special deal on copies of the Good News Bible version of the Gospel of John with a view to encouraging gospel distribution.

On 21 March 1969, while he was still president of the union, he took the theme of 'Evangelising the Post-Christian Man' for the Diamond Jubilee Lecture of the London Baptist Preachers' Association. In this lecture he sought to encourage preachers to learn how to preach the gospel in terms which make sense to people outside the church.

---

16   *Renewed For Mission* (Baptist Union, London, 1968), 5, 12 and 15.

J.C. Hoekendijk cited a one-time prisoner of war from Russia who gave his impressions of the church as he found it on returning to freedom: 'There is a preacher talking from behind the pulpit. We don't understand him. A glass cover has been put over the pulpit. This smothers all the sound. Around the pulpit our contemporaries are standing. They, too, talk and they call. But on the inside this is not understood. The glass smothers all sound. Thus we still see each other talk, but we don't understand each other any more'. Hoekendijk's comment on this is that it is too complimentary a picture. It's not ordinary glass that separates people on the inside from those on the outside, but distorting glass! The people outside receive the strangest images of what is going on inside the Church, and alas the Church all too often is simply not communicating with the man outside.[17]

My father went on to note that Americans call evangelistic services 'revival meetings'.

But is it not imperative to provide ways of evangelising men who have nothing to revive? I would plead for attempts to be made to present the Gospel to contemporaries of ours who think that Christianity is dead and ought to be buried, who never sing hymns and never intend to do so, and never want to hear anyone else sing them either, but who would be prepared to enter a meeting that had no frills but was arranged for the sole purpose of presenting the belief that Christianity works in twentieth century everyday life; such a meeting would include testimony and proclamation and perhaps provide opportunity for questions and discussion.[18]

During that year the council made the decision to appoint a separate chairman of the Baptist Union Council—up to that point it had always been the president for the year, but not all presidents turned out

---

17 *Evangelising the Post-Christian Man* (London Baptist Preachers Association, London, 1969), 8.
18 *Evangelising the Post-Christian Man*, 9.

to be good chairmen. The tenure of the new chairman
of council was three years. My father was made the first
chairman of the council (1968–71). This caused him a
great deal of extra work and slowed him up with his
writing.

Baptism

Along with all the demands of college principal, as also
with the demands of being the chairman of the Baptist
Union Council, my father continued to write. In
particular it was while he was Principal of Spurgeon's
that he produced his three most significant contributions to baptism: his article on 'Baptism in the
Epistles of Paul', published in *Christian Baptism*, a
collection of essays by British Baptists, edited by Alec
Gilmore;[19] and his two books, *Baptism in the New
Testament*[20] and *Baptism Today and Tomorrow*.[21]

It was also while he was at Spurgeon's that he made
the time to translate two German books on baptism: *Did
the Early Church Baptize Infants?* by the distinguished
Lutheran New Testament scholar, Kurt Aland;[22] and
Baptism in the Thought of St Paul by the equally distinguished Roman Catholic scholar, Rudolf Schnackenburg.[23] With regard to the former, this was essentially a
detailed critique of Joachim Jeremias' *Infant Baptism in
the First Four Centuries*.[24] Although Kurt Aland
regarded the practice of infant baptism as both necessary
and legitimate, over against Jeremias he believed that
there was no historical evidence for the practice of
infant baptism before the last years of the second

---

19 'Baptism in the Epistles of Paul', in Gilmore (ed.),
Christian Baptism, 128-149.
20 Macmillan, London, 1962.
21 Macmillan, London, 1966.
22 SCM Press, London, 1963.
23 Basil Blackwell, Oxford, 1964.
24 SCM Press, London, 1960.

century. Needless to say, the reason for my father wanting to translate this book into English must be self-evident! My father, however, did more than simply translate. He also wrote a lively and provocative introduction entitled 'The Baptismal Controversy in the British Scene'.[25] As for the motive for translating Schnackenburg, my father was keen for a wider English-speaking audience to become aware of the way in which New Testament scholars of widely varying traditions were coming to an increasingly common view on the question of baptism—so much so that even a Baptist could find himself in substantial agreement with a Roman Catholic. As my father wrote in his 'Translator's Preface':

> The author has stated in his preface that he has endeavoured to follow the historical-critical method 'which all scholars in the New Testament field are obliged to observe'. The results obtained by a distinguished Roman Catholic scholar, using this common method of Biblical scholarship on a theme of importance to all Christian people will be of interest to Protestants and Roman Catholics alike: the former may be surprised that a Roman Catholic theologian should express himself in the manner found at times in this book; the latter will undoubtedly be stimulated by the freshness of approach to the subject.
>
> Inevitably I myself would find it necessary constantly to express myself differently from the author. Yet my first impression on reading this book remains, that no treatment known to me of Paul's teaching on baptism is so profound as that contained within these pages.

The significance of my father's work on baptism has been dealt with at length by Anthony R. Cross, himself a former minister of Zion Baptist Church, Cambridge, in a massive tome, entitled *Baptism and the Baptists:*

---

25   *Did the Early Church Baptize Infants?*, 17-27

Theology and Practice in Twentieth-Century Britain.[26] There Cross writes: 'Beasley-Murray...wrote what are undoubtedly the most eloquent, theologically balanced and important contributions any Baptist has made to the baptismal debate.'[27] With regard to my father's essay on baptism in Paul, Cross calls it 'the most controversial work on baptism by any Baptist this century'.[28] He describes *Baptism in the New Testament* as 'the single most important and detailed study of baptism by any Baptist this century'.[29]

In the light of Anthony Cross' very full exposition of my father's work on baptism, there is less need for me in this biography to go into every detail and refer to every paper he wrote on baptism.[30] Nonetheless, some things need to be said.

'Baptism in the Epistles of Paul' proved to be so controversial amongst Baptists because of the overt sacramentalist position my father adopted. It offended those for whom baptism was primarily an act of witness. The key passage in the essay comes in the conclusion:

> With his predecessors and contemporaries, Paul saw in baptism *a sacrament of the Gospel*... Behind and in baptism stands the Christ of the cross and resurrection, bestowing freedom from sin's guilt and power, and the Spirit who gives the life of the age to come in the present and is the pledge of the resurrection at the last day. Beyond his predecessors and contemporaries, however, Paul saw in baptism the *sacrament*

---

[26]   Paternoster, Carlisle, 2000.

[27]   *Baptism and the Baptists*, 227. This assessment is supported by Stanley K. Fowler, *More Than a Symbol: The British Baptist Recovery of Baptismal Sacramentalism* (Paternoster, Carlisle, 2002), 141. See the whole of Fowler's discussion, 141-147.

[28]   *Baptism and the Baptists*, 227.

[29]   *Baptism and the Baptists*, 464.

[30]   See also the detailed discussion throughout Fowler's *More Than a Symbol*.

of union with Christ. Because it was that, it involved union with Him in His redemptive acts, both in the rite and in subsequent life which should conform to the pattern of the passion and resurrection (Phil 3.10f). And because it was that it involved union with His Body, making the believer a living member, partaking of the life of the whole. Baptism was thus an effective sign; in it, Christ and faith come together in the meeting of conversion.[31]

Such a conclusion smacked of baptismal regeneration to some. Dr Beattie, for instance, a medical doctor who was a member of my father's first church at Ashurst Drive in Ilford and who had assisted at my birth, joined in the correspondence in the *Baptist Times* and declared that the writers of *Christian Baptism*, by giving the impression that the outward symbolic act played even some part in conversion, were guilty of pandering to the popular superstition that something done to us, for us or by us, was essential or demanded, so that we might be saved.[32] In a subsequent article my father made it clear that in no way did he and his fellow con- tributors to *Christian Baptism* believe in baptismal regeneration. However, were they to be asked, 'Do you believe that baptism is a means of grace?', the answer would be, 'Yes, and more than is generally meant by that expression. In the Church of the Apostles (please note the limitation) the whole height and depth of grace is bound up with the experience of baptism. For to the New Testament writers baptism was nothing less than the claims of God's dealing with the penitent seeker and of the convert's return to God.'[33]

The same position was adopted in *Baptism in the New Testament*, which was an expansion of his

---

[31] 'Baptism in the Epistles of Paul', 148.

[32] N. Beattie, 'Christian Baptism', *Baptist Times*, 12 November 1959, 6.

[33] 'Baptism Controversy: "The Spirit Is There"—Declares Dr G.R. Beasley-Murray', *Baptist Times*, 10 December 1959, 8.

Whitley Lectures delivered at Regent's Park College, Oxford, and at University College, Bangor, North Wales, over the winter of 1959–60. Just before it was published my father commented that he would have no friends when it came out, as it was too Baptist for the sacramentalists and too sacramental for the Baptists! It is no exaggeration to say that it was a 'magisterial' work. Originally published by Macmillan, it was reprinted numerous times by the Paternoster Press and was in print until the year of my father's death—this was quite an achievement for a book which was first offered to the now defunct Carey Kingsgate Press, at the time the publication house of the Baptist Union, which turned it down on the grounds that 'it will not sell'! It became the standard textbook on baptism not just in Baptist colleges and seminaries, but in colleges and seminaries of every tradition, Roman Catholic included. One of the reasons for its wide acceptance was to be found in the approach adopted by my father. As he stated in the preface:

> I have striven to interpret the evidence of the New Testament as a Christian scholar, rather than as a member of a particular Christian confession... For this reason the controversy concerning infant baptism has been rigorously kept from the body of the work and has been reserved for the last chapter. That section inevitably reflects a frankly confessional standpoint and I cannot but expect dissent from many who may conceivably sympathise with much of the exposition contained in the earlier part.[34]

Of great interest to many was the 'Postscript' entitled 'Baptismal Reform and Inter-Church Relationships'. There my father challenged the churches practising infant baptism to put their house in order by at the very least 'exercising discipline with respect to families whose infant children receive baptism. It is to be doubted whether any single factor has weakened the Church

---

[34] *Baptism in the New Testament*, vi.

in its history so gravely as the practice of indiscriminate baptism.'[35] A little later he posed the question: 'Is a return to believers' baptism as the normal Christian baptism really inconceivable?'[36]

But the challenge was not limited to Paedobaptists. 'Baptists, too must consider their ways.' Although unable himself 'to recognise in infant baptism the baptism of the New Testament Church', he made this plea:

> In respect for the conscience of our fellow-Christians and the like charity, which we trust will be exercised towards us, could we not refrain from requesting the baptism of those baptised in infancy who wish to join our churches and administer baptism to such only where there is a strong plea for it from the applicant?[37]

Furthermore, with regard to the administration of baptism in Baptist churches, he called for 'reform according to the Word of God' in three respects: there should be an endeavour to make baptism integral to the gospel, to conversion and to church membership. In addition, he pleaded for the laying on of hands to become an integral part of the service.

> All of us in all the Churches need to consider afresh our ways before God, with the Bible open before us and a prayer for the guidance of the Holy Spirit and a preparedness to listen to what the Spirit is saying to all the churches.[38]

It was a powerfully argued case.

As a result of persistent requests to produce a non-technical version of *Baptism in the New Testament* my father wrote *Baptism Today and Tomorrow*, particular-

---

35   *Baptism in the New Testament*, 388.
36   *Baptism in the New Testament*, 389.
37   *Baptism in the New Testament*, 392.
38   *Baptism in the New Testament*, 395.

ly with lay-people in view. The content of this popular book is indicated by the chapter headings:

1. The Significance of the Baptismal Controversy
2. Baptist, a Symbol or Sacrament?
3. The New Testament Teaching on Baptism
4. Baptism in Baptist Churches Today
5. The Debate Concerning Infant Baptism

Particularly in the chapter on 'Baptism in Baptist Churches Today' my father refused to pull any of his punches:

> For where the cry goes out, 'Only a symbol', emphasis is placed on the obedience and witness expressed in baptism. But this obedience is for the carrying out of a rite with virtually no content—and what is that but ritualism? And even the confession is robbed of its significance, for in Baptist Churches baptism is commonly administered *after* confession—and that a confession made in public! The rite then becomes a public ratification of a confession already publicly made. This problem is rendered yet more acute by the methods of mass evangelism that none are so forward in supporting as Baptists; for the essence of the method is conversion by confession, which in the New Testament is expressed in baptism. Carefully handled, this appeal could prepare for baptism. Badly handled, and with a low view of baptism, it could render baptism superfluous...
>
> If Baptists were to grapple with their favourite proof-text relating to baptism (Rom 6.3-4) and really come to terms with it, their commonly held notion of baptism as a purely symbolic event would itself have to be buried in the grave.[39]

In the section on 'The Debate Concerning Infant Baptism' he commented on the misleading nature of the title of the report of the Faith and Order Commission of the World Council of Churches on baptism, *One Lord, One Baptism*, as if there were agreement on

[39]   *Baptism Today and Tomorrow*, 85, 86, 91.

the subject of baptism. He went on to make the astute observation, which in ecumenical circles still needs to be heard:

> If it be asked, wherein the unity of the Church does lie, if not in one baptism, the answer, surely, must be: in the common confession of that to which Biblical baptism points, namely the redemption of God in Christ and participation in it through the Holy Spirit by faith.[40]

Over the succeeding years my father lectured all over the world on baptism. As indicated by Anthony Cross, he continued to write many an article on baptism. His lecturing and his writing caused him to remain a *cause célèbre* amongst Baptists. Indeed, for many Baptists his chief claim to fame was his work on baptism. Yet, if the truth be told, while my father has had a great influence amongst Christians of other traditions, his influence amongst Baptist has been limited even amongst British Baptists. At a popular level most Baptists remain non-sacramentalists in their approach to baptism, as indeed to the Lord's Supper.

My father's final contribution to the subject of baptism came in a paper, 'The Problem of Infant Baptism: An Exercise in Possibilities', written for a collection of essays in honour of Günter Wagner, a German New Testament scholar who succeeded him as Professor of New Testament at the Baptist Theological Seminary in Rüschlikon.[41] There my father revealed that he had softened his attitude by recognising in certain circumstances the 'possibility' of acknowledging the legitimacy of infant baptism:

> I make the plea that churches which practise believer's baptism should consider acknowledging the legitimacy of infant baptism, and allow members of the Paedobaptist

---

40   *Baptism Today and Tomorrow*, 160.
41   Faculty of Baptist Theological Seminary, Rüschlikon (ed.), *Festschrift Günter Wagner* (Peter Lang, Berne, 1994), 1-14.

churches the right to interpret it according to their consciences. This would carry with it the practical consequence of believer-baptist churches refraining from baptising on confession of faith those who have been baptised in infancy.

...It [this position] is at least in harmony with variations in the experience of baptism among the earliest believers recorded in the New Testament (cf. Acts 2.37-38; 8.14-17; 10.44-48; 11.1-18; 18.24-19.6). The great lesson of those variations is the freedom of God in bestowing his gifts.[42]

My father ended the article with a reference to the appeal in the Book of Revelation to 'hear what the Spirit says to the churches!' (Rev. 2.7):

I leave it to my fellow believer-baptists to ponder whether the 'possibilities' expounded in this article in any sense coincide with what the Spirit is saying to the churches today.[43]

If the truth be told, the response is likely to be minimal—and not simply because the article was published in a Swiss Festschrift, not easily accessible to a wider Baptist audience. Why this surprising change of heart? Is it in part to be accounted for by the ageing process, which causes us to see issues in increasing 'greys' rather than in 'blacks and whites'? My father was very conscious of the fact that he had changed his mind and unusually sent me a draft of the essay for my comment. Although myself not sharing his perspective, I encouraged him to proceed with publication. After all, it was, as he said 'an exercise in *possibilities*'.

Children and the Church

Inevitably in dealing with baptism my father found himself dealing with the related issue of children and

[42]   'Possibilities', 13-14.
[43]   'Possibilities', 14.

the church. His very first article on this subject, dealing specifically with the meaning of the 'dedication' service, dated back from his days at Ashurst Drive.[44] The article began with a wonderful example of Cockney humour:

'Why don't you baptise children, the same as other churches?' asked a Lambeth woman of her Baptist friend. 'Oh, there's not much difference', replied her friend, 'only we give' em a dry christening!'.

In *Baptism and the New Testament* considerable space was given to 'the rise and significance of infant baptism'. There my father showed that children, far from being models of passivity, are in fact models of receptivity. To receive the good news of the kingdom of God as a child is to respond to God's call of grace—just like 'children respond at once to a call from people they know and they run and throw themselves into their arms'.[45]

My father elaborated more fully on the place of children in the church in *Baptism Today and Tomorrow* which has a sub-section devoted to the subject of 'Children and membership in the church'. He drew attention to 1 Corinthians 7.14 where Paul speaks of children with a believing mother (but an un-believing father) being 'holy'.

The saying is significant as supplying a mode of expressing the importance of being within the sphere of the Church, or, if you will, its outer circle, *even in the case of those who are not actually members of the church.*[46]

In other words, children in Christian families are in a different position to children in non-Christian families. They may not be in the church, but on the other hand

---

44   'The Church and the Child', *Fraternal* 50 (April 1943), 9-13.

45   *Baptism in the New Testament*, 326.

46   *Baptism Today and Tomorrow*, 102.

they are not totally outside the church either. With regard to the baptism of children, in so far as the New Testament witnesses to believer's baptism (as distinct from 'adult' baptism), children as well as adults may be baptised.

> There is no theological bar to a child with faith being baptised. In a secularist world that is loaded against a life of faith in God there is much to be said for taking the yoke of Christ in early days.[47]

The 'proper age for a declaration of faith' will vary from child to child. My father went on to argue for the establishment of a Christian 'catechumenate' leading up to baptism and then following baptism in which children could be nurtured. This Christian 'catechumenate' he distinguished from a church's Sunday School and saw the minister of the church having particular responsibility for such children. I wonder whether my father would make such a distinction now, at a time when Sunday Schools tend to be made up almost exclusively of children from church families?

Much of the argument in *Baptism Today and Tomorrow* is lifted from an earlier paper on 'A Baptist Interpretation of the Place of the Child in the Church', given by my father as a paper in Hamburg to the Commission on Baptist Doctrine of the Baptist World Alliance in August 1964.[48] In this paper, however, my father deals also with the issue of children, as distinct from children born into Christian homes. In such a

---

[47] *Baptism Today and Tomorrow*, 105.

[48] Subsequently published as 'A Baptist Interpretation of the Place of the Child', in *Foundations* 8 (April 1965), 146-160, and as 'Church and Child in the New Testament', *Baptist Quarterly* 21.5 (January 1966), 206-218. See also the paper given by my father to the 1986 Evangelism and Education Conference of the European Baptist Federation, 'The Bible and the Child', 1-8, in the privately produced collection of papers: *The Child—A Challenge to the Church*.

context he admits that 'the Bible gives us too little data to enable us to define with precision the relation of children to God'. He rejected as 'a slander on God' the idea of 'babes a span long in hell'—'they belong to a race that is not only fallen but redeemed'. However, he does not really deal with the issue of at what stage a child becomes a responsible person before God.

In a later article entitled 'The Child and the Church', my father expanded a little more on his previous writings by highlighting the issues involved.[49] He pointed out, for instance, that 'there are Baptists who virtually deny that children have any real place in the church at all'.[50] On the other hand, he noted with a hint of disapproval that it was not unknown in Southern Baptist churches for children to be baptised as young as five and even four years of age (there were 1,146 cases reported in 1966).[51] Writing as a New Testament scholar, as distinct from a psychiatrist dealing with child development, my father was concerned to assess the New Testament evidence, limited as he acknowledged it to be. He concluded:

> It would seem that the apostolic church viewed the children of Christian parents as standing in a unique relation to the church. They were not regarded as born-again children of God for such an experience must await the opening of the life to Christ in faith. But neither were these children regarded as part of the world that lies in the power of the evil one (1 John 5.19). They were seen rather as lying under the care of God, in the bosom of the church, committed by the Lord to its tender care and nurture, in hope of their ultimate entry into the life of faith in Christ.[52]

---

[49] 'The Child and the Church', in Clifford Ingle (ed.), *Children and Conversion* (Broadman Press, Nashville, Tennessee 1970), 127-141.
[50] 'The Child and the Church', 128.
[51] 'The Child and the Church', 129.
[52] 'The Child and the Church', 133.

Children: At School and University

Needless to say, my father did not simply 'theologise' about children, he also—together with my mother— had children to bring up. This included family prayers —at one period they were held after breakfast, at another period after the evening meal. It was always a relaxed time, when we children could air our views. During these years my parents had the joy of seeing all their four children baptised and become church members during their early teenage years. Although not all of us have remained within the Baptist 'fold', in our differing ways we have all sought to continue to go the way of Christ.

It was during his period as Principal of Spurgeon's College that all four of us children received our secondary education: Elizabeth, Stephen and I went to local schools in nearby Croydon, and so did Andrew after a spell at boarding school. From school we then moved on to university: I left for Cambridge and eventually moved on to Manchester; Elizabeth went on to Nottingham, and later studied at Birmingham; Stephen went up to Liverpool, and after a break followed my parents to Kentucky where he did doctoral studies at the Southern Baptist Theological Seminary; initially Andrew went with my parents to the States, but he returned to do a first degree at Coleraine in Northern Ireland and later gained a London MA.

Ecumenism

A convinced evangelical and also a convinced Baptist, my father was also convinced that neither evangelicals nor Baptists have a monopoly of the truth. Right from the beginning of his ministry he abhorred what he termed the 'pharisaism' of the 'orthodox'. He had a breadth of vision which in 1950 was unusual amongst evangelicals. In an address given to the college branch of the Theological Students Fellowship he declared:

The attitude adopted by many Fundamentalists towards the World Council of Churches is nothing short of scandalous. It is regarded as the first stages of the church of Antichrist. The worst motives are imputed to its enthusiasts; all are tarred with the same brush, and all are tools of the devil, including Karl Barth, the Archbishop of Canterbury and Dr Percy Evans! One is reminded of Hitler's attitude to the Jews; he gained unity by rousing indignation against them; and some Christians evidently find it easier to unite on the basis of hate than love.[53]

For a number of years my father was a member of the Commission of Christ and the Church set up by the Faith and Order Committee of the World Council of Churches. He became the commission's secretary in 1957 and it eventually produced the report *One Lord, One Baptism*. He worked alongside such well-known scholars as Anders Nygren, Geoffrey Lampe, Oscar Cullmann, Edmund Schlink, Tom Torrance and John Marsh. As a member of this commission he was a member of a delegation to Russian Orthodox Church theologians in August 1962. The next year he was an advisor and Bible study leader in the Montreal Faith and Order Conference in July 1963. It was a most enriching experience for him personally. He often said that it was 'humbling to be amongst such spiritual giants of faith'. His involvement in ecumenical circles also proved helpful to Baptists generally.

I suppose I could say with some truth that I have been able to clear up some misunderstandings concerning our Baptist views, and have helped to rehabilitate in some manner our church in the eyes of some ecumenical figures. For example, I learned that Bishop Nygren has adopted a much more

---

53 'Vulnerable Points in the Christian Armoury', *Spurgeon's College Students Magazine*, Summer Issue 1950, 4.

cordial attitude to Swedish Baptists since my participation in the group of which he is chairman.[54]

He was well aware that he could not please everyone by serving on this committee. Some very close friends were aghast that he should take on this work. On the other hand there were those who were thrilled that he had taken on this responsibility.

In 1962, P. Gardner-Smith, my father's former director of studies at Jesus College, Cambridge, invited some of his former students to contribute to a volume of essays entitled *The Roads Converge: A Contribution to the Question of Christian Re-Union*.[55] In his preface Gardner-Smith stated: 'Unity cannot be brought about merely by the cultivation of a spirit of goodwill. It must have some definite basis in common beliefs, common practices, and common ideals.'[56] My father's brief was to write an essay on 'The Apostolic Writings'.[57] It proved to be a magnificent broad-sweeping review of 'the primitive traditions that formed a common basis for reflection and instruction in the early church' and deserves to be much better known. The essay abounds in quotable quotes. For example: 'The spiritual unity of the Church is intended to be expressed "bodily"; so long as it is "bodily" denied, the Church contradicts its nature and calls in question its right to preach the reconciliation of all things in Christ.'[58] From my own perspective its prime significance lay in the recognition of the importance of pre-Pauline hymns, confessions and creeds, a theme which I was to take up some years later in my own Manchester doctoral studies.[59]

---

[54] Letter to Dr Cawley 31 December 1962.
[55] Edward Arnold, London, 1963.
[56] *The Roads Converge*, vii.
[57] 'The Apostolic Writings', in *The Roads Converge*, 75-112.
[58] 'Apostolic Writings', 102.
[59] 'The Lordship of Christ over the World in the Corpus Paulinum' (Manchester University, 1970) explores the way in which this theme is taken up in the pre-Pauline material.

Reflections on the Ecumenical Movement[60] was a 'tract for the times' in which my father, as an evangelical leader, urged his fellow evangelicals in the Baptist Union to take a more positive attitude toward ecumenism. He was at pains to stress that the World Council of Churches was not about compromise but about convictions:

> If any one imagines that Faith and Order discussions on Christian doctrine are genteel conversations in which theological platitudes are analysed with a view to producing agreed statements on milk-and-water Christianity, I should like him to have witnessed some of the encounters in which I have participated, wherein steel has met steel; when debate has been sustained for hours between diametrically opposed parties; when Old Testament and New Testament, Fathers and the whole gamut of the history of theology has been called into play; when breathless, bloody but unbowed has more fittingly described the participants than sleek hair, conviviality and back-slapping.[61]

The booklet ended with a rallying call for Baptists to 'cry to God for a fresh experience of His power in every respect—for cleansing and for a spiritual revising such as the Church has not known since Pentecost. Disunity is a symptom which calls for radical renewal by the Spirit of the Lord.'[62]

The Ipswich Meeting

On Tuesday 24 January 1967 my father participated in a Christian Unity Meeting in Ipswich. At the time of the invitation my father had not known that along with the Anglo-Catholic Bishop of St Edmundsbury and Ipswich, he would be sharing a platform with Father

---

[60] Baptist Union of Great Britain and Ireland, London, 1965.
[61] *Reflections on the Ecumenical Movement*, 8.
[62] *Reflections on the Ecumenical Movement*, 13.

Agnellus Andrew, a Roman Catholic priest on the staff of the BBC. Indeed, the first he knew of it was on the Saturday before the meeting when he received a leaflet issued by the Protestant Truth Society with the headline 'Ipswich Heroes Betrayed!'. The reference was to nine Protestant martyrs who were burned more than 400 years ago by the Roman Catholic Church for their faith. The leaflet continued: 'A meeting has been arranged in Ipswich, at the Baths Hall, to seek to unite the Protestant Churches under the Church of Rome.' My father was incensed and publicly took issue with the Protestant Truth Society. His sermon notes for that evening reveal that after giving his own testimony of how he came to faith, he asked Father Agnellus three questions:

> Has Christ found you in the sense of which I have spoken and you found Christ?
> Do you confess Christ as your Saviour and Lord?
> Do you believe that through his birth into unity with us men, his dying for us on the cross, his glorious resurrection and his intercession for us—i.e. through Christ as your Mediator—you are a forgiven man and reconciled to God in Him?

On receiving affirmatives to each of these three questions, my father said:

> Then I humbly own you as a brother in Christ. There are many elements in the creed of your Church I cannot accept, for I believe them to be wrong. But you and I have been made one with God in Christ, and we cannot be one in Christ with the Father and not be one with each other.

A little further in his sermon my father went on:

> Here is the ground of the unity of the people of God: We are sinners for whom Christ died. We have confessed our sins and have been brought out of our disunity with God in a

unity of guilt into unity with Christ our Saviour, who makes us one in Him and with each other by his Holy Spirit.

The Ecumenical Movement is a call to the people of God, not to become one, but to recognise that they are one in Christ, and to endeavour to give this unity a better expression than they have done in history. That's what this meeting is for.

I differ from Mr Spurgeon. In the College he founded we teach and preach the Gospel that he loved and preached as few men in all history did. But Spurgeon was a pessimist with regard to the Churches. And I'm not. I believe in the Holy Ghost! He believed the Church of England and the Roman Catholics as Churches alike to be manifestations of the spirit of Antichrist. Spurgeon was a man of his age, who shared its intolerance as well as its convictions. We keep the convictions and leave the intolerance.

As if preaching such a sermon were in itself not enough, he then had published an article in *The Christian and Christianity Today*, an article in which he repeated much of his sermon.[63] He himself entitled the article: 'Evangelical Irresponsibility and the Ecumenical Movement'. The paper used as its banner headline a quotation from the article itself: 'How sad that believers in Christ should do the Devil's work for him'! In this article my father did not mince his words.

I'm not ashamed of the Gospel, No. But I confess to being ashamed of some of its defenders. In particular I find myself at a loss to comprehend the tactics of some preachers in their relations with other preachers of the Gospel. There appears to be a competition among Evangelicals to see who can vilify most effectively the people of Christ who believe it is the will of God to end the hostilities within the church.

He attacked the Protestant Truth Society for their 'deliberate untruth' in pretending that the purpose of the

---

63　10 February 1967, 12.

meeting in Ipswich was 'to seek to unite the Protestant Churches under the Church of Rome'. 'This kind of propaganda', declared my father, 'has more in common with the propaganda of Mao Tse Tung than with the Gospel of Jesus Christ'. He ended his article with an appeal:

> I appeal to Evangelical believers to manifest less the attitude of the Inquisition and more the Calvary love of the Lord. Where we differ from other Christians, let us do so in a manner befitting the children of God. If we believe that we have a message for *the whole world*, let us share it with *the whole Church*. For this is the hour when the Churches are ready to listen to men of Evangelical persuasion. We have an unparalleled opportunity to help in the reformation of the Church and to form a spearhead of the Church's evangelistic thrust. Let us not repeat Israel's sin, and fail to recognise the hour of our visitation.

Needless to say the article provoked a flood of varying responses. Many were supportive of the stance he chose to take. But many others disagreed—some courteously and others less courteously.

The *Protestant News-Letter* for March-April 1967, issued by the National Union of Protestants, had as its main headline 'The Menace of the Beasley-Murrays'. The 'literary editor', Charles Alexander, wrote:

> It is a highly suspicious thing when anyone professing himself to be an evangelical lashes out in anger or in contempt against fellow evangelicals. Dr Beasley-Murray is not alone in this. He is representative of the generation of new-evangelicals who are arising all over the English-speaking world and emerging even in the most highly rated evangelical organisations.
>
> They are usually distinguished by their hatred of 'Fundamentalism' and their high regard for the enemies of the gospel. Dr Beasley-Murray's love for Agnellus Andrew is

not only naive; it is sincere, and perhaps not too truthfully expressed...

Dr Murray's attitude to Spurgeon and to Spurgeon's warnings indicates how far the rot has gone in the College over which he rules and which is still graced with Spurgeon's name...

If Spurgeon's is now being managed by a self-professed ecumenicalist, who is also an obvious Neo-Evangelical, the question must arise, 'Whither the British Baptist Union?'...

We can foresee a campaigning for the Millennium at break-neck speed, in which every weight is jettisoned and the little Baptist barquentine will scud before the ecumenical gale, under bare poles. True evangelicals in the Baptist Church should take heed. Their duty is plain; protest or get out...

Today in most evangelical circles such sentiments may seem extreme, if not bizarre. But in the 1960s this was not the case. Many evangelical Baptists had deep suspicion of the World Council of Churches. Francis Dixon, for instance, the minister of one of the largest Baptist churches in the country, Lansdowne, Bournemouth, then still in the Baptist Union, wrote an article in his church magazine, which was then reprinted and widely distributed, in which he disassociated not only himself and his church from the World Council of Churches, but also called for others to do the same. The temperature began to rise amongst many evangelical Baptists. In particular pressure was being put on my father to stem the 'ecumenical tide' in which it was feared 'evangelicals will be drowned'. [64]

---

64   A letter from the Rev Theo Bamber, Chairman of the Baptist Revival Fellowship, sent to my father on 9 February 1967.

Baptists and Unity

The above is the context in which my father's role with
regard to the *Baptists and Unity* report must be seen. My
father at that time was chairman of the Baptist Union's
Advisory Committee on Church Relations. It was
under his chairmanship that the report entitled *Baptists
and Unity* was prepared and presented to the Baptist
Union Council in March 1967. This report was drawn
up in response to a challenge presented by appointed
representatives of the major Protestant denominations
in Britain, meeting at the Nottingham Conference on
Faith and Order in 1964, and directed to the Protestant
churches of Britain. The conference called on the
member churches of the British Council of Churches
(therefore excluding the Roman Catholic Church) to
covenant to work and pray for the inauguration of
union by an agreed date, and it was hoped that this date
would not be later than Easter 1980. It further asked that
any member church that could not join in such a
covenant should state the conditions under which it
could do so.

The Advisory Committee on Church Relations
declared its conviction that it would be wrong for the
Baptist Union to press the idea of organic union by 1980,
'lest it endanger denominational unity and thereby
seriously weaken the witness Baptists have to make'. It
also declined to attempt to state the conditions on
which it would be possible for Baptists to covenant to
work and pray for organic union with other churches.
Instead in its report it described the areas of study that
demanded attention: specifically baptism, the autonomy
of the local congregation, the Lord's Supper, the
ministry (especially in relation to episcopacy), creeds
and confessions, church and state.

It was my father's task to present these issues for
study at the 1967 Baptist Assembly. He ended his
presentation with a personal story:

Twenty years ago I had a long telephone conversation with an honoured minister of our denomination, who in recent years has felt it his duty to oppose the ecumenical movement uncompromisingly.[65] At that time I was involved in a storm in a tea cup that had arisen over certain of my views on eschatology and the tea was splashing violently into the saucer, and I wanted some advice. At the end of the conversation my honoured friend said to me, 'George, I know that many people in our denomination think I'm narrow and harsh in my views, but you know, if a man is right on the person of our Lord, he's all right with me'. I never forgot those words. If my honoured friend is here this morning, I remind him of them, and assure him that sentiment is the beating heart of this report. Let us explore its implications together and endeavour to act on it in our relations with one another. Possibly we shall learn how to extend it beyond our borders.

Needless to say, my father in his role as chairman of the Advisory Committee was not idle during the period set aside for the churches to study the report. He was involved in a good deal of diplomacy, acting as a bridge between conservative evangelicals and the wider denomination. For instance, in response to a suggestion from the Rev Ronald Luland, a member of the committee of the Baptist Revival Fellowship,[66] my father agreed to host a small informal 'meeting of Baptists concerned for our denomination but who are known to entertain different judgements upon the

---

65　The friend was Theo Bamber.

66　The Baptist Revival Fellowship was formed in 1938 by a group of London Baptist ministers who were burdened by the low level of spiritual life in their churches. However, along with their concern for spiritual renewal, was also their concern at what they perceived as theological liberalism within the leadership of the Baptist Union. See McBain, *Fire over the Waters*, 24-26, who draws attention to the unhelpful influence of Martyn Lloyd-Jones on this group.

Ecumenical Movement'.[67] This meeting eventually took place on 13 December 1967. After almost four hours of discussion, it was felt to be so helpful that the group met again in the following February. At the same time my father was involved in the more formal 'Ad Hoc' Committee set up on 12 September 1967 by the General Purposes and Finance Committee of the Baptist Union to look at 'causes of dissension within the denomination leading to the withdrawal of some churches', of which a chief cause was the difference of attitude to the ecumenical movement.[68] In addition my father was involved in much correspondence with individual ministers and churches, who had deep concerns about the *Baptists and Unity* report.

After two years of study, during which 655 churches, seventeen associations, several ministers' fraternals and a number of individuals submitted written comments, my father, at the Baptist Assembly of 1969, moved a resolution to the effect that Baptists should continue to share in the exploration and discussion of ecumenical issues both within the denomination and with those of other denominations. The resolution went on to recognise the differences of conviction among Baptists regarding inter-church relations and the right of members to engage in or to refrain from participation. It called upon all members to maintain in their differences a mutual trust and love which accords with their fellowship in Christ.

---

[67]   Letter to Ronald Luland dated 27 October 1967.

[68]   Ecumenism, however, wasn't the only issue. Other concerns included 'doubts of the adequacy of the declaration of principle in the constitution of the Union'; suspicion of the activities and designs of the union and desire to preserve inviolate the independence of the local church; and apparent reluctance of the union to give place to evangelicals in Baptist Union matters and on Baptist Union platforms' (Interim Report of the Committee on Causes of Dissension within the Denomination).

As J.J. Brown, himself a former President of the Baptist Union, noted: 'The fact that the resolution was approved by a large majority was due in no small measure to the tone and content of the proposer's presentation of this delicate subject.'[69] Similarly David Coffey, the present General Secretary of the Baptist Union, commented at my father's funeral: 'From our vantage point on the ecumenical journey, this was a clearly prophetic stance to adopt at the end of the 1960s, but he was trusted and the report was received by the Assembly.'

I believe that Bamber was right, my father was the man who, more than any other leader of his generation, combined evangelicalism with ecumenism. My father was in a unique position. I found it interesting that at the time of my father's death, the *Scottish Baptist Magazine*'s editorial highlighted not his writings or his past addresses, but rather his ecumenical contribution.[70]

Bultmann's John

To many evangelicals it seemed extraordinary that the Principal of Spurgeon's College should be responsible for the translation of the commentary on *John* by Rudolf Bultmann, which was published in Britain in 1971.[71] For Bultmann was an extreme sceptic of the historicity of the Gospels—he once said that all we can know about Jesus is '*that* he lived and died'—and insisted that the Gospels needed to be 'demythologized' of all its extraneous superstition and mythological elements. However, my father was unconcerned by the astonishment of his fellow evangelicals. In his search

---

[69] 'Denominational Leader', *Spurgeon's College Record* 47 (December 1973), 10.

[70] Mary Sinclair, *Scottish Baptist Magazine* (April 2000), 1.

[71] Rudolf Bultmann, *The Gospel of John: A Commentary* (Basil Blackwell, Oxford, 1964) edited and supervised with assistance from R.W.N. Hoare and J.K. Riches.

for truth he believed it to be important to look at every viewpoint. As he wrote in an article for ministers:

> Investigation of the Scriptures which by hook or by crook reaches predetermined conclusions is a denial of the Spirit of truth who is behind them and does no honour to our Lord or His Gospel. The minister who is afraid of truth contradicts alike his calling and his credentials.[72]

He was convinced that he could always learn something, even from those with whom he disagreed. Furthermore, he believed that those with whom one disagreed should always be treated courteously. As he said in his Drew lecture: 'Where scholars divide one has to make one's own decision and maintain it with respect for the opinions of others.'[73]

People would have been less surprised by his decision to head the translation of Bultmann's *John* if they had listened to a Third Programme BBC talk given by my father in 1955. On that occasion he had taken issue with Bultmann's approach to the Gospel, and yet at the same time was prepared to acknowledge that Bultmann had made a very positive contribution to Christian thought, and not least in his emphasis on the cross: 'However absurd it may sound, in his desire to make men see their only hope of redemption in the Cross, Bultmann shares the evangelistic aim of a Billy Graham, even though the methods of the two men have no contact'.[74]

---

[72] 'The Minister and his Bible', *The Fraternal* 92 (April 1954), 14.

[73] 'The Contribution of the Book of Revelation to the Christian Belief in Immortality' (The Drew Lecture on Immortality), delivered at the Whitefield Memorial Church on 27 October 1972, printed in *Scottish Journal of Theology* 27 (1974), 79, and later in C.S. Duthie (ed.), *Resurrection and Immortality* (Bagster, London, 1979), 108.

[74] 'Bultmann and "Demythologising"', *The Listener* Vol. 54 (13 October 1955), 601.

Christology

Christology—the doctrine of the person of Christ—
provided yet another area of contention, where once
again my father proved to be 'fearless for truth'. An
address given by the Rev Michael Taylor, the then
recently appointed Principal of the Northern Baptist
College, at the Baptist Union Assembly of April 1971
sparked off a major controversy that lasted a full year
until the following assembly. The development of the
controversy could form the subject of a whole book and
the many details are important to evaluate the stance
my father took. It is therefore necessary to give a
detailed account of the way in which matters were
handled.

On the Tuesday night of the Baptist Union Assembly
Michael Taylor, at the invitation of Dr Henton Davies,
Principal of Regent's Park College, Oxford, and the
newly installed President of the Baptist Union, gave an
address which caused much consternation. The title of
the address, which had been given to him by Henton
Davies, was 'The Incarnate Presence; how much of a
man was Jesus Christ?' That night Michael Taylor
appeared to question the very basis of the Christian
faith.

In an attempt to restate in a contemporary manner
the Nicene Creed he put forward the following 'draft'
statement:

> The story of Jesus makes such an overwhelming impression
> that I am not content to say that he was an extraordinary
> man. I believe that in the man Jesus we encounter God. I
> believe that God was active in Jesus, but it will not quite do
> to say categorically: Jesus is God. Jesus is unique, but his
> uniqueness does not make him different in kind from us. He
> is the same sort of animal. He is fully and unambiguously a
> man. The difference between him and ourselves is not in the
> manner of God's presence in Jesus. The difference is in what

God did in and through this man and the degree to which
this man responded and co-operated with God.

A little later he went on to say:

> However remarkable this life, I think I must stop short of
> saying categorically: Jesus is God, and I understand the New
> Testament probably stops short of it as well. This is the
> most troubling aspect of some of the old creeds which keep
> insisting that Jesus is truly God and truly man, of one
> substance with the Father and one substance with us—as if
> the more you shout about it the more convincing it becomes.
> But it sounds like a contradiction to me.

My father, aware of the strong feelings this address
was already beginning to arouse and of the implications
which it could have for the ministers and churches of
the Baptist Union, at the Thursday afternoon meeting
of the Baptist Union Council asked that a notice be put
in the *Baptist Times* assuring people that the views of
speakers at the assembly were not necessarily representative of the Baptist Union Council. This deliberately
non-judgmental suggestion was made over against the
plea by another council member, Rev Stanley Voke,
that the council should immediately repudiate the exposition of Christology given by Michael Taylor. Dr
Ernest Payne, the distinguished former General
Secretary of the Baptist Union, argued that it was the
wrong thing to do because that particular council
meeting was not a full council meeting—it was held
simply for the purpose of co-opting new council
members. The council was persuaded by Ernest Payne
and other denominational leaders to do nothing.

For the next few months my father made no public
statement about the address. He was involved in
considerable correspondence and discussion with concerned ministers and lay-people. A small representative
group met with Michael Taylor in mid-September with
a view to elucidating some of the problems of

interpreting his address, but my father felt no progress was made at all. Michael Taylor refused to enter into the conversation about the issues of concern. The following week the Baptist Union's General Purpose and Finance Committee held their monthly meeting to discuss matters further. My father expressed himself very strongly, declaring his conviction that such an exposition of Christology was irreconcilable with the historic Christian faith—but to no avail. For, as my father reported, 'every strong figure' on that committee was 'active in advocating their support for Michael Taylor',[75] not because they necessarily agreed with his views, but because they wished to support the principle of religious liberty.

Many of the ministers and churches in membership with the Baptist Union were becoming increasingly perplexed and troubled at the unwillingness of its leadership to make any comment upon the assembly address. A well-attended public meeting, for instance, took place at Bloomsbury Central Baptist Church on Saturday 2 October, at which the Rev David Pawson gave an address on 'How much of a God is Jesus?'[76]

When the matter of the assembly address came to a meeting of the Baptist Union Council held on 9

---

[75]   Private letter to Sir Cyril Black, 22 September 1971.

[76]   My father was not present at the meeting, but listened to a tape of the address. In a private letter of 11 November 1971 to the Rev Andrew McKie, my father commented: 'David Pawson has one of the clearest minds that I know, and has a most extraordinary gift of lucidity. I felt that this was particularly observable in his attempt to draft out a confession of faith. In so far as it is possible to do that in a child's language, I think that David succeeded in doing it here. Naturally on a number of points I would express myself differently from David, and if one compares his address with that of Michael Taylor one has to admit that it suffers by comparison in as much as Michael Taylor had the opportunity of thinking for months over his address and doubtless prepared it with the utmost care.'

November 1971, in spite of my father's pleading to the contrary, the council, by a very large majority, recognised the right of Michael Taylor to express himself in the way he did. At the same time the council asserted its adherence to the Declaration of Principle contained in the constitution of the Baptist Union in which Jesus Christ is acknowledged as both 'Lord and Saviour' and 'God manifest in the flesh'. The council stated:

> The Council recognises that the address on the humanity of Jesus given at its invitation by the Rev Michael Taylor was an individual attempt made, with integrity, by a member of the Baptist community expressing faith in the living Christ as a contribution to the ongoing theological task...
>
> The Union has always contained within its fellowship those of different theological opinions and emphases, believing that its claim for toleration involves tolerance and mutual respect within its ranks.[77]

In the light of the passing of such a resolution my father felt that he had no option but to resign as chairman of the council because he could no longer associate himself with its position. In a letter to Dr David Russell, the General Secretary of the Baptist Union, dated 17 November he confirmed his resignation. It was circulated at my father's request to members of the council. He wrote:

> I tried to explain to the Council my conviction that what was expressed was not faith in the living Christ of the Bible, and

---

[77]   In actual fact the council had not given the invitation to Michael Taylor, nor had it given him the subject. The responsibility for this lay on the shoulders of Henton Davies. Henton Davies, however, in a lengthy statement published in December 1971, not only disassociated himself from the address, but also made it clear that Michael Taylor in his address provided 'something radically different from what I anticipated'.

that its implications demand radical changes in Baptists' attitudes to the New Testament, to the God we worship and the Gospel we preach. Not least on such a basis our understanding of baptism would be an anachronism, and therefore the continued existence of our denomination unwarranted.

He concluded that his resignation would now free him from 'the restraint which I felt laid upon me since the assembly'.[78]

At the same time he also wrote a personal letter to Michael Taylor, with whom he had had a three-hour private conversation in his home at Spurgeon's College the previous Sunday. Two of its paragraphs read as follows:

You and I have been placed in positions that are burdensome to endure. You will need great grace to forgive me for my apparent intransigence. It is a question of the Gospel being in my sight of greater account than either you or me. I hope that it may be possible speedily to dissociate discussions from your name and person. That may be difficult at first, but I shall do all in my power to see that it is achieved.

On Sunday evening last we tried to be open to each other. You thought we had not got very far. If we reached deadlock in our discussions at least we came (I believe) to a fuller understanding of each other. This has made it more difficult for us both in coming days in a way that is right, for it will temper our words. Perhaps that applied to me even more than you—though you may be tempted to hard thoughts and words about me at times. The discussion cannot possibly end at this point. You have set in motion forces that will continue to move for a long time. My concern will be to try to direct some of them at any rate in a right direction. If the end of it all is a greater understanding of Christ and the Gospel

---

78   The letter was held back by David Russell and not actually circulated until after the meeting of the General Purposes and Finance Committee on 7 December 1971.

and a better communication of our message to the world, that will be a wonderful gain. But in the process there will certainly be hurt, for many feel that their faith and the Baptist Denomination in particular is threatened, and people in that situation are not used to quiet speaking. They feel above all that the honour of the Lord is at stake, and they must see that we give him his rightful place in our thought and message...[79]

The pressure on the Baptist Union leadership continued to grow. On the very day Dr David Russell received my father's letter of resignation he also received a resolution from the Baptist Revival Fellowship indicating that the vast majority of those who had put their names to the resolution were contemplating resignation from the accredited list of ministers and were determined to encourage others to do likewise. This was followed by a letter sent on behalf of the November Swanwick Conference of the Baptist Revival Fellowship to all ministers, deacons and churches of the Baptist Union, which stated:

> We cannot in conscience remain associated with the life of a Union which has decided to tolerate the denial of the Deity of our Lord Jesus Christ amongst its accredited ministers. The details of the way in which we translate this conviction into action will be a matter of individual judgment. We understand that some of our members will resign in the immediate future from the BU Accredited List and that some will do so later.[80]

On 12 January 1972 David Russell wrote to all ministers and church secretaries to reassure the churches of the Baptist Union's commitment to its Declaration of

---

[79]   Letter dated 17 November 1971.

[80]   The statement was passed with 155 votes in favour, 14 against and 24 abstentions. Although the conference met in Swanwick from 15-18 November, the actual letter with the statement was not sent out until 31 December 1971.

Principle with regard to the deity of our Lord. However, in so far as David Russell failed to distance the union from Michael Taylor's address, his letter was not able to pour oil on troubled water. In this climate Frank Fitzsimmonds, President of the Spurgeon's College Conference, wrote to all past students of the college urging patience on those considering secession: 'I beg you to hold back at least for a while longer, from precipitate action, however strongly it may be provoked.'[81]

Throughout these months my father was in constant touch with Sir Cyril Black, a former Conservative Member of Parliament for Wimbledon and a prominent Baptist layman, who, less than two years earlier in his role as President of the Baptist Union, had chosen as his presidential theme 'Reconciliation'. Together they formed a small unofficial group with a view to coming to a common mind on a resolution to be brought to the 1972 Assembly of the Baptist Union, which would make it possible for ministers and churches contemplating secession to remain in the union. It was in this context that in January my father submitted an article for publication in the *Baptist Times* entitled 'The Controversy Cannot End—Yet', which in essence urged the forthcoming assembly to confess its faith in Christ and to disassociate itself from any Christology which does not recognise Christ's full deity as well as his complete humanity. My father began his article in this way:

> Recent correspondents in the *Baptist Times* have pleaded that a halt be made to the endless disputing that has been going on in the denomination of late. A cry has gone out, 'Let's end all argument, and let's get on with the job'.
>
> I understand the reaction. I, too, hate controversy, especially with my own people, and above all with my own colleagues. But may I in turn plead that those who have so

---

[81] Letter dated 12 November 1971.

understandably expressed themselves take time to sit and think? What are they wanting to get on with? Preaching the Gospel? But it is precisely the Gospel which is at stake in the present discussion! My great fear is that at this juncture we may be so desirous of seizing on peace at any price that we may be prepared to pay the price of Christ.

Let us face it: a torch has been thrust into the forest, and a blaze has been started. Nobody wanted it, but it's spreading. To demand that we may be quiet about it is to ask that we sit and watch destruction. And that's crazy.

I believe that our denomination does not realise what has taken place in its midst. The issues are of such importance, we must make time to look at them, steadily and clearly.

The editor, Rev Walter Bottoms, refused to publish the article, pleading 'In a matter where expert opinion is divided I believe it would be both unjust and a breach of fundamental principle for the council or assembly to pass a vote of censure.'[82]

My father was dismayed by the rejection and replied to Walter Bottoms that he would find another avenue for the publication of his views.[83] With the encouragement of friends and with the financial backing of Sir Cyril Black, he turned his article into a booklet entitled *The Christological Controversy in the Baptist Union* and sent it to all Baptist ministers together with an accompanying letter on 20 March 1972. At no point did my father use Michael Taylor's name; as far as he was concerned this was not a personal vendetta but an issue of principle in which the gospel was at stake. In the letter he wrote:

The last meeting of the Baptist Union Council illustrated yet again that Baptists who share my disquiet about the theology propounded among us are seriously misunderstood. It is being maintained that our troubles are due to a division in

---

[82] Letter dated 21 January 1972.
[83] Letter dated 25 January 1972.

the Union between an outmoded right wing theology and a progressive theology which takes account of the realities of our time (the former was actually described by one Council member as 'nineteenth century revivalistic theology'). The difference could be more objectively described as between a small group of theologians maintaining a theological novelty and the consensus of theologians past and present. Such a characterisation does not settle the rightness or wrongness of the views in question, but it sets the identification in perspective...

The enclosed article suggests the seriousness of the theological issues involved and these require more prolonged consideration. Surely we shall not shirk to give this? If my interpretation of the issues is false, let it be shown by reasoned statements. I am always very anxious to learn!

In the booklet my father sought to spell out the implications of the so-called 'new' approach to the incarnation developed by 'process' theologians such as Norman Pittenger and embraced by the American New Testament scholar, John Knox. Not only the doctrine of the Trinity was at stake, my father maintained, but also the doctrine of salvation, Christian worship, the church and its sacraments. He brought his argument to an end in this way:

It is my settled conviction that the logical end of this theology is the reduction of Christianity to a Reformed Judaism...

Christ and the Gospel are inseparable. A Christ who is man but not God entails a different religion from that of the New Testament. Admittedly the New Testament presents us with diverse elements with which to construct a Christology rather than a finished product. The great issue is whether in its pages there is a reality corresponding to the declarations about the Paraclete in the Fourth Gospel (John 14–16). Have we or have we not testimony to Christ from the Spirit of Truth which conveys an understanding of who He really was and who He is. The Church through the ages has answered that question with an affirmative. Baptists can claim a place in that Church only in so far as they join in that affirmation. If otherwise, they become a 'sect' in the worst sense of the term, as their adversaries have so often regarded them...

We must declare where we stand. If we fail to do so we call in question our existence as a Christian denomination today. And there may be no tomorrow.

This letter brought scores of letters supporting my father. It also provoked strong reaction among the more liberal members of the denomination, who sent strong letters of protest to my father. Probably the strongest letters of protest came from Ernest Payne.

It is instructive to quote extracts from the exchange of letters in order to gain a feel for how things were. In his first letter Ernest Payne, wrote:

I feel impelled to let you know how shocked and grieved I have been to receive the letter and article which you have sent to all Baptist ministers.

He accused my father of having misunderstood Michael Taylor, and went on:

Christian history is littered with examples showing how impossible it is to expect a popular Assembly of our kind 'to clear the air'. By your action you have, I fear, pushed the denomination nearer disaster at a moment when your friends hoped you were going to exercise the kind of restraining influence which we surely have the right to expect from you... You have spent a lot of time and energy translating Bultmann. What if I publicly criticised you for spreading the views of one who is regarded by many as being extremely arbitrary in his treatment of evidence and who reduced the reliable information about Jesus and his teaching to a few verses only?[84]

---

[84] Dated 6 April 1972.

In response my father sent Ernest Payne a strong but courteous letter back:

> If you think that an unprejudiced reader could not read into Michael's address the kind of denials with which I have charged him, I have evidence to the contrary. I submitted that manuscript of mine to two theologians to ask their views of it, and they both concurred with what I had written.

The two theologians in question were Professor Tom Torrance of Edinburgh University, and Dr Charles Duthie, the Principal of New College, London. With regard to the views of Rudolf Bultmann, my father went on:

> I wonder whether you have read his exposition of the Gospel of John. I wish with all my heart that Michael had it in him to declare the gospel in the kind of terms that Bultmann makes of John 3.16 and other related sayings within that gospel... Naturally I do not accept Bultmann's historical scepticism, but you ought to know Bultmann well enough to realise that he is an exponent of the Lutheran doctrine of justification by faith, despite his absurd limitation of the authentic teaching in the Synoptic Gospels. The extraordinary thing is what he does manage to make of the amount of the teaching of Jesus which he does recognise as authentic.[85]

Dr Payne was not mollified. Instead he sent a second letter which ended:

> You have been stirring up trouble instead of calming it, and have contributed therefore, more than perhaps any other single individual, to the very difficult and dangerous situation we now face. Is not 1 Cor 3 relevant to our present distress. I beg you to think again and, if you speak next

---

[85] Letter dated 12 April 1972.

week, to choose your words with greater care than I think you showed in your recent letter and article.[86]

My father wrote back:

A discussion of this kind, particularly between ourselves, is particularly distasteful to me. I think, however, that you have allowed yourself not merely unwise but almost violent charges to be laid against me, in virtually accusing me to be a troubler of Israel. This doubtless is because you do not concur with my kind of tactics. They are that differences of theological judgment should be openly acknowledged and not hidden. The more so when they are of vital importance. I did my utmost to prevent a fire raging in the denomination. You will remember that on the occasion of the Council meeting that was at the end of the last assembly I pleaded with the Council members then present to issue a statement with regard to the address of Michael Taylor embodying the perfectly obvious observation that speakers at our assembly bear the responsibility for their utterances themselves, and that the Union is neither responsible nor implicated in them... You yourself were above all responsible for the Council declining that advice... I believe that you made a grave mistake, and that you thereby made possible the escalation of the discussion to a denominational controversy... If the Baptist Union were to be characterised by the theology uttered and implied by Michael Taylor I could have no part with it. That perhaps is of minor consequence, but so long as I am a part of our Baptist Union I feel it my duty to prevent the Union from moving in a direction away from essential Christianity. Invective against such a decision is wholly out of place. So far as I am concerned I have endeavoured and shall continue to endeavour to keep this discussion in a spirit that is consonant with our Gospel. It is my earnest hope that such a spirit will prevail in the discussion on Tuesday next.[87]

---

[86] Letter dated 18 April 1972.
[87] Letter dated 20 April 1972.

Matters reached a climax at the Baptist Union Assembly on Tuesday 25 April 1972. Delegates from the churches who had come for the debate packed Westminster Chapel from floor to ceiling as they debated and then voted upon the resolution, proposed by Sir Cyril Black, and seconded by my father. Great care had been taken in the drawing up of the resolution that Michael Taylor was not mentioned by name.[88] The issue was about principles, not personalities. It read as follows:

> This Assembly of the Baptist Union of Great Britain and Ireland places on record its deep sadness that during the past year divisions and misunderstandings have arisen among us that have disturbed our fellowship, caused the withdrawal of certain ministers and churches, and may possibly cause the withdrawal of others. We earnestly seek at this critical time for the removal, by God's help, of these divisions and misunderstandings, so that unitedly we may labour more effectively together for the extension of the Redeemer's Kingdom.
>
> Following the example of the council, we gladly and explicitly reaffirm our wholehearted acceptance of and belief in the Declaration of Principle set out in the Constitution. We thereby unreservedly assert of our belief in God the Father, Son and Holy Spirit, into whose Name are baptised those who have professed repentance towards God and faith in our Lord Jesus Christ, who 'died for our sins according to the Scriptures, was buried and rose again the third day'. We acknowledge this Jesus Christ as both 'Lord and Saviour' and 'God manifest in the flesh' (understanding these words as expressing unqualified faith in His full deity and real humanity). We recognise Him as the sole and absolute authority in all matters pertaining to faith and practice as revealed in the Holy Scriptures, and acknowledge

---

[88] It is perhaps of note that following his address at the 1970 Assembly Michael Taylor made no further public utterance on the subject.

the liberty of each Church under the guidance of the Holy Spirit to administer and interpret His laws.

We firmly and unhesitatingly place on record our conviction that the Declaration of Principle represents the basic requirements for fellowship in the Baptist Denomination and that we attach high importance to the loyal and wholehearted acceptance of it. In particular we assert the unacceptability of any interpretation of the person and work of Jesus Christ Our Lord which would obscure or deny the fundamental tenet of the Christian Faith that Jesus Christ is Lord and Saviour, truly God and truly Man.

We recall that a rule of Ministerial Recognition stipulates that 'all persons who become or remain Ministers or Probationers accredited by the Union are required to accept the Declaration of Principle as contained in the Constitution of the Union'.

We earnestly desire that these emphatic reassurances may be effective in removing all misapprehensions and may make it possible for Ministers and Churches contemplating secession to remain in the Union, and for ministers and churches of the Baptist Faith and Order who have departed from, or never belonged to, the Union, to enter into discussion with us with a view to entry or re-entry into our Fellowship.

We are profoundly convinced that the unity together of all who can sincerely and wholeheartedly subscribe to the Declaration of Principle will enable us to witness and work more effectively in these challenging days, so that God may be glorified and His Kingdom extended.

Four amendments were presented, all of which were thrown out by large majorities.[89] Instead, when the

---

[89] Significantly this included the amendment proposed by Dr Leonard Champion, Principal of Bristol Baptist College, which would have deleted paragraphs 3 and 4 concerning the words 'We firmly and unhesitating place on record...' and ending with the words '...as contained in the constitution of the Union' on the ground that these paragraphs were an 'interpretation' of the deity of Christ as referred to in the

resolution was put to the assembly, it was over-whelmingly carried. Of the several thousand delegates present, only forty-six voted against it, and seventy-two abstentions were recorded, being the expression of those who wished to be associated with the positive statements in the resolution but not with paragraphs three and four. The vote brought astonishment to the leaders of the Baptist Union as indeed to others. Only the previous week one leading Baptist minister had commented that 'he felt the Assembly would be swamped by the rising tide of apathy about this issue, which would lead to a resounding defeat for Sir Cyril's resolution and the vindication of the Council's position'.[90]

It was a historic vote. In the words of my father: 'We have never had a debate on this magnitude in the present century, and the delegates by their vote made abundantly plain their faith in Christ and the Gospel and their dissociation from liberal views of Christ and a liberal Gospel.'[91] Sir Cyril Black for his part commented: 'Most of our Ministers and lay people are much more conservative than are what might be described, not unkindly, as the "professional" Committee men who

---

Declaration of Principle. He, along with Dr Ernest Payne and others, feared that, if passed, they might open the door to action leading to the 'excommunication' of Michael Taylor. Dr Raymond Brown, in a private letter dated 17 May 2000, commented: 'I think the top brass knew only too well that it was not your father's wish (nor Sir Cyril's, I believe) to organise a heresy trial for Michael Taylor, but they knew that, such was the intensity of feeling at that time, there were plenty of people who would have given anything to have him drummed out, if only as a warning to others.' For further details of the proposed amendments see *The Baptist Union Directory 1973–1974* (Baptist Union, London, 1974), 41.

[90] Quoted anonymously by John Capon in his report for the *Christian Record*, 12 April 1972.

[91] Letter dated 11 May 1972 from my father to the Editor of *Die Gemeinde*, the German Baptist magazine.

tend to dominate the Finance and General Purposes Committee and the Council of the Union. The strength of this conservative opinion in the denomination cannot any longer be ignored.'[92]

From that moment things began to settle down. True, not immediately. There were still rumblings from the 'right' wing, represented by the Baptist Revival Fellowship, and the 'left' wing represented by the Baptist Renewal Group. However, the resolution had been passed and the widespread anxiety in the churches had been allayed. It was not to be long before the tide began to turn and the losses which the Baptist Union had suffered from secession of ministers and churches began to be made up. Indeed, there are those who see 1972 as the moment when the tide actually began to turn even though it was some years before the tide began to come in. The ethos of the denomination began to change. Evangelicals began to get more involved in Baptist Union structures. The ginger group, 'Mainstream—Baptists for life and growth', was formed, and the Baptist Union began to experience new life and new growth.[93]

How then are we to evaluate the controversy? The first thing to be clear about is that a Christological matter can never be less than important. As my father wrote at the time:

---

[92] Letter to David Russell dated 25 April 1972.

[93] One of the aims of this ginger group, which arose as a result of Douglas McBain and myself coming together, was to get 'Mainstream'-minded people into office in the Baptist Union, and as the 1980s and 1990s were to prove, the group had great success in this particular respect. Douglas McBain himself became an Area Superintendent. Other members of the first Mainstream Executive included David Coffey, the present General Secretary of the Baptist Union, and Peter Grange, a current Area Superintendent. See McBain, *Fire over the Waters*, 82-85.

Here was no secondary issue for theologians to argue over through having nothing better to do. Nothing in the universe is more important than the truth of Jesus Christ and the proclamation of the Gospel. It seemed necessary for drastic action to be taken...to ensure that these supreme truths should not be endangered among us.[94]

Hindsight is always a wonderful thing, but it does seem that repeatedly the denomination was not at that stage well served by its leaders and its council members. It is possible that the subsequent troubles might well have been avoided had the Baptist Union Council at its meeting at the 1971 assembly taken the action my father proposed. Although much of the blame for this might be laid on the shoulders of the leadership of the union, it did not help that some of the more evangelical members of the council failed to perceive what the consequences for the denomination would be if prompt action were not taken. Similarly had the council at its meeting in November 1971 disassociated itself from the views expressed by Michael Taylor, the trouble might have been defused. Sir Cyril Black, perhaps unfairly, put much of the blame on the shoulders of David Russell: 'I think that he started out on this matter seeing himself as what might be described as the "great adjuster" and in the belief that the various people who expressed concern had not understood the matters properly and that it would only be necessary for him to explain it for everything to be all right.'[95]

Matters were not helped by the more 'hard-line' members of the Baptist Revival Fellowship, who almost seemed to be looking for trouble; nor were matters helped by certain people in the *Evangelical Times* constituency, who were looking to recruit members of the Baptist denomination for the Fellowship of Independent Evangelical Churches. The *Baptist Times*

---

94   *Spurgeon's College Record* 54 (June 1972), 5.
95   Private letter to my father dated 21 July 1971.

was equally unhelpful and, from the perspective of the evangelical wing, inflammatory in its coverage of the controversy.[96] The fact is that many 'loyal' Baptists were deeply perturbed too.

As for my father's role, evangelicals generally have seen him as the saviour of the union, without whom the denomination would have split irretrievably. Dr Derek Tidball, for instance, the Principal of London Bible College, states that my father's part in that controversy 'was one of the things that kept me in the denomination at a time when many of my friends were looking elsewhere'.[97]

On the other hand, others felt my father got things out of proportion, and so went 'over the top' unnecessarily. Dr David Russell, for instance, reflecting on my father's resignation from the chairmanship of the Baptist Union Council wrote:

> As General Secretary, sitting by his side, I confess I was greatly taken aback by this unexpected announcement, given without warning. I tried to reason with him, but to no avail. I recognised that he had acted out of deep conviction, demonstrating that same fearlessness in pursuing what he believed to be the truth. There was nothing vindictive about his protest, but it did accentuate the division that had already shown itself. I continue to believe, as I did back then, that his action in resigning in the way he did tended to increase the tension within the denomination, not least when it would appear, some people thought he had resigned, not

96 For example, in its issue of 11 November the editorial contained a highly critical report of David Pawson's address. As Sir Cyril Black, in a private letter of 12 November 1971, said to my father: 'Large numbers of people regard the *Baptist Times* as the voice of the establishment at the Church House, and they will bitterly resent the terms of these criticisms of David Pawson... If ever there was a case of pouring fuel on the flames, this is it. It is quite obvious to me that there is no possibility of the Michael Taylor controversy dying down.'
97   Email dated 28 March 2000.

from the chairmanship of the Council but from the Union itself.[98]

Bernard Green, who succeeded Dr David Russell as General Secretary of the Baptist Union and who had great admiration for my father, likewise felt his actions were not helpful:

> As the controversy increased he obviously found himself under tremendous pressures from different groups and individuals within the evangelical wing of the denomination and beyond. I wonder if this became so intolerable that he did what was not typical of him. His letter to all Baptist ministers, dated 20th March 1972, together with his booklet, 'The Christological Controversy in the Baptist Union' added fuel to the fire... I wonder if your father now uncharacter- istically looked over his shoulder at those who were pressing their case more and more, and struggled with what he ought to say and do to satisfy them. Yet, to his credit, he would not go as far as some of them were demanding, and he still publicly upheld Michael Taylor's integrity.[99]

Alec Gilmore, a long-standing member of the Baptist Union Council, had a particular friendship with Michael Taylor, who had entered ministry from his first church in Northampton, had also over the years become a friend of my father's, differed also from my father's perceptions:

> At the time I felt George over-reacted rather and I put it down to the fact that he was more acutely aware than most of the tendencies for splitting in the Baptist churches of the States and feared that something similar would be happen- ing here, but I think he failed to take sufficient account of the differences between the USA and the UK and also of the

---

98   'Recollections and Reflections', a private communication sent to me in June 2000.
99   Letter dated 31 July 2000.

fact that neither Michael nor any of those who may have gone along with his views were in a mood for division.

I think it is true that he was not the only one among Baptist leadership at that time to overreact and I had much sympathy with him. It seems to me he was somewhat unfortunate at that time to be in a position for which he was not ideally equipped. His major gifts were in other spheres and though he could handle the job well as long as things ran smoothly, handling that kind of crisis was not his forte. The fact that the issues were ones on which he had such strong convictions did not help, but for that and for the timing neither he nor anyone else could be responsible.[100]

Throughout that year of controversy I was out of the country serving with the Baptist Missionary Society in the Democratic Republic of Congo (Zaire). On returning to the UK and then accepting a call to minister in Altrincham, on the south side of Manchester, I quickly discovered that for many people in 'Northern pews' the controversy was seen, in part at least, in geographical terms, of 'South' against 'North', of 'them' against 'us'. While this may have been true to a degree, in no way was this a root cause. It was in essence a theological controversy.

Looking back over the controversy I am convinced that my father took the right course of action. He was right in seeing the dangers posed by Michael Taylor's address. There is little doubt that had my father not take the courageous and costly stand he took, the denomination would have been damagingly split. He was right not to personalise issues, but to focus on the theological issues that were at stake. As a result of focusing on those theological issues, the denomination, in a way which had not been true previously, took a distinctively evangelical turn of direction. This change in direction may well be one of the reasons why in the late twentieth century Baptist churches in Britain held

---

[100] Private communication dated 25 May 2000.

their own over against other denominations which lost substantial numbers of people.

Travel

In 1971 my mother was elected President of the Baptist Women's League. Whereas previously my mother had always driven up to central London to meet my father at one of the mainline stations after a preaching engagement, now it was my father's turn to meet my mother. He was very supportive of her.

For the most part, however, it was my father who was the traveller. As a preacher and lecturer he travelled all over the country—and beyond too. At times this led to tension in the college. My father remembered well how when he was first appointed principal, the college officers made it clear that they wanted a man to represent the college overseas and as far as they were concerned they could always get other men to lecture. But just a year or two later after his appointment a well-known minister said that the college needed a principal who would be in the classroom—it didn't matter if the principal was not able to travel. Different expectations!

In February 1973 my father was invited by the Senate of McMaster University, Hamilton, Ontario, Canada, to accept the honorary degree of Doctor of Divinity and to address the Divinity College Convocation on 1 June 1973.

In authorising this award, members of Senate were keenly appreciative of your distinguished career as a teacher, scholar and administrator. They recognised the excellence of your service to the Baptist Church which culminated in your election to the presidency of the Baptist Union of Great Britain and Ireland in 1968–69. They had before them the impressive list of your publications which have gained you such high esteem and eminence among your peers.

An Invitation to Louisville

My father had often received invitations to serve in other colleges and seminaries around the world. Although grateful for these offers, he never hesitated to decline them. He knew that his work was at Spurgeon's. But in March 1973 when yet another invitation came from the Southern Baptist Theological Seminary in Louisville, Kentucky, my father realised that maybe this was the time to lay down the principalship.[101] He was frustrated by the fact that he had got behind with his writing and doing the things that God had laid on his heart to do. So he felt at this time he should accept the invitation. He explained his acceptance in this way:

> In recent years various friends have urged me to consider setting aside a few years of my working life to increase my contribution to the wider constituencies of Baptists by being more productive in writing. From the commencement of my time as principal here requests have pressed upon me to serve other Colleges and Christian institutions, and always I have had the conviction that the time was not right for any such move. Now, however, the situation has changed. The College is in a position of strength under God, we have young men able to serve it well, and a very insistent call has come for service in a challenging situation. The Lord's hand seems unmistakably to beckon us on, and my wife and I feel that we have to respond to that leading.[102]

The timing may well have been of the Lord. My father had already given twenty-two years of his life—six as tutor, and sixteen as principal—to the college, and it could well be argued that both he and the college needed a fresh start. The college itself was in good heart.

---

[101] It was in September 1955 that Dr Duke McCall, the President of Southern Baptist Theological Seminary, first sought to invite my father to spend a year as a visiting professor at Louisville.

[102] A circular letter sent to friends in April 1973.

There were a good number of students, and there was a faculty composed of some very capable men—Dr Raymond Brown, Stanley Dewhurst, Frank Fitzsimmonds, Dr Rex Mason and Dr Bruce Milne.

Of the many letters my father received wishing him well, one of them in particular needs to be recorded. Michael Taylor, then still Principal of the Northern Baptist College, wrote:

> It was kind of you to include me in the list of friends whom you have notified about your move to Louisville. It sounds right to me. I want you to know that I shall be genuinely sorry to see you go from a personal point of view, but you both have my warmest good wishes. I hope this opening will provide you with ample opportunity to make an even greater contribution to our common life.[103]

His old friend, Professor F.F. Bruce, expressed a similar wish in his tribute at that time to my father:

> It is a pity that a man of his calibre cannot get an opportunity in his own country for the uninterrupted pursuit of biblical scholarship, but we can only applaud the vision of Louisville Seminary in providing him with a post in which the necessary leisure will be forthcoming.[104]

A Pleasant Man to Live With

Among all the tributes given to my father the most personal came from one of his colleagues, Frank Fitzsimmonds, which appeared in the *Baptist Times* when my father was called to Louisville, and was later reproduced in the *Spurgeon's College Record* after his death. It bears reprinting in full, for it conveys something of his character.

---

[103] Letter dated 27 April 1973.
[104] 'Biblical Scholar', *Spurgeon's College Record* 57 (December 1973), 9.

I remember years ago hearing Pearce Carey lecture enthusiastically on the subject of William Carey. When the lecture concluded an opportunity was given for questions and these enabled still more of Carey's life and character to be unfolded.

At last a little old lady rose to put her question. She said, 'I know that he was a great man. I know that he was a good man. But tell me, was he a pleasant man to live with?'

I thought it was the most sensible question of the evening, and I was delighted to hear Pearce Carey give a clear affirmative reply.

Perhaps there are those in the wider circle of the churches who would like to put the same question concerning George Beasley-Murray. His academic gifts are beyond dispute attested by the universities of London and Cambridge and exemplified in the quality of his lectures and writing over the years. The influence of his character is similarly beyond question for who could fail to be inspired by his steadfastness and singleness of purpose.

But has he been pleasant to live with? That is the question!

I write as one who has known him intimately over many years. Consequently I can make a clear unequivocal, unqualified affirmation that he has indeed been very pleasant to live with and interesting into the bargain!

The principalship embraces such an enormous span of duties. Ten times each day he switched his agile mind from one area of interest to another and in the process has never ceased to be a person, intensely human and full of understanding sympathy.

Blessed with a complete lack of self-consciousness he could address the largest assembly without outward signs of strain and then join with equal readiness and embarrassment in a hilarious game at the church social. At other times he has given himself without stint to keenest theological debate and then shared a joke with his colleagues as if he had no care in all the world. His has been a sublime confidence born of natural temperament but reinforced by the conviction of a destiny decreed in the divine purpose for the service of Christ and the Church.

In the college he has ruled with a light hand, never claiming precedence but accepting it by virtue of an authority which was inherent. In other people's lectures the students might occasionally display casual attitude and a few red herrings would by no means be unknown. But when the principal lectured there was never the slightest doubt but that serious business was afoot and if humour intruded it came only to sharpen and emphasise an important point.

One of his outstanding characteristics has been an astonishing vitality. How could we fail to admire and envy his unflagging energy and fierce determination, and what could we do but come panting behind ever trying to catch up?

When George Beasley-Murray closes the door of a car, he grasps the handle firmly, then hurls himself with furious vigour towards the opening. The impact is enough to shake the heavens, and one fears for the survival of the car. But what determination, and what a sense of purpose. So it has been with everything to which he has put his hand.

I suppose that the thing which has brought the greatest delight to the heart of his friends has been his unfailing enthusiasm for the gospel and his ability to hold it constantly in mind.

How often we have sipped coffee together and discussed the affairs of the college, and the fortunes of our families and then we have prayed together for each other's children and for ourselves. It has seemed such a natural thing to do with one who not only proclaimed the truth, and taught the truth, but who believed it himself and lived by it day by day.

It would be foolish to pretend that in 20 years we have always seen perfectly eye to eye. His ecumenical eagerness was always more optimistic than mine. But it was just such rare occasions which provide proof of the strength of our friendship. I've never had to consider what was prudent. I've never needed to disguise my feelings. The cards have always been face upwards on the table and that is a thing that can only be done where there is mutual trust and respect and love.

We at Spurgeon's will never forget him, and we have no need to hide the fact that his going has made us feel terribly sad.

He has stood in the finest tradition of our college and has served it wonderfully well. It has been a privilege to serve by his side.[105]

---

[105] *Spurgeon's College Record* 117 (June 2000), 6.

Chapter 9

Southern Baptist Theological Seminary: James Buchanan Professor of New Testament Interpretation (1973–1980)

The Seminary

The Southern Baptist Theological Seminary is based in Louisville, Kentucky. With its four 'Schools' of Theology, Church Music and Worship, Christian Education and Leadership, and its School of Mission, Evangelism and Church Growth, it is one of the world's major seminaries. At the time my father was teaching at Southern there were over 2,000 students preparing for a wide variety of Christian ministries. Its James P. Boyce Centennial Library, containing over 872,000 'items', is a wonderful facility for students and scholars alike. By comparison Spurgeon's College with some sixty students and a library of some 30,000 volumes seemed very small indeed.

My father really enjoyed his time at Louisville. Not being the Dean or the President of the Seminary, but only an ordinary professor,[1] he was able to catch up on his reading which he had had to put aside because of the administrative load at Spurgeon's. He felt that while at Spurgeon's he had become 'theologically illiterate'. Now at last he was able to get abreast with the latest developments in New Testament scholarship. As a result he was eventually able to start writing again. True, it took a while for the publications to come on stream. Indeed, some of them had to wait until he was back in Britain. But none of those later publications

---

[1]   He was appointed the James Buchanan Harrison Professor of New Testament Interpretation. On his retirement and return to England he was named Elrod Senior Professor.

would have been possible without his time in Louisville.

Southern Baptists and Evangelism

In my father's day Southern Seminary, as its name implies, used to be one of the four main seminaries of the Southern Baptist Convention of the USA. The Southern Baptist Convention itself claims to have some 18.5 million members belonging to some 40,000 churches, and is therefore easily the largest Baptist grouping in the world. One of the reasons for its strength is its commitment to evangelism. Almost every service, whatever the content of the sermon, concludes with an invitation to people to come forward to find Christ or to renew their faith in Christ. To other Christians such regular 'altar calls' may seem overdone. However, there is no doubt that the weekly appeal reminds church members what the purpose of the church is.

This emphasis on evangelism is also reflected in the convention itself. Growth and expansion are the names of the game. Plans are drawn up accordingly for Southern Baptists to win their nation—and indeed the world—to Christ. For other Baptists—let alone other Christians—Southern Baptists may seem incredibly arrogant and insular. At times it may appear that salvation is only to be found in a Southern Baptist church—as distinct from only in Christ! Likewise the emphasis on numbers is undoubtedly overdone—so much so, in fact, that the membership of an average Southern Baptist church often needs to be divided by three to gain a realistic number of committed members: for one third of the membership may be non-resident; a further third may be local but non-attending; and only one third may be active! Yet, for all the faults of the Southern Baptist Convention, one has to admit that evangelism is more to the fore than in many a Christian denomination elsewhere.

Not surprisingly, therefore, my father felt at home amongst Southern Baptists, even though he was not really one of them. He too shared their evangelistic fervour and regarded his teaching at Southern Seminary as being a contribution to the training of pastor–evangelists who would forward that mission.

The Authority of the Bible

Inevitably a convention of this size encompasses a wide diversity of views. Always theologically conservative, in recent years its leadership has become much more 'fundamentalist' in outlook. This swing to the right theologically inevitably has had an impact on its seminaries, which in turn have become increasingly conservative themselves.

Initially my father had little difficulty in feeling at home with his colleagues in Southern Seminary. He, like them, was a committed evangelical. However, although by comparison with New Testament scholars in general, he was regarded as a conservative theologian, he was not a conservative evangelical, and most certainly not a fundamentalist. There is no doubt that had he stayed on for a further decade, he would have felt distinctly uneasy—indeed, his post might even have been terminated.

Unlike many evangelicals—and certainly unlike fundamentalists—my father welcomed the advent of biblical criticism. His approach is well illustrated in a popular talk he gave on the overseas service of the BBC in 1963:[2]

> Biblical criticism is as necessary for Fundamentalists as for every one else. For criticism of the Bible is not a process of pronouncing judgment on the Bible, but the investigation of

---

2   'The Bible Comes Alive: 4. Through Great Argument', broadcast on 3 and 5 November 1963.

the circumstances of its making—who its authors were, their time and place of writing and why they wrote...

It is hard to exaggerate the gain that has come to our understanding of the Bible through the application of critical methods to its study. The Old Testament prophets and their books have come alive through appreciation of their historical situation. The life and teaching of Jesus have become far more clearly understood through our better knowledge of the nature of the Gospels. The distinctive contributions of the New Testament Letters have been freshly grasped, as also the common faith that bound together all the apostolic writers. And the Book of Revelation has become vastly more comprehensible now that we have been able to put it into its literary genre.[3]

In regard to the infallibility of the Bible, my father identified himself with the general position of the great Reformers:

They [the Reformers] distinguished between the Word of God and the Scripture which presents it; the word of God is to the Scripture what the soul is to the body... Now it is this Word of God to which final authority belongs; it attaches to the writings only as they convey that Word.

The life of the kingdom comes not from the Scriptures, but from Christ to whom they testify. He who submits to him in faith knows how infallibly true it is that God has given us eternal life and this life is in his Son.

Almost twenty years later my father elaborated on his view of scripture in a closely-argued paper entitled 'Recovering the Authority of the Bible'.[4] For him 'the Bible may be referred to as the Word of God, namely in

---

3   My father developed a similar argument in 'The Minister and His Bible', *The Fraternal* 92 (April 1954), 13: 'Critical questions are matters of fact, to be investigated in a spirit of adventure not of fear. We need the guidance of the Spirit, not bludgeons to defend it.'

4   Written in 1982, but never published.

its function as witness to the Gospel'. With Luther and Calvin he 'affirmed the trustworthiness of the Bible as an infallible authority in matters of salvation and the life of faith'; and with them too he acknowledged that it 'contains normal human flaws and failings' which can be sorted out by scholarly study. The final two paragraphs of the paper helpfully illuminate his understanding of the Bible:

> We should clearly recognise that the concept of inerrancy is concerned with the *form* of the Bible rather than its *message*. Those who formulated it were concerned with the grounding of faith in a rational concept of the Bible. Well meaning as this idea is, especially in connection with a formulation of Christian apologetics, the Bible gives us a different account of its function: it is to present the Word of God to the mind and conscience of the hearer, and by the Holy Spirit's operation to make it the means of salvation, whether entrance into it or continuance in it. The authority of the Bible no more depends on rational proof than the God of salvation does. That authority is self-evidencing to all whose hearts become open to the Holy Spirit. Through the Spirit's operation the revelation of God was given initially (for the Spirit is God at work in the world); through the Spirit the revelation is grasped, and through him its truth and power are known. The Spirit of truth is the life-giving Spirit. The unbeliever who lets the Word of God reach his heart discovers the truth of the Bible by its power to convince and renew, and such a one experiences the life.
>
> In conclusion we affirm that the authority of the Scriptures resides in God in Christ who works through the Holy Spirit with the Scriptures. The Word of God in the Bible claims its hearers and readers as the Holy Spirit burns its message into their hearts...

Unfortunately this approach to scripture, although common among many evangelical scholars in Britain and elsewhere, no longer finds much favour today with the leadership of the Southern Baptist Convention.

Happily this was not the case in the 1970s with the result that my father was able to teach in Southern Seminary and exercise a wide preaching ministry, as also to write for the Broadman Press, the publishing arm of the Southern Baptist Convention.

St Matthew's

Initially my mother found it difficult to accept the decision to go to the States. At that stage in life she had no wish to leave her family and friends. However, she never doubted that this was absolutely right for my father, and so therefore she accepted that it must be God's will for them both. But when they got to Louisville, things became easier for my mother, for she and my father quickly found themselves surrounded by new friends and a new life started for them.

This process of making friends was helped above all by my parents joining St Matthew's Baptist Church, a large three-thousand membership 'Southern Baptist' church near to the seminary, situated on Grandview Avenue. They were amazed by the friendships they made in the church, friendships which lasted through the years. They were very grateful for the close-knit circle of friends who enriched their lives immensely.

My father enjoyed his all-age Sunday School class made up of men similar in age to himself. Whenever he was not preaching, he was there. Indeed, if the truth be told he preferred attending Sunday School to attending some of the worship services. The teaching may not have been all that helpful, but the fellowship was greatly attractive. My mother was also in an all-age Sunday School class with women in their forties. As an aside we may note that although some attribute the growth of Southern Baptists to their evangelistic preaching, the secret of their growth may in part at least be found in the all-age Sunday School system with its emphasis on small-group work.

Writing

My father was very aware that while he had been Principal at Spurgeon's he had not been able to keep up with his theological reading as he would have liked. He often said that the quickest way to illiteracy was being appointed a college principal! Much of his early days in Louisville were spent catching up on developments in New Testament scholarship with a view to writing his book on the kingdom of God.

Nonetheless he still found time to do some writing on a variety of New Testament issues. He was, for instance, a frequent contributor to Southern Seminary's own theological journal, *Review and Expositor*, as also to other scholarly journals elsewhere.

It was toward the beginning of his time in Louisville that my father's commentary on *The Book of Revelation* was published in 'The New Century Bible Commentary' series.[5] To the delight of his four children, this commentary was dedicated to them 'in gratitude for their affection, understanding and encouragement in all my labours'. In essence an expansion of his commentary on the book of Revelation in the *New Bible Commentary*, my father received a one-off payment of £75 for his pains! The commentary, however, sold exceedingly well and went through a number of editions. Although now finally out of print, it is in fact still one of the best standard commentaries for preachers.

My father made apocalyptic literature understandable. Many, for instance, have appreciated the parallel he drew between such literature and political cartoons:

---

5   *The Book of Revelation* (Marshall, Morgan & Scott, London 1974, rev. edn 1978). It was published in a softback edition in 1981 and 1983.

The purpose of a cartoon is to embody a message relating to a contemporary situation, whether it be of local, national, or international import. Many of the symbols employed by cartoonists are stereotyped. Some of their representative figures are human (like John Bull and Uncle Sam), others are animals (e.g. the lion for Britain, the bear for Russia, the eagle for USA), and occasionally the animals are given human faces, identifying leaders of the nations in their representative actions. Frequently the situations depicted are deliberately exaggerated, and even made grotesque, in order that the message may be made plain... The book of Revelation uses the cartoon method more consistently than any other work of this order.[6]

While still working on this commentary my father had given a series of lectures on the book of Revelation to a conference organised by the Southern Baptist Sunday School Board in 1971. These lectures were expanded and published under the title of *Highlights of the Book of Revelation*.[7] The lectures themselves were fairly basic and the exposition somewhat limited. However, for the preacher the closing section of each lecture, although somewhat dated, still contains much grist for the mill. For example, in his conclusion to the lecture on 'The Judgment of Nations' my father has a fascinating quotation from Martin Buber on the contribution of the Jewish people to the Christian church: 'Divided from you, we have been assigned to you for your help'. My father goes on: 'In what way can the Jew help the Christian? By reminding the church that it has not all in its possession and that there is a future before it. He [Buber] cites his fellow Jew Rosenzweig: "You who live in an 'ecclesia triumphans' need a silent servant who reminds you every time you believe you have partaken of God in bread and wine,

---

6   *Revelation*, 16-17.
7   Broadman Press, Nashville, Tennessee, 1972; and Lakeland, London, 1973.

'Sir, remember the last things'. That is *remember the judgment!*" This service Israel can do for the Church, for Israel has borne judgement, and yet is still in the hand of God.'[8]

Equally thought-provoking is his conclusion to the final lecture on 'The Coming of Christ and His Kingdom' where he contrasts at length Marxism and Christianity. Whereas 'the inspiration of Marxism is the biblical hope drained of God', the church by and large 'has lost its message of hope' by its relegation of the kingdom of God to beyond history. It is at this point that we need to heed the book of Revelation, which 'teaches that Christ's coming will bring that kingdom which is among men in this world now to decisive expression among men in this world then'.[9]

In 1976 my father was asked, along with Herschel H. Hobbs and Ray F. Robbins, to speak at a conference on the book of Revelation organised by the Southern Baptist Sunday School Board. Each of the three speakers represented different perspectives on the book of Revelation. These addresses were subsequently publish-ed under the title of *Revelation: Three Viewpoints*.[10] There was little new in what my father had to say: he continued to maintain his belief in God's establishing of a kingdom on earth. His premillennial views, however, did contrast quite sharply with the other two speakers, who adopted 'amillennial' (Hobbs) and 'apocalyptic' (Robbins) approaches to the book of Revelation. Nonetheless, the sharpest contrast was to be found in the viewpoint which was not represented at all at the conference: namely the 'dispensational' or 'post-millennial' view, popularised in the 1970s by Hal Lindsey, which interprets world events against the backcloth of the book of Revelation.

---

8   *Highlights*, 62.
9   *Highlights*, 74, 77, 79.
10 Broadman Press, Nashville, Tennessee, 1997.

Wider Ministry

My father was in constant demand as a guest lecturer. His views on baptism never failed to stimulate controversy amongst his American audiences, and in doing so clearly pleased the then President of Southern Seminary, Duke McCall: 'I was never more proud of him than when he rebuked Southern Baptists for "infant baptism". He insisted that the New Testament required an understanding of sin and redemption to which a commitment to Jesus Christ as Lord is required. He objected to evangelism which brought very young children into the church before they were old enough to make such a life transforming commitment.' My father also had many opportunities to preach all over the USA and to conduct the January Bible Studies in a good number of churches in the convention.

As the years passed, so did the invitations to lecture increase—and not least to lecture beyond the USA. My father eventually realised that if he could retire a year early he would then be free to fulfil a number of these engagements. So in 1980, after seven happy years at Louisville, he and my mother returned to England.

Expressions of Appreciation

Before he left the service of the seminary my father was presented with a collection of fifty-four letters of greeting and appreciation from colleagues and friends around the world. Three in particular are of interest since they illustrate the title of this book. First, James Dunn, now Professor of New Testament at the University of Durham, for whom my father had been the external examiner when he submitted his Cambridge doctoral thesis, referred to *Jesus and the Future* and *Mark 13*:

> I have greatly admired the tremendous courage and honesty you showed in tackling that so sensitive and difficult issue

of Jesus' own expectation of what was to happen. When I treat of this question in my own lectures I always make a point of referring students to your study as one of the best models of Christian scholarship wrestling with difficult texts in a spirit of proper subservience to the text.

Secondly, Charlie Moule, the former Lady Margaret Professor of Divinity in the University of Cambridge, who had examined my father in the Cambridge Theological Tripos, wrote of how his books had not only 'made a notable contribution to the understanding of the New Testament', but also 'all exemplify the combination of rigorous and scholarly honesty and warm Christian faith for which you are well known'.

Thirdly, Kingsley Barrett, then at the University of Durham, wrote helpfully of the approach to scripture which he and my father shared:

> I believe it would be true to say that for both of us the New Testament has never been a mere repertory of intellectual puzzles but the Word of God, and that the use of all the methods of literary and historical criticism has served rather to underline than to obscure that truth. From a task understood in these terms there is of course no retirement, nor would you desire one. The pattern of our activities changes, and perhaps the rate of striking drops, but the old search for truth, and the will to communicate it will last; long may you continue to enrich us in both respects!

The Board of Trustees of the seminary also passed a formal 'resolution' of appreciation. Although inevitably marked by that warmth of spirit which is so characteristic of Southern life, it seems to me that this resolution truly gets to the heart of the contribution my father made, and for that reason it is worth quoting in full.

RESOLUTION

WHEREAS, George R. Beasley-Murray has served on the faculty of The Southern Baptist Theological Seminary for almost a decade, bringing a wealth of spiritual and intellectual commitment to the study of New Testament; and

WHEREAS, he has distinguished himself through his scholarly writings and participation in academic societies both in the United States and internationally; and

WHEREAS, he has been an effective interpreter of the message and meaning of the New Testament to churches and groups both in the United States and in England; and

WHEREAS, he has communicated the meaning of the New Testament and guided hundreds of students both at the professional and graduate levels in the acquisition of those skills necessary to interpret the New Testament; and

WHEREAS, he now returns to England to continue his work as scholar, teacher, and churchman;

THEREFORE, BE IT RESOLVED that the Board of Trustees in the 1980 annual session express appreciation to Dr George R. Beasley-Murray for his insight, courage, and commitment in furthering the cause of Christ and the understanding of the New Testament and our best wishes for his continuing service in the Kingdom of God.

In the light of the title of this book, *Fearless for Truth*, it is surely noteworthy that the word 'courage' features in the resolution.

Chapter 10

Beckenham: 'Retirement'
(1980–1986)

Before leaving Spurgeon's my parents had bought a house in Beckenham, Kent, a middle-class south London suburb, in the area in which my mother had grown up and where her mother at that time still resided. It was therefore to Beckenham that my parents returned from the States. Within a matter of months my parents invited Daisy Weston (my mother's mother) to come and live with them—she had been living on her own since being widowed in 1962.

Almost immediately on their return from the States, they set off for Australia and New Zealand where my father had been invited to lecture. This in fact set a pattern for my father for much of his time in Beckenham. An examination of his diaries for that period reveals that he was frequently away preaching and lecturing—including normally two trips a year to the States.

On coming back from 'down-under' my parents soon became members of the Beckenham Baptist Church. The minister when they arrived was Michael Walker, a most colourful and thought-provoking preacher. My father thoroughly enjoyed Michael's biblically-based preaching—as also his sensitive leading of worship. On those Sundays when he was free of other engagements my father was there—and was also a regular attender at the church meeting. When Michael left to teach at the South Wales Baptist College, my father was a natural choice to become moderator of the church.

Moderating

A 'moderator' of a Baptist church in England is
normally an ordained minister, who is appointed by the
church to chair deacons' meetings and (important)
church meetings during a pastoral 'interregnum' or
'vacancy'. In addition the moderator will often take any
weddings and funerals, and will from time to time
preach on a Sunday. The moderator is not normally the
equivalent of the 'interim minister', a role which is
often exercised in churches in North America. For the
most part the moderator simply enables the church to
carry on and is particularly appreciated for his help in
finding the new minister.

My father's ministry at Beckenham had been
marked by a good deal of happiness. His departure was a
matter of sadness to the members and was occasioned
by a strong sense of call to exercise ministry elsewhere.
My father's duties as moderator at Beckenham were
therefore relatively straightforward and not particularly
onerous.

My father's experience at Beckenham, as also subsequently when he was moderator at Woodmansterne,
a small church on the outer edges of south London, and
even later, on his removal to Hove, at Seaford, a lively
Baptist church further along the south coast, was in
stark contrast to a later period when my father was
moderator of Duke Street Baptist Church situated in
Richmond, south west London, very close to the River
Thames. Duke Street, for many years a very strong and
staunchly evangelical church, had lost its previous
minister in the unhappiest of circumstances. Relationships within the church were at rock-bottom. It was an
extraordinarily difficult situation. Few other moderators would have been up to the challenge. Indeed, few
other moderators would have been willing to give so
much time. Thankfully, the difficulties were eventually
resolved and the church was then able to call a new
pastor. Looking back on that period, one of the former

deacons wrote: 'At that time we were a bitterly divided church... It was George's job to sort us out and to restore harmony, trust, respect and love between us... It took months, but George achieved the reconciliation he so earnestly desired.'[1]

Needless to say, reconciliation only comes about as people learn to forgive one another. For my father, such forgiveness lay at the heart of the gospel. This is exemplified in a letter he wrote to a minister who was struggling with this very issue. 'The prayer, "Father forgive them..." was prayed in the act of crucifixion— and persisted in the resurrection. "Beginning at Jerusalem", the place of rejection, was part of the missionary commission, implying, "for I love them still, though guilty".' He went on to refer to the memorial altar of Coventry in the old ruins of the original cathedral. 'When it was first erected the words were, "Father forgive them", I saw them with my own eyes. The next time I went, the word "them" was erased. This was clearly due to recognition that *we* are all sinners, for whom Christ died, and having been forgiven for our sins we are called to unconditional love. The Sermon on the Mount illustrates the principle before the world saw it in action. It's extraordinarily presented in Luke 6.27-36. The last sentence is instructive: whereas Matthew has it, "Be perfect as your heavenly Father is perfect"—an impossible standard to attain— Luke has "Be merciful as...", and that is *chesed, grace* to enemies and sinners, as God shows us all.'

Writing

My father never regarded himself as 'retired', but rather 'self-employed'. His attitude to growing old is well illustrated in a sermon he preached to mark the sixty-fifth birthday and therefore 'official retirement' from Baptist ministry of Harry Young. 'I warn you Harry,

---

1   Sir Eric Richardson 7 July 2000.

when Caleb was 85 years old, he said to Joshua "I am still this day strong...as my strength was, even so is my strength now...now give me this mountain...the Lord shall be with me!" (Josh. 14.12). Who knows what mountains you may still possess...and you are only 65 years!'[2]

His life-style remained disciplined and devoted to the end. Retirement as far as he was concerned simply gave him more time to engage in serious writing as also to give guest lectures at various colleges and seminaries. Much as he would have liked, for instance, to have been like many other retired ministers and taken up golf, he felt he just could not spare the time. My father did, of course, play the piano. However, even playing the piano was largely restricted to those times when he felt too tired to think. This, incidentally, did not mean to say that music was not on his mind at other times. Indeed, my mother maintains that music was on his mind most of the time. So much so that in conversation with others my mother would notice that his fingers would be moving—they were tapping out music even while he was conversing.

Over the years my father had regularly written Bible reading notes for Scripture Union[3] and for the International Bible Reading Association.[4] His last pop-

---

2   Private letter 19 July 2000.

3   *Bible Study Notes*: Revelation (6–30 December 1951); James (11–18 June 1952); Ezekiel 10–48 (1 March–8 April 1953); 2 Corinthians (24 May–8 June 1953); Ezekiel 1–9 (21–29 February 1956); Ezekiel 10–48 (1 March–8 April 1956); 1 Thessalonians (3–10 June 1962); 2 Thessalonians (30 November–3 December 1962).

4   *Daily Bible Studies*: Mark (1 March–20 April 1954); Acts 1–12 (1–30 June 1954); Acts 13–28 plus selections from the Epistles of Paul (1 October–15 December 1954); The Church of the Holy Spirit—readings in John, Acts, 1 and 2 Corinthians (15 May–30 June 1956); Matthew (1 September–30 November 1956); Acts of the Holy Spirit—selections from the Old Testament and from Acts (1–30 June 1962); Revelation (21

ular series of notes appeared in *Matthew* as part of Scripture Union's Bible Study Commentary.[5] Intended to provide material for three months of Bible reading, it offers a very straightforward commentary on the Gospel, blending lightly assumed scholarship with devotion. In this latter respect some of the quotations included 'to think about' still repay thought: for example, with reference to Matthew 22.23-33: 'If there were no Creator, we would fall into nothing in death. But because God is, we fall into the arms of God' (Karl Heim); with reference to 26.17-30: 'It is the Last Supper which makes Calvary sacrificial' (A.E.J. Rawlinson); 17.1-14: 'The difference between remorse and repentance is that between death and life' (G.R. Beasley-Murray).

For many years my father had been intending to write on the kingdom of God. Indeed, as we have seen, it was his intention to do this when he moved to Switzerland in 1956. But other commitments intervened. Finally, however, he was able to put his mind to his long-chosen subject. Much of the work for this was undertaken in the USA, but it was not until he was in Beckenham that he was able to bring his studies and his writing to a successful conclusion, when *Jesus and the Kingdom of God* was published.[6] The sheer breadth of this work combined with the attention to detail is quite staggering.

The first seventy pages of the book set the context to the teaching of Jesus and are devoted to 'The Coming of God in the Old Testament' and 'The Coming of God in the Writings of Early Judaism'. The remaining three

April–18 May 1963); James and 1 and 2 Peter (13 August–14 September 1963); Luke (31 January–24 April 1965); Romans 12–16 (7–20 November 1965); Matthew (14 January–20 April 1968).

5   *Matthew* (Scripture Union, London, and Christian Literature Crusade, Fort Washington, Pennsylvania, 1984).

6   *Jesus and the Kingdom of God* (Eerdmans, Grand Rapids, and Paternoster, Carlisle, 1986).

hundred or so pages are devoted to a meticulous examination of every saying and parable of Jesus related
to 'The Coming of God'. This examination includes a
careful assessment of and interaction with previous
work undertaken by a broad range of New Testament
scholars. The lengthy notes and the many pages of
bibliography are all testimony to the massive scholarship which underlies the main text. My father's old
friend, F.F. Bruce, was not exaggerating when he
described *Jesus and the Kingdom of God* as 'an
exegetical treasure-house'.[7]

The surprising feature of this work of scholarship is
how eminently readable it is. Furthermore, although
there is a serious engagement with the Greek text, the
English translations provided ensure that it is accessible
to readers without knowledge of Greek. For my father
scholarship was not an end in itself—it was there to
serve the wider church. This 'down-to-earth' approach
is reflected in the concluding chapter, where my father,
reflecting on the way in which Jesus freely used
metaphorical, symbolic and mythic images, poses the
question: 'What significance can it have then for our
outlook on life? More specifically, to what extent does
the teaching of Jesus determine our expectations of our
future and of mankind as a whole?'[8] The reply comes
three pages later:

> The symbol related to divine intervention that brings about
> judgment and redemption... The coming of God for the
> initiation of his kingdom in the ministry of Jesus took place
> in historic, concrete action, which led to a deed at Golgotha
> and to an apocalyptic event of the third day. Jesus depicted
> all these acts in eschatological terms, supremely at the Last
> Supper, which anticipated the feast of the kingdom of God.
> These provide our chief clues to what the parousia means: it

---

7   *Baptist Times*, 13 March 1986.
8   *Kingdom of God*, 338.

is an act of God in Christ for the salvation of the world and its judgment.[9]

The book ends with the message to the churches from the Evanston Assembly of the World Council of Churches:

> We do not know what is coming to us. But we know who is coming. It is he who meets us every day and who will meet us at the end—Jesus Christ our Lord. Therefore we say to you: Rejoice in hope.[10]

The book received many favourable critical reviews. R.T. France, for instance, then at London Bible College and later the Principal of Wycliffe Hall, Oxford, ended a lengthy review in the *King's Theological Journal* by declaring: 'This is a book full of good things for all who appreciate rigorous exegetical discussion. Its breadth of scholarship is impressive, and it is unusual to find an English author who pays far more attention to German scholarship than to British.' At a more popular level, Terry Griffith, then a pastor of a tough inner-London Baptist church, wrote in the *Mainstream Newsletter*: 'This is a magnificent book. We are led through the jungle thickets of New Testament scholarship. Our guide's machete cuts through the views of others efficiently. The difficult and circuitous route is made manageable and leads to an El Dorado... Jesus' teaching on the kingdom is opened up in a penetrating way which must surely aid the preacher in the task of exposition... Serious preachers cannot fail to benefit from studying this book which yields pure gold.'[11] But not all reviewers were so complimentary. For while I. Howard Marshall of Aberdeen University wrote in the *Baptist Quarterly* that 'This is conservative scholarship

---

9   *Kingdom of God*, 341.
10 *Kingdom of God*, 344.
11 *Mainstream Newsletter* 25 (April 1987), 16.

at its best',[12] an American fundamentalist paper charged my father with 'liberalism' and with 'the rankest, subtlest kind of unbelief... Needless to say, we do not, in any sense, recommend this dangerous book.'[13]

While still engaged in researching for *Jesus and the Kingdom of God*, my father was invited to Nigeria to give the Emmanuel Ajahi Dunsi Memorial New Testament Lectures for 1981. Later published under the title of *The Coming of God*,[14] the four lectures anticipated the later work, albeit in a more popular form. Here my father was concerned less to interact with other scholars as to give some of the distilled fruits of his scholarship. However, although the lectures themselves bore the marks of a scholar, the context in which they were introduced shows every sign of the preacher. Let me quote the introductory two paragraphs:

'What oxygen is for the lungs, such is hope for the meaning of human life'. So wrote Emil Brunner at the beginning of his book on the doctrine of the last things. He was right. Without oxygen a human being cannot live, and without hope he has no reason to live. People who have no hope see no point in living, and their meaningless lives ebb away to the grave. That is happening to millions of our contemporaries today. That is why Brunner saw the recovery of hope to be of primary importance for the world of our time and the urgency of the Church declaring its message about it. 'A church which has no clear and definite message on this point', he said, 'has nothing to say at all... A church which has nothing to say concerning the future and then life of the world to come is bankrupt'.[15]

How strange that one can even talk about 'a church which has nothing to say about hope', when the Bible is the book of

---

12   *Baptist Quarterly* 32 (April 1987), 99.
13   *Sword of the Lord*, 10 February 1987.
14   *The Coming of God* (Paternoster Press, Exeter, 1983).
15   Emil Brunner, *Eternal Hope* (Lutterworth, London, 1954), 7, 211, 219.

hope! It tells us what a world without God cannot possibly know: why the world exists, why we are here, what God has planned for His world, and how we can have part in those plans. And this is not a forlorn hope. It has nothing in common with the classic picture of hope: a blindfolded woman stooping over a lyre, out of which to make music to inspire the soul! That is in truth *desperate* hope. By contrast Christian hope is healthy and vigorous. It is faith directed to the future, a future which is in the hands of the almighty God who has worked in love and power through Jesus Christ our Lord for our salvation, the God who has a purpose for the future and who is able to bring it about through that same Jesus Christ our Lord. The hallmark of that purpose and the evidence of its sure accomplishment is the cross and resurrection of Jesus. The God who initiated his saving rule for mankind with such immeasurable love and with such signal power will surely complete it.[16]

During this period my father began to write his Word Biblical Commentary on John,[17] although it was not actually finished until he moved to Hove. At the time when he was commissioned to write this particular commentary, his instructions were to contain his material within one volume. When subsequently multi-volumed commentaries in the series appeared,[18] my father often expressed the regret that he had not been allowed more space. However, the fact is that my father by limiting himself was remaining truer to the original vision of the series, which was to meet the needs not just of professional scholars and teachers (who would have easy access to libraries), but also the needs of working ministers (who would not normally be able to afford to buy more than one commentary per

---

16   *The Coming of God*, 7-8.

17   *John* (Word, Dallas, Texas, 1988).

18   The Word commentaries on *Matthew* and *Mark* run to two volumes, while the Word commentary on *Luke* and *Revelation* run to three volumes.

book of the Bible). Furthermore, the content of his book also remains true to the original aim of the Word series, which was less concerned to provide scholars opportunity to break new ground as to provide 'a theological understanding of Scripture that is grounded in the best of today's biblical scholarship'. My father understood this aim. So although he addressed technical issues of interest to scholars, he was not obsessed with the minutiae of scholarship, but is rather concerned to expound the meaning of the Gospel for pastors.

The spirit with which he approached this work of scholarship comes to clear expression in his Author's Preface:

> Why...yet another commentary on it [John]? One supreme consideration weighed with the writer in his decision to embark on this work. He knows well that average ministers are far too busily engaged in their diverse responsibilities to attempt to cope with Hoskyns and Bultmann, with Barrett and Dodd, with Schnackenburg and Haenchen, etc.—still less to examine the endless stream of articles and monographs on varied aspects of the Fourth Gospel. It seemed that there was room for an attempt to pass on some of the treasures of modern study of this Gospel and with them to combine one's own findings and convictions. It has been an immeasurable enrichment of mind and heart to prepare for and write this exposition of the so-called 'spiritual Gospel'. To study the book with integrity, openness and with expectation of the guide of the Paraclete-Spirit can and should be a spiritual adventure for anyone. It will lead the reader to a more profound understanding of him of whom it tells—Jesus, the Christ, the incarnate Son of God, Word of God, Son of Man, and Saviour of the World; and, if the purpose of its composition is fulfilled in him, it will lead to a deeper faith in and knowledge of that same Jesus, and a more adequate witness to him before the world.[19]

---

19   *John*, xi.

The result is that, in my judgment, his commentary is the most useful to preachers of all the Word commentaries. Its usefulness is perhaps reflected in the fact that it has been one of the best-selling volumes in the series.[20] The sad fact is that today so many commentaries are written for scholars. My father's commentary on John was written for preachers. This comes to expression time and again, both in the detailed 'Comment' sections as also in the more general words of 'Explanation'. It comes to expression too in the very final sentence of the commentary: 'Happy is the congregation whose shepherd interprets the word of the Lord for today's world in its truth and power.'[21]

From my own perspective as a working pastor it is his commentary on John which I have appreciated most. Certainly it is the book which I have used the most. For while many, for instance, reckon that his *Baptism in the New Testament* may have been his most significant book, even as a Baptist pastor I am not preaching many sermons on baptism, whereas I am often preaching sermons from John's Gospel.

---

[20] Another explanation for the success of his commentary on John is that my father was well known both in North America as also in the UK and elsewhere.

[21] *John*, 418.

Chapter 11

Hove: The Closing Years (1986–2000)

Holland Road, Hove

My parents moved from Beckenham to Hove, together with my grandmother, Daisy Weston. Sadly my grandmother lived only a further eighteen months, dying in the August of 1987, not long before her ninety-fifth birthday. She was a wonderful lady—much loved by all the family.

Hove in the county of Sussex and on England's south coast, has traditionally been regarded as a little quieter than Brighton, the town immediately adjacent to it. However, there is not much to choose between them— indeed, recently the two towns have been joined together to form a city. There in Hove my parents lived in a delightful house in Holland Road, less than 300 yards to the north of the sea front and only some 400 yards or so south of Holland Road Baptist Church.

My father enjoyed living near to the sea. Not for him a deck-chair on the beach. Rather he enjoyed being able to walk along the promenade for his daily 'constitutional'. Even on the morning of his final stroke he was out 'striding' along the Brighton promenade. Many would say that they enjoyed a day with my parents, but were exhausted by the speed with which my father set off walking!

Although at the time some of us wondered whether my parents had left it somewhat late to move again, our fears were groundless and it proved to be a good move. Very quickly they made friends—with people both within and without the church.

My parents were no strangers to Holland Road Baptist Church. Over the years my father had preached there many times. For many years the church had been profoundly suspicious of the ecumenical movement and was one of a handful of Baptist churches who asked for it to be made clear in the Baptist Union Directory that it wished to have nothing to do with any unity process. Nonetheless, in spite of these theological differences, my parents quickly became active members of the church, supporting the ministry not only on a Sunday but during the week too. Within a relatively short-time my father was elected a deacon—which was one office he had never previously held in any church.

The modesty of my father was such that most people in the church had no idea of the various positions he had held prior to his retirement. If they knew anything at all, then they knew that he was a retired Baptist minister who loved to play the piano.

The Neighbourhood

Holland Road is a fairly busy road, in which most people do not know their neighbours. Nonetheless, my parents made a real effort to get to know their neighbours. They made friends with neighbours to the left, neighbours to the right, and neighbours across the road. Many Christians tend to live a kind of ghetto-like existence, but this was not true of my father at Hove. He talked to everybody he met. What's more, he happily talked to people about his Christian faith.

One of the difficulties which he faced in sharing his faith was that only on rare occasions did he feel free to invite his new friends to church. For my father felt that his church, like far too many churches, was too 'churchy'—particularly for people who had never darkened the door of a church. Long sermons and worship with lots of modern songs emanating from charismatic renewal, seemed to him to create an unnecessary barrier to faith.

For my father sharing the faith was of the essence of Christian living. So long as he had breath, he wanted to tell others of the Saviour. Unlike some ministers who urge their members to tell their neighbours and friends of Jesus, but themselves never actually do so, my father lived out his passion for evangelism to the end. In the words of Dr Raymond Brown, his successor as Principal of Spurgeon's College: 'It would not be far wrong to use of George the words which Geoffrey Nuttall wrote of Philip Doddridge—"Evangelism was the thread on which his multicoloured life was strung".[1] Evangelism was for George a controlling passion which gave purpose, shape and impetus to everything he did.'[2]

The Study

My father remained the perpetual student almost to the end. In his mid-seventies he bought himself a computer and, unlike many of his contemporaries, soon mastered the art of word-processing. Although never a technical wizard, he enjoyed the facilities which email and a scanner have to offer.

In 1991 his *Gospel of Life: Theology in the Fourth Gospel* was published.[3] It represented an expansion of the 1990 Payton Lectures delivered at Fuller Theological Seminary, and offers a non-technical introduction to some of the main themes of the Gospel. 'Christian theology is the story of Jesus interpreted by the aid of the Spirit of God', he began, and then went on to relate this statement to John's Gospel in particular: 'The unique representation of Jesus in the Gospel of John' is accounted for 'in terms of the illumination of the evangelist's mind by the Holy Spirit, the "other

---

[1]   G.F. Nuttall, *Calendar of the Correspondence of Philip Doddridge* (Historical Manuscripts Commission JP26, London, 1979), xxxv.

[2]   Tribute given to my father at Spurgeon's College, 15 June 2000.

[3]   *Gospel of Life: Theology in the Fourth Gospel* (Hendrickson, Peabody, Massachusetts, 1991).

Paraclete" promised by the Lord to follow on his own ministry.'[4] In essence the approach adopted is identical to that found in his Word commentary. However, at one or two points the application is more direct. For example, at the end of his chapter on 'Sacraments in the Fourth Gospel', where he has been expounding the discourse on the Bread of Life in John 6, he draws attention to the tendency amongst Baptists in general (and Baptist churches in North America in particular) not to make the Lord's Supper the central feature of worship each Sunday.

> Without doubt this total faith and dependence upon Jesus Christ, the crucified, risen, and exalted Lord, the assurance of forgiveness and his sustaining grace and oneness with us as the Saviour and Lover of our souls may be known in life's ordinary ways. But there is equally no doubt that such experience is known and 'enjoyed' more intensely, and even uniquely, in the fellowship of Christ's people as they gather about the table of the Lord and share in the bread and the wine...
>
> In my own experience, whenever a congregation chooses to adopt a weekly celebration of the Lord's Supper, its members never go back; they 'enjoy' the Lord's fellowship in ever fresh ways at his table. If this is the Lord's ordaining, that should be no surprise.[5]

Similarly in his chapter on 'Church and Ministry in the Fourth Gospel', in the course of expounding the 'Prayer of Consecration' in John 17, he commented on 'the grievous divisions of our time':

> It is one of life's mysteries to me that relatively so few Christians are concerned about this issue, above all in North America, where the church scene is nothing less than chaotic. Paradoxically, the more 'evangelical' churches are, the less they are concerned about brothers and sisters in Christ in

---

4   *Gospel of Life*, vii, ix
5   *Gospel of Life*, 98-99.

denominations other than their own—I say 'paradoxically', for it is *Jesus*, in the beloved Gospel of John, who prayed for the church's unity, and through our disinterest *we* obliterate its manifestation to the world.[6]

It was while he was in Hove that my father had the joy of completing his last major project, *Jesus and the Last Days*.[7] It is a work of meticulous scholarship. Forty years after writing *Jesus and the Future* and his *Commentary on Mark 13*, he was able to integrate the two books into one and update his history of the interpretation of Mark 13 into the 1990s. Such a major revision was necessary, since in those forty years no less than twenty works on 'the little apocalypse' had appeared, most of them on Mark 13, but some on the versions in Matthew 24 and Luke 21. Furthermore, in those years the new discipline of redaction criticism[8] had emerged and been applied in particular to Mark 13.

Significantly on the question of whether or not Jesus understood the 'parousia' and the triumph of the kingdom of God as taking place within the life-time of his own generation, my father indicated that he had changed his mind, believing that the saying of Jesus in Mark 13.30 relates primarily to the prophecy of the destruction of the temple in Mark 13.2. The factors which caused him to change his mind were the following:

(1) The significance of the connection with the Q saying of Matt 23.36/Lk 11.51. It is one of the pointers to Jesus

---

6   *Gospel of Life*, 114.

7   *Jesus and the Last Days: The Interpretation of the Olivet Discourse* (Hendrickson, Peabody, Massachusetts, 1993).

8   'Redaction criticism' concentrates on the Gospel writers as 'redactors' or editors, and sets out to determine why they chose what they did to include or omit, how they arranged their material, and what distinctive theological emphases they wanted to stress.

viewing the catastrophe to which Israel was heading as the day of the Lord on the nation of its city.

(2) In the OT prophetic literature the day of the Lord on a city or people most commonly signifies an act of God in judgment, not the immediate precursors of the kingdom of God.

(3) It is Mark himself who placed 13.32 in this context. He presumably found it as an independent saying... When viewed by itself the verse's meaning is unambiguous: the time of the end, therefore of the parousia and consummation of the kingdom of God, is unknown to all humanity, including the Son of God: only the Father knows it. This I earlier failed to take as seriously as the saying demands, for I viewed v32 always in the light of v30, as though Mark (and Jesus) meant that while the end would fall within the contemporary generation its closer definition of time is beyond the bounds of knowledge. But that is an illegitimate interpretation of v32...

(4) The interpretation of v30 as affirming that the time of the end is to fall within the generation of Jesus entails Mark in a contradiction of interests. If he was writing during the Jewish–Roman War, ca. AD 68, the generation of Jesus and the apostles was already at its limit; accordingly, if he was representing that the parousia was to happen before the end of that generation, then he was looking for it to take place in the very near, if not immediate, future. But to oppose that notion was one of Mark's primary emphases in his redaction of the discourse; whereas he sought to diminish the eschatological fever of his contemporaries, and of the false prophets in particular, on this reading of the evidence there was little or no difference between his 'near expectation' and that of the people he was opposing.[9]

Here we have yet again more evidence of my father's fearless pursuit of truth. He was not afraid to say publicly that he had changed his mind.

---

[9]   *Jesus and the Last Days*, 448-449.

Three years later his revised and expanded *Preaching the Gospel from the Gospels* was published in which my father sought to take account of developments in recent Gospel scholarship.[10] Whereas the first edition amounted only to 127 pages in a small format, the second had 282 pages in a large format. The first edition had hardly any footnotes, the second edition abounded in them. Whether or not he was wise to expand the original work in this way is open to question. What was essentially a 'popular' book for lay-preachers had become a more 'serious' book for ministers.

His last project was to revise his Word biblical commentary on the Gospel of John.[11] Sadly toward the end of that project his powers of concentration began to decline, with the result that it was only with the greatest of difficulty that it was completed. But the task was finished, and just a few weeks before he died he received a copy of the new second edition. It includes an additional fifty pages, in which the developments of Johannine scholarship over the intervening eleven years or so are reviewed.

Of his other writings, a contribution to *Ministry Today*, the journal of the Richard Baxter Institute for Ministry, is of interest. There, under the heading of 'Ten books to rescue from the fire', my father listed— with appropriate comments—the ten 'seminal' books (two of which were multi-volumed) which he would wish to rescue if his house were on fire.[12] The selection was not made easily. My father commented: 'If I tried to take all I wanted to keep, I'd stagger under the weight and be overcome by smoke and flames and perish with the books!' The books were as follows:

Gerhard von Rad, *Theology of the Old Testament*

---

10   *Preaching the Gospel from the Gospels* (Hendrickson, Peabody, Massachusetts, 2nd edition, 1996).

11   *John* (Thomas Nelson, Nashville, second edition, 1999).

12   *Ministry Today* 12 (February 1998), 31-32.

Joachim Jeremias, *A New Testament Theology*
Wolfhart Pannenburg, *Jesus God and Man*
P.T. Forsyth, *The Cruciality of the Cross*
Walter Künneth, *The Theology of the Resurrection*
C.H. Dodd, *The Parables of the Kingdom*
W.G. Kümmel, *Promise and Fulfilment*
Rudolf Schnackenburg, *The Gospel according to St John*
A Dictionary of Jesus and the Gospels
Dictionary of Paul and the Gospels[13]

My father's perspective on his approach to his work as an author and preacher is found in a draft of his final address given in the summer of 1999 to students of Spurgeon's College on the occasion of their graduation. It is worth quoting in full:

A.M. Hunter at the conclusion of a brief book on the writings of the New Testament offered a final word of advice to the student: 'Do not', said he, 'expect too much from commentaries. Commentaries are often incredibly dull and useless affairs, as inspired commentators are few and far between'. That observation went right home to me, for at that time I was writing a commentary on the Book of Revelation, and it compelled me to face the question whether I was adding to the number of these 'incredibly dull and useless' volumes... Yet how can Christian authors ever write dull books about the cross of Christ, the love of God and his wrath, the resurrection of the dead and the life of the age to come?

The issue comes nearer home if we ask how it is that sermons on the same themes are also frequently 'incredibly dull and useless'? 'Inspired commentators are few and far between', said Hunter; are inspired preachers more common? It is to be hoped so, but I'm not sure that they are. I

---

13   When my father wrote this article, *A Dictionary of the Later New Testament and its Developments* (Leicester, IVP, 1997), edited by R.P.Martin and P.H.Davids, had yet to be published. My father commented: 'This...I shall hope to secure when my house is rebuilt!'

beg not to be misinterpreted here. There is no question of passing judgment on my fellows... Yet after many years of involvement in this work [of writing and preaching] I am burdened with the mediocrity of our ministry. Men—and women—who set the minds and hearts of their fellows aflame, who capture their imagination and flood their lives with the light of heaven are exceedingly rare.

Perhaps the question may be raised to what extent the mediocrity of much of our ministry is due to what goes on in the study. I do not have in view alone the degree of diligence in our studies, although that is important, but of the spirit in which we carry them out. Years ago I heard Tom Torrance, who spent most of his years in Edinburgh University as a professor of dogmatics, state that in his view theology ought to be done on our knees, i.e. in dependence on God, looking for that grace without which neither reflection nor writing nor preaching is of any avail. The thought is not original. Helmut Thielicke pointed out that Anselm begins his demonstration of God in his Prologue with a prayer, so that his theology was 'prayed theology'. A [more] modern example of that spirit has been recorded of P.T. Forsyth's exposition of the atonement in his work *The Cruciality of the Cross*. It is impossible to miss in Forsyth's writing his awesome sense of the holiness of God and the love of Christ which unite to redeem us.

Listen to what one wrote of Forsyth in his study when writing this book: 'At these times he was wrestling with thought almost beyond human expression; and he wrote with a physical and nervous intensity which shook the desk, and which after an hour or two left him utterly spent, stretched out white and still upon his study couch, until the Spirit drove him back to pen and paper'.

This surely represents the theologian's counterpart to the sacrificial toils which have been rendered to the Lord through the ages by men and women who are prepared to feel the weight of the cross as well as preach it. And this, I believe, is the spirit demanded of all Christ's servants, whether they are in the heart of a jungle or in the quieter paths of a theological college or in a suburban pastorate. It is the costly response of the man or woman of God to the 'costly grace' of the Redeemer. Intelligence without it is like tongues and prophecy and miracle-working faith without love—nothing, absolutely nothing.

Wider Ministry

Although my father had begun to slow down and no longer raced along in his presentation, he still was preaching effectively in this final stage of his life. A lovely example of this was when in his eightieth year he preached at Canterbury Baptist Church on the parable of the Prodigal Son. Subsequently a woman in the church gave her testimony: 'You all thought me to be a devout Christian. Until Dr Beasley-Murray came to preach I was a prodigal daughter. That morning I returned to the Waiting Father.'[14]

As a former President of the Baptist Union of Great Britain, he was a life-member of the Baptist Union Council, and in this role continued to keep in touch with the heart of Baptist Union life. Although by now an elder-statesman, he was never satisfied with the 'status quo'. His watchword was that of Luther's: 'ecclesia reformata et reformanda'—the church was both reformed and to be reformed. In this respect he was supportive of the efforts of 'Mainstream', a 'ginger-group' concerned for 'life and growth' within the Baptist Union, expounding the scriptures at one of the annual Mainstream conferences and also taking part in a Mainstream consultation on Baptist identity. At this latter consultation my father gave a paper on 'Confessing Baptist Identity'[15] in which he urged his fellow Baptists to 'pluck up courage and do for our day what our Baptist forefathers did for theirs, namely produce a

---

14 Private letter from Rev R.W.F. Archer of 7 August 2000.
15 'Confessing Baptist Identity', in D. Slater (ed.), *A Perspective on Baptist Identity* (Mainstream, 1987), 75-85.

contemporary Baptist Confession of Faith'.[16] The word 'courage' was significant. Although Baptists in the seventeenth and eighteenth centuries had been happy to produce confessions of faith, in the twentieth century the leadership of the Baptist Union had become very wary of producing a contemporary confession of faith, fearing that it might become divisive rather than unifying. My father begged to differ. Such a confession of faith, he maintained, was 'desirable for God's sake, for our sakes, for the sake of other Churches, and for the sake of the world'.[17]

It was desirable for God's sake, in so far as it would enable Baptists to 'have an understanding of God by which their praise and thanksgiving may rise to genuine adoration'. It was desirable for the sake of Baptists, because it 'could transform the understanding of their faith which many people hold to be dead. It could also become an excellent basis for instructing new converts.' It was desirable for the sake of other Christians, because 'there are surprisingly few members of other denominations who have a reasonable accurate knowledge of what Baptists believe'. And it was desirable for the sake of the world, in so far as it would help Christians to bear an effective witness to the gospel. 'Mission is supposed to be in our blood: it needs to be in our head and in our heart.'[18]

He drew his paper to a close with these words:

A Confession of Faith for today...does not need to have negative effects. They could be wholly positive when slanted in the direction of vision for action. We are not wanting a ten point creed corresponding to the Ten Commandments, to which signatures will be demanded from those who camp around the Baptist Mount Sinai! We belong to the city of God. We celebrate with our fellow-citizens beneath an open

---

16   'Confessing Baptist Identity', 78.
17   'Confessing Baptist Identity', 78.
18   'Confessing Baptist Identity', 78-81.

heaven in the presence of the God of glory and Jesus the Mediator of the New Covenant.

We want to catch a fuller glimpse of the reality to which we belong. We need to let it inspire us to action in keeping with his new world of God's kingdom. Theology is thinking and talking about God. It is dead only when it comes hundredth hand from dusty volumes that got it hundredth hand from even dustier libraries. Theology is done on our knees, our faces turned towards God, our ears attentive to hear from God's Word and what the saints have learned from it. From that mountain top we can see the needy multitudes below. When this is done, visionary theological thinking becomes possible.[19]

My father continued with his lecturing up to the last couple of years of his life. A frequent lecturer for Fuller Theological Seminary in California, he gave guest lectures at other seminaries too. For the most part he lectured on the New Testament. However, in 1989 he gave the Newell Lectures on 'The Imitation of Christ in Christian Leadership' at the Centre for Pastoral Studies of the Anderson University School of Theology.[20] These lectures were wide-ranging in content, and were more practical rather than academic. They for the most part lacked in depth, but he again showed his gift in drawing upon stories to illustrate his point. He referred, for instance, to coming across a church in Toronto with the extraordinary name of 'St James Bond Church', formed as a result of two churches joining together (St James Church and Bond Street) and went on: 'I fear...there are not a few churches whose minister is a kind of St James Bond, drawing a great congregation

---

19   'Confessing Baptist Identity', 84.

20   Subsequently published together with a series of lectures by Walter Brueggemann on Jeremiah in Timothy Dwyer (ed.), *Newell Lectureships Vol. II* (Warner Press, Anderson, Indiana, 1993), 81-163 [NB the concluding chapter is wrongly attributed to the editor!]

ready to offer their leader hero worship and complete obedience.'[21]

Together with my mother, he spent the academic year 1995–1996 at the 'new' International Baptist Theological Seminary, which had moved from Switzerland to the Czech Republic a year or two previously. Situated in Jeneralka on a fourteen acre site on the north-western edge of Prague, it is almost as idyllic in setting as the former site in Rüschlikon. Two other retired professors, Dr John Watts and Dr John Kiewit, were also invited to come back and help the new seminary. All three were there basically as volunteers, in the sense that although they received board and lodging, they were not actually paid for their services. Not only did this save money, it also gave the seminary time to make new full-time appointments following the loss of most of their faculty at the time of the move. Eduard Schweizer, the great New Testament scholar who taught at the University of Zurich, wrote to him: 'It's good that you teach in Prague, because people speak of a danger that the Baptist Seminary might descend from its academic level it had reached (recently much more recognised here!) in Rüschlikon.'[22]

Further Honours

He was elected President of Spurgeon's College Conference for 1986 as an accolade for his service and devotion to the College.[23] Significantly, my father chose as his presidential theme 'Christians and Jews, yesterday and today'. As a long-standing and enthusiastic supporter of the work of the Council of Christians and Jews, this was a natural choice. Ever since seeing a film of the Nazi concentration camp at

---

21   *Newell Lectureships Vol. II*, 97.
22   Letter dated November 1995.
23   'College Conference' is made up of all past and present members of the college.

Bergen-Belsen just after the war, he felt burdened by the failure of the churches to stand up for the Jews. As a guest speaker he invited Dr Pinchas Lapide, an orthodox Jewish Rabbi from Frankfurt, who spoke on 'The Creed of a Jewish New Testament Scholar'. Here, commented J.J. Brown, was 'another instance of the breadth of George's interest and of his eager desire to build bridges of understanding firmly based on truth and love'.[24]

In 1988 my father was presented with his first Festschrift, *Eschatology and the New Testament*, in which eight leading biblical scholars came together to write an essay each and thereby honour my father: Eduard Schweizer, Ronald E. Clements, James D.G. Dunn, F.F. Bruce, C.K. Barrett, Günter Wagner, Ralph P. Martin and I. Howard Marshall.[25] The editor of the Festschrift, W. Hulitt Gloer, who had served my father for two years as his 'Graduate Fellow' at Louisville, paid this fitting tribute: 'As a scholar, teacher and preacher Professor Beasley-Murray has offered countless persons, including myself, a distinctive model of how careful biblical scholarship and the service of the church not only can but must go hand in hand.'[26]

In May 1989 my father was awarded the earned Cambridge Degree of Doctor of Divinity for his book on *Jesus and the Kingdom of God*. As he wrote to his old friend, Jack Brown: 'My time there as a student had a tremendous effect on me. It's good to have this particular imprimatur on my work.'[27]

At Spurgeon's College's Graduation Ceremony on Wednesday 22 November 1989 my father received the Honorary Degree of Doctor of Letters (DLitt) conferred

---

24　'A personal appreciation', in *Mission To the World*, 19.

25　W. Hulitt Gloer (ed.), *Eschatology and the New Testament: Essays in Honor of George Raymond Beasley-Murray* (Hendrickson, Peabody, Massachusetts, 1988).

26　*Eschatology and the New Testament*, ix.

27　Letter dated 12 May 1989.

by the Council of National Academic Awards. This was the first time that the CNAA had ever conferred such a degree on a College-sponsored candidate. The statement in support of the college's nomination of the degree was drawn up particularly for the approval of a secular academic institution, and therefore says nothing, for instance, about his passion for evangelism. Nonetheless it is a fair summing-up of the academic side of his ministry:

There is no doubt that George Beasley-Murray is the leading British Baptist New Testament scholar of his generation. There can equally be no doubt about the significance of his contribution to theological education both within the United Kingdom and beyond it. As a teacher, no less than as a scholar, he has exercised a profound influence on the life of the churches.

Dr Beasley-Murray's academic writing has been prolific and wide-ranging... He has published three major works on biblical eschatology (the early *Jesus and the Future*, the *Commentary on Mark 13*, and the more recent compendious survey in *Jesus and the Kingdom of God*. The latter work in particular shows the enormous breadth of reading which has always informed his scholarship). His major commentaries on Revelation and the Gospel of John are certain to prove of abiding importance. However, his academic reputation perhaps owes most to his *Baptism in the New Testament*, which has become a standard work of reference on the subject far beyond the confines of the Baptist denomination. Dr Beasley-Murray's appreciation of the importance of continental biblical scholarship is evidenced by his English translation of Rudolf Bultmann's magisterial commentary on the Fourth Gospel.

The internationalism of George Beasley-Murray's outlook is further demonstrated by his acceptance of teaching posts in Zurich and Louisville, Kentucky, and his frequent lecture tours of North America, Europe and Australasia. He participated in the important consultation on baptism convened by the Faith and Order Commission of the World

Council of Churches at Louisville in 1979, and has maintained a broad range of ecumenical contacts. He has also played an active role for many years in the study commissions of the Baptist World Alliance.

The greater part of George Beasley-Murray's teaching career has been dedicated to raising the standards of theological education, in order to achieve a combination of academic excellence and practical vocational training. It was under his Principalship (1958–1973) that Spurgeon's College became increasingly committed to the attainment of high levels of academic achievement. He encouraged growing numbers of students to enter for, and obtain, the BD degree of the University of London. Above all, in the later years of his Principalship he initiated the College's successful approaches to the Council for National Academic Awards. This pioneering step by a small denominational college established the subsequent education orientation of the College, and encouraged other theological colleges to follow suit. Since Dr Beasley-Murray's return to this country from the United States, he has maintained a lively interest in the College's developing relationship with the CNAA. He has also acted as supervisor of a significant number of research students from a variety of institutions, some of whom have now become familiar names in the world of New Testament scholarship.

Another honour which came my father's way was the presentation of a British Festschrift to mark the fiftieth anniversary of his ordination to the Christian ministry. In addition to a personal appreciation by his old friend and batch member, J.J. Brown, it consisted of seven essays on the theme of 'Mission to the World' by some of his former students at Spurgeon's College: Michael K. Nicholls, Colin Marchant, Athol Gill, John E. Colwell, Bruce Milne, Nigel G. Wright and Derek Winter. In addition there was a comprehensive bibliography of his writings drawn up by one of his former Louisville students, Larry Kreitzer. In the brief Foreword I wrote:

As I have reflected on my father's past fifty years of ministry, no theme seemed to be more appropriate for a collection of essays in his honour than 'Mission to the World'. It was no accident that on 29 April 1968, in his Baptist Union Presidential Address, he chose to speak on the subject 'Renewed for Mission', for down through the years my father has been passionately concerned to see the lost won for Christ. Even in his retirement, along with his writing, he is still seeking to befriend those who know not the Saviour. As he declared on that Presidential evening, 'There is a Name under heaven given among men by which we must be saved, *and that Name must be heard*. To make Him known is to give men and women the possibility of life from the dead in the here and now; to withhold the News of Him is to withhold this life from them.[28]

The delight of the presentation was that my father had no idea of what lay behind the evening, only that for some reason his batch were having their fiftieth anniversary of ministerial service curiously early!

Warts and All!

It is said of Oliver Cromwell that he told an artist to paint him 'warts and all'. Although I did not set out to eulogise my father, I am very conscious that I have highlighted those things which the Apostle Paul termed 'true, noble, right, pure, lovely and honourable' (Phil. 4.9). The question inevitably comes to mind: 'But what were his failings?'

My mother's immediate reply to this question was: 'No towel rail George put up ever lasted a week.' He was an impossible handyman. My mother tells the story of how some five months before my birth he had enthusiastically painted some old furniture to go into the 'baby's room'. Five months later, on the night of my birth, the midwife stuck to the painted chair. I believe

---

[28]　*Mission to the World*, 7.

that he had forgotten to stir the paint first. In similar vein I can vividly remember another occasion when Heinrich Greeven, a distinguished German professor, was stuck in our bathroom—my father had failed to nail down the lino which in turn had jammed the door.

Along with his failure to master DIY matters was also his failure to master the financial side of running a home. In the end it was my mother who looked after the household finances. In this respect my mother tells of the occasion when just before their wedding he bought a scarf costing £5 to match her 'going away' dress. In 1942 £5 was a large sum of money, in present terms probably equivalent to well over £200—certainly not a sum which a Baptist minister in war time could rightly afford.

There were times when my father's self-confidence could be perceived as a failing. Frank Fitzsimmonds, a colleague and close friend, once dryly commented to me that 'the thought didn't come very easily to George that he might be wrong!' At times there was perhaps a lack of self-awareness in my father. This was also exemplified in the way in which my father was never shy in coming forwards when in company with others. If, for instance, he knew the answer to a question, he would immediately speak up and offer the answer. He rarely gave time to those with slower minds to have their say.

If the truth be told, there were times when my father could be impetuous in his decision-making. He wasn't a man to waste time making up his mind. His decision to bring forward his wedding day is one such example. Similarly his decision to move down to Hove was born very much of an impulse. It is possible that this impetuosity was in fact linked with his self-confidence.

Perhaps precisely because my father was always a very motivated, if not goal-orientated, man, there were times when he could easily forget what he perceived to be lesser matters. My mother tells of a time in Cambridge when twice he failed to remember to turn up to tea at the home of Newton Flew—it was only the third time, when my mother was included in the invitation, that the appointment was kept.

My father, however, was never 'one-eyed' in the sense of only having one goal. Indeed, from the point of view of New Testament scholarship, this was perhaps a weakness. For although his writings were prolific, there is no doubt that he could have achieved more in the area of New Testament scholarship had he devoted all his energies to his studies. As it was, while he was at Spurgeon's he devoted a good deal of his energies to the Baptist Union. Both in London and in Louisville and then back in London he was constantly among the churches preaching or speaking at ministers' conferences. None of this was absolutely necessary. The truth is that my father was not first and foremost a scholar—had he been, then he would never left Rüschlikon; nor later would he have left Louisville with all its wonderful facilities. First and foremost, he was a minister of the gospel.

Another 'weakness' well-remembered by his grand-children was his fondness for ice-cream. It didn't matter the time of day or the time of year, he was always eager to eat ice-cream. It is scarcely an exaggeration to say that 'heaven' for him was an ice-cream cornet.

From my perspective, at least, these are but minor failings and pale into insignificance compared to all the positive side of his character. I, for instance, never remember him ever running a person down by speaking behind his or her back. If my father had something to say, then he said it like a gentleman, face to face.

The Golden Wedding

It was in April 1992 that my parents were able to celebrate their Golden Wedding. Along with members of the wider family, all four children were present together with their wives, and some of their grandchildren. My parents often quipped what an international family they had—for I married a Welsh girl, Stephen an American, Andrew had a Japanese wife, whilst Elizabeth married an Englishman.

At a time when so many marriages fail and Silver Weddings are becoming increasingly rare, a Golden Wedding is a special achievement. However, it needs to be said that my parents did not just achieve longevity in their marriage, they also enjoyed great happiness together. In their differing ways both my parents were strong characters—and yet I was never aware of an argument between them. Disagreements, yes, but arguments, no.

Throughout the years my mother was totally committed to my father's ministry. Indeed, as far as she was concerned, she was in the ministry with him. Not that she ever wished a public role—although later she gained such a role first as President of the Baptist Ministers' and Missionaries' Wives' Prayer Fellowship and then as the National President of the Baptist Women's League. Her ministry was first and foremost the ministry of encouragement.[29] For example, when my father was engaged in one of his frequent writing projects, she would always be encouraging him to write a few more pages before the evening was out. Although my father certainly made time for her, I do not remember her demanding time of him. Not every wife would have been as supportive as she was. But she saw her commitment to my father as part of her commitment to her Lord. Indeed, this commitment was well expressed on the occasion of their wedding, when

---

[29] We may also note that she also had particular roles of her own: e.g. at Zion, Cambridge, she founded a Girls Covenanter Class; at Spurgeon's College she began regular meetings ('soirees'!) for the wives and fiancées of students; at Holland Road, Hove, she led a senior-citizens luncheon club ('The Hand of Friendship') and then later transformed a traditional women's meeting into the more outgoing 'Open Windows'.

they changed the wording of one of their hymns from the first person singular to the first person plural (a custom of the Plymouth Brethren, from which my mother came):

> Were the whole realm of nature ours,
> that were an offering far too small,
> love which the highest thought o'erpowers
> shall have our souls, our lives, our all.

Like most ministers' wives of that day, my mother never went out to work. She was a full-time home-maker for my father, both with and without children. The home was very much a place of warmth and love. What is more, this warmth and love were shared with others. A gracious hostess and a gifted cook, hospitality from the beginning of their marriage was the order of the day. My mother loved to entertain guests—and my father for his part would happily join in, often playing the piano as part of the entertainment. This was true even of their time in Hove. On many a Sunday after church my parents would bring a stranger back home for lunch. There was always sufficient food, because in anticipation of inviting somebody home my mother would have already cooked what would otherwise have been an unnecessarily large piece of meat.

Something of the affection my father had for my mother is revealed in a long letter he wrote to her on 23 April 1989 to be opened up at the time of his death. It is an intensely personal love-letter and therefore it would not be right to reproduce it in full. Nonetheless, I have my mother's reluctant permission to allow a few of the paragraphs to see the light of day

> I've been passing in review our years together... One thing impresses me—almost depresses me when I think about it—and that is the sacrifices that you made in the early years of our marriage, especially with our children, to enable me to get on with my ministry in the churches and my studies.

Indeed, the sacrifices didn't cease when we went to Spurgeon's—if anything they became greater, as life became more complicated for us. We had the trials of war, and the difficulties of accommodation at Zion, and the strange situation at Spurgeon's for a number of years. It changed from the period when I was a tutor to the time I was principal, but no one knew just what we endured in those times, and the extent to which you yourself were burdened. I really expected a lot from you in all those years, more than I should have done, and you went through it all without complaining. I was too dim-witted to realise at that time what was happening. At *this* time I realise that every book I've ever written has been at the cost of your blood, as it were, as well as mine. We've had much less time together than a husband and wife should have. You know that early on I was stirred with the challenge of the need for men of evangelical convictions to write expositions of the Bible and the Christian Faith, but the cost of doing that was beyond my imagining—still less could I guess what it would mean to you. The old adage that behind every man who has achieved anything stands a woman who has made it possible is extraordinarily true in our case...

Of course, there has been another aspect of the story that we have written together. We have been wonderfully blessed in a multitude of ways. We had some lovely friendships in both our churches, and it's been a privilege to serve in the various ways that came our way in Spurgeon's College. And we've travelled far and wide in our later years, making many friendships along the way. Who would have dreamed in 1973 how our lives were to be entwined with the folk at St Matthew's? And how doors would be opened all over the USA?...

Our lives have become entwined in a love that is of God and that only death can break. But I've come increasingly to feel that death *won't* break that love. Why should it? The main difference is that it won't be exclusive as it is here. We're incapable of sharing ourselves in depth with many people in life here, but we shall surely be able to extend it to others on the other side without losing it for each other. I didn't notice till I wrote my commentary that the last word of the prayer of Jesus for the Church in John 17 is 'that the love with which you loved me may be in them, and I in them'. That refers to our life beyond! So we shall have *more* love than now, and we'll be able to share it with others—and each other!...

You have been a wonderful wife, and a wonderful mother to your children, just as you were a wonderful daughter to your parents—especially to your mother through the many years of her widowhood. I'm grateful to you my dearest, *deeply* grateful, and I love you for it, and always will—yes *always*!

God will sustain you through the rest of your years. He will surely comfort and strengthen you in the days immediately ahead, just as he will continue to give you his peace and joy...

My love to you once more. And as I used to say to you when writing to you in Glasgow—Yours with *all* my heart, George.

Final Days

At all times my father was grateful to God for his health. In this respect he was certainly blessed, for he had experienced little illness in his life. However, in 1998 my father told my mother that he was beginning to experience some memory loss. At first my mother was not convinced, but in the autumn of 1999 it was confirmed that my father had suffered some mini-strokes. Indeed, it was probably the result of a small stroke which caused my father to have a nasty fall when visiting my brother Stephen in the States in November 1999. Gradually my father began to become confused and needed to be constantly cared for by my mother. It was a very testing time for her. Then on 9 February he suffered a major stroke and was rushed to the Royal Sussex County Hospital in Brighton. For two weeks he hovered between life and death. Finally on Wednesday 23 February 2000, at the age of eighty-three,

Hove: The Closing Years 217

he passed into the presence of his Lord whom he had loved and served for so many years, and now enjoys that salvation which is ours in Jesus. As my father wrote in the penultimate paragraph of the final chapter of *Christ is Alive!*:

> Salvation is...a vital process bound up with the activity of a living Lord. We have been reconciled through His death and resurrection. We are justified in Him. We share His risen life and by His Spirit are being transfigured into His likeness. Death for us will be the introduction of a fuller communion with him. His return will accomplish our resurrection into His image so that our body will be 'fashioned anew that it may be conformed to the body of his glory' (Phil 3.21). The resultant state is life 'for ever with the Lord' (1 Thess 4.17). It is all one process in which no element can be dispensed with. It is God in action in the Person of our Lord Jesus Christ, the Lord that died, the Lord that lives, the Lord that shall come again. If he is ours we have the utmost that even God knows how to give, which is God himself—God in all His fullness, God the Father, Son and Spirit, Three in One, and *One in us*. O marvellous grace, that such salvation should be given to sinful man![30]

Or in the words of Paul with which we concluded the announcement of my father's death in *The Times*: 'Thanks be to God who gives us the victory through our Lord Jesus Christ' (1 Cor. 15.57).

Farewells and Thanksgivings

A service of committal took place at the local crematorium and, with the exception of the Area Superintendent and the pastor of the church, attendance was restricted to family members only.

This was then followed by a well-attended service of thanksgiving at Holland Road Baptist Church, at which

---

[30] *Christ is Alive!*, 177-178.

three generous tributes were given—the first by David Coffey, a former student of my father and now General Secretary of the Baptist Union; the second by Lewis Drummond, a former colleague who flew in from the States for the occasion; and the third by Rhys Stenner, my father's pastor. At my father's request each one of us children took part by reading the scriptures. The preacher was Dr Brian Haymes, now minister of London's Bloomsbury Central Baptist Church, and a former Principal of Baptist colleges in both Manchester and Bristol, for whom my father had developed a great respect. Brian preached on the resurrection hope which is ours, and in doing so used as an illustration the great 'Credo' in Beethoven's 'Missa Solemnis'. You can tell the sermon had an effect, because a number of people immediately bought the CD.

Obituaries were published in *The Times*[31] and *The Independent*,[32] as well as in a wide range of Christian papers and magazines. The *Baptist Times*, in one of its editorials, commented:

> Of all the generous tributes paid to the Revd Dr George Beasley-Murray, who died last week, none conveys more accurately or succinctly the essence of the man than that contributed by his friend and contemporary (and fellow-President of the Union), the Rev J.J. Brown. 'The mind of a scholar; the heart of an evangelist' sums up in ten words one whose contribution to the life of the denomination is almost impossible to measure, not least because of the courageous stand he took with others at a time of denominational unease in the early 1970s. Earth is the poorer, heaven the richer for his passing. Let us hope that he is even now taking advantage of a whole new musical career opening up for him in the heavenly orchestra.[33]

---

[31]   15 March 2000.
[32]   18 March 2000.
[33]   *Baptist Times*, 2 March 2000

A few months later Spurgeon's College held a 'celebration' of my father's life on Thursday 15 June 2000, with tributes by three former colleagues, Dr Raymond Brown, Rev Frank Fitzsimmonds and Dr Bruce Milne. I too was given the opportunity to make a brief tribute, in which I sought to honour my father on three counts:

> First of all, I want to honour my father as *a man who loved his family*... He loved my mother, he loved his four children, and he was proud of all his grandchildren. He always had time for us. As a child, as a teenager, and later as an adult, I knew that his door was always open for me. For this reason I miss him deeply.
>
> Secondly, I want to honour my father as *a man who loved truth*. It was this love of truth which lay at the heart of all his scholarship. This love of truth could be costly —it meant that he did not conform to any particular evangelical mould. When it came to issues surrounding baptism and ecumenism, Christology or eschatology, my father's thinking was determined not by the understanding of others, but by his understanding of the Scriptures.
>
> Thirdly, I want to honour my father *as a man who loved his Lord*. It was his love for the Lord which was the over-riding motivating force in his life... It was his passion to give his all for his Lord which caused him to work so hard. He was very conscious that unlike many of his contemporaries he had been spared to survive the war—if God had spared him, he reasoned, then he had spared him for a purpose.

A Final Testimony

Let me end this biography with the notes of the final section of a 'Testimony' my father once gave.

> *Conclusion: 'What I owe to Christ'*
> Everything! More specifically
> • *a) A decisive change of direction of life for good.*

- This is very obvious to me when I see how the rest of my relatives have gone through life.
- *b) An enrichment beyond measure.*
- Through my relationship with God: I belong to Christ, Christ belongs to me.
- I am a forgiven child of God. I belong to his people.
- I have a place in his kingdom. These are things beside which the world is small.
- *c) I have a faith now that sustains me in life and a hope for the future.*
- That hope is centred in Christ and his promise.

I have felt his power already in my life. I shall know it in death.

When God completes his purpose in his universe, I shall be there. For Christ my risen, almighty Lord will bring me.

Be sure you have Him too!

Bibliography of the Writings of George Raymond Beasley-Murray[1]

A. BOOKS

1. *Christ is Alive!* (Lutterworth Press, London, 1947).

2. *Jesus and the Future: An Examination of the Criticism of the Eschatological Discourse, Mark 13, with Special Reference to the Little Apocalypse Theory* (Macmillan: London, 1954).

3. *Preaching the Gospel from the Gospels* (Lutterworth Press, London, 1956).

4. *A Commentary on Mark Thirteen* (Macmillan, London, 1962).

5. *Baptism in the New Testament* (Macmillan: London, 1962).

6. *The Resurrection of Jesus Christ* (Lakeland Series, 48, Oliphants, London, 1964).

7. *The General Epistles: James, 1 Peter, Jude and 2 Peter* (Bible Guides, 21, Lutterworth Press, London, 1965).

8. *Baptism Today and Tomorrow* (Macmillan, London, 1966).

9. *Highlights of the Book of Revelation* (Broadman Press, Nashville, Tennessee, 1972).

10. *The Book of Revelation* (New Century Bible Commentary, Oliphants, London, 1974).

11. *The Coming of God* (Paternoster Press, Exeter, 1983).

12. *Matthew* (Bible Study Commentary, Scripture Union, London, 1984).

13. *Jesus and the Kingdom of God* (Paternoster Press, Exeter, 1986).

---

[1] This bibliography is an expansion of that compiled by Dr Larry Joseph Kreitzer, which appeared in *Mission to the World*, 62-68, supplemented by Dr Anthony R. Cross and Mrs Judy Powles, Librarian of Spurgeon's College.

14. *The Gospel of John* (Word Biblical Commentary Series, 36, Word Books, Waco, Texas, 1988).

15. *John* (Word Biblical Themes, Word Books, London, 1989).

16. *The Holy Spirit* (Christian Training Programme Course C-7, Baptist Union, London, n.d.).

17. *The Gospel of Life: Theology in the Fourth Gospel* (Hendrickson, Peabody, Massachusetts, 1991).

18. *Jesus and the Last Days: The Interpretation of the Olivet Discourse* (Hendrickson, Peabody, Massachusetts, 1993).

19. *Preaching the Gospel from the Gospels* (Hendrickson, Peabody, Massachusetts, 2nd edn, 1996).

20. *The Gospel of John* (Word Biblical Commentary, Thomas Nelson, Nashville, 2nd edn, 1999).

B. CONTRIBUTIONS TO BOOKS, COLLECTIONS AND FESTSCHRIFTEN

1. 'The Apocryphal and Apocalyptic Literature', 'Ezekiel' and 'Revelation', in F. Davidson (ed.), *The New Bible Commentary* (IVF, London, 1953), 52-57, 645-667 and 1168-1199.

2. 'Baptism in the Letters of Paul', in A. Gilmore (ed.), *Christian Baptism: A Fresh Attempt to Understand the Rite in Terms of Scripture, History, and Theology* (Lutterworth Press, London, 1959), 128-149.

3. 'Philippians', in Matthew Black and H. H. Rowley (eds.), *Peake's Commentary on the Bible* (Thomas Nelson & Sons, Sunbury-on-Thames, 1962), 985-989.

4. 'The Baptismal Controversy in the British Scene', Introduction to Kurt Aland, *Did the Early Church Baptize Infants?* (trans. G.R. Beasley-Murray, SCM Press, London, 1963), 17-27.

5. 'The Apostolic Writings', in P. Gardner-Smith (ed.), *The Roads Converge: A Contribution to the Question of Christian Reunion by Members of Jesus College, Cambridge* (Edward Arnold, London, 1963), 75-112.

6. 'Introduction to the New Testament', in H.H. Rowley (ed.), *A Companion to the Bible* (T. & T. Clark, Edinburgh, 2nd edn, 1963), 90-122.

7. 'Die Taufe der Gläubigen', in J.D. Hughey (ed.), *Die Baptisten* (Evangelisches Verlagswerk, Stuttgart, 1964), 27-36.

8. 'The Diaconate in Baptist Churches', in *The Ministry of Deacons* (WCC Studies, 2, World Council of Churches, Geneva, 1965), 72-81.

9. 'Baptists and the Baptism of Other Churches', in J. Nordenhaug (ed.), *The Truth That Makes Men Free: Official Report of the Eleventh Congress Baptist World Alliance, Miami Beach, Florida, USA, June 25–30, 1965* (Broadman Press, Nashville, Tennessee, 1966), 261-273.

10. 'My Call to the Ministry', in C.A. Joyce (ed.), *My Call to the Ministry* (Marshall, Morgan & Scott, London, 1968), 35-41.

11. 'The Holy Spirit and the Church', in A.H. Chapple (ed.), *Sermons for Today. 1. Ministers* (Marshall, Morgan & Scott, London, 1968), 91-105.

12. 'The Child and the Church', in Clifford Ingle (ed.), *Children and Conversion* (Broadman Press, Nashville, Tennessee, 1970), 127-141.

13. 'Jesus and the Spirit', in Albert Descamps and R.P. André de Halleux (eds.), *Mélanges Bibliques: en hommage au R.P. Beda Rigaux* (Duculot, Gembloux, 1970), 463-478.

14. '2 Corinthians', in C.J. Allen (ed.), *The Broadman Bible Commentary: Volume II* (Broadman Press, Nashville, Tennessee, 1971), 1-76.

15. 'How Christian is the Book of Revelation?', in Robert Banks (ed.), *Reconciliation and Hope: New Testament Essays on Atonement and Eschatology Presented to L.L. Morris on his 60th Birthday* (Paternoster Press, Exeter, 1974), 275-284.

16. 'The Clue to the Meaning of Life', in C. Frazier (ed.), *What Faith Has Meant To Me* (Westminster Press, Philadelphia, 1975), 11-18.

17. 'Premillennialism', in G.R. Beasley-Murray, Herschel H. Hobbs and Ray Frank Robbins, *Revelation: Three Viewpoints* (Broadman Press, Nashville, Tennessee, 1979), 9-70.

18. 'Faith and the Parousia', in Robert Patterson (ed.), *Science, Faith and Revelation: Festschrift for Eric Rust* (Broadman Press, Nashville, Tennessee, 1979), 127-143.

19. 'Abomination of Desolation', 'βαπτίζω', 'λούω, wash', 'νίπτω, wash', 'ῥαντιζω, sprinkle', in Colin Brown (ed.), *The New International Dictionary of New Testament Theology* (4 vols, Paternoster Press, Exeter, 1979), I, 74-75, 144-150, 150-153, 153-154 and 224-225. (An earlier German version of these articles appeared in L. Coenen, E. Beyreuther and H. Bietenhard [eds.], *Theologisches Begriffslexikon zum Neuen Testament* [Theologischer Verlag Rolf Brockhaus, Wuppertal, 1971]).

20. 'Jesus and Apocalyptic: With Special Reference to Mark 14,62', in Jan Lambrecht (ed.), *L'Apocalypse johannique et l'Apocalyptique dans le Nouveau Testament* (Leuven University Press, Leuven, 1980), 415-429.

21. 'Preaching from Eschatological Texts', in James W. Cox (ed.), *Biblical Preaching* (Westminster Press, Philadelphia, 1983), 352-368.

22. 'The Promise of a New Kingdom of Light', in Lewis Drummond (ed.), *From Darkness into the Light of the Kingdom* (Baptist World Alliance, Washington, DC, 1985), 15-20.

23. 'John 12, 31-32: The Eschatological Significance of the Lifting Up of the Son of Man', in *Studien zum Text and zur Ethik des Neuen Testaments: Festschrift zum 80 Geburtstag von Heinrich Greeven* (Walter de Gruyter, Berlin, 1986), 70-81.

24. 'Confessing Baptist Identity', in D. Slater (ed.), *A Perspective of Baptist Identity* (Mainstream, London, 1987), 75-86.

25. 'Baptism. 1. Biblical Theology', in D.F. Wright and J.I. Packer (eds.), *New Dictionary of Theology* (IVP, Leicester, 1988), 69-71.

26. 'Matthew 6:33: The Kingdom of God and the Ethics of Jesus', in Helmut Merklein (ed.), *Neues Testament and Ethik: Für Rudolf Schnackenburg* (Herder, Freiburg im Breisgau, 1989), 84-98.

27. 'The Word Comes To Us', in James W. Cox (ed), *Best Sermons* (Harper, San Francisco, 1991), 3-9

28. 'Persecution and Eschatology: Mk 13.9-13' and 'The Mission of the Logos Son', in F.Van Segbroeck, C.M. Tuckett, G.Van Belle and J. Veheyden (eds.), *The Four Gospels 1992* (Festschrift for Frans Neirynck) (Leuven University Press, Leuven, 1992), 1141-1159 and 1854-1869.

29. 'The Kingdom of God in the Old and New Testaments', in George L. Klein (ed.), *Reclaiming the Prophetic Mantle: Preaching the Old Testament Faithfully* (Broadman Press, Nashville, Tennessee 1992), 179-201.

30. 'The Imitation of Christ in Christian Leadership', in Timothy Dwyer (ed.), *The Newell Lectureships* (Warner Press, Anderson, Indiana, 1993), II, 81-163

31. 'Baptism' and 'Dying and Rising with Christ', in G.F. Hawthorne, R.P. Martin and D.G. Reid (eds.), *Dictionary of Paul and His Letters* (IVP, Leicester, 1993), 60-65, 218-222.

32. 'The Gospel Baptists Preach from the Bible', in Walter B. Shurden (ed.), *Proclaiming the Baptist Vision: The Bible* (Smith & Helwys, Macon, Georgia, 1994), 131-137.

33. 'The Kingdom of God and Christology in the Gospels', in J.B. Green and M. Turner (eds.), *Jesus of Nazareth, Lord and Christ: Essays on the Historical Jesus and New Testament Christology* (Paternoster, Carlisle and Eerdmans, Grand Rapids, 1994), 22-36.

34. 'Revelation', in D.A. Carson, R.T. France, J.A. Motyer, G.J. Wenham (eds.), *The New Bible Commentary* (IVP, Leicester, 1994), 1421-1455

35. 'The Problem of Infant Baptism: An Exercise in Possibilities', in Faculty of Baptist Theological Seminary Rüschlikon (eds.), *Festschrift Günter Wagner* (Inter-

national Theological Studies: Contributions of Baptist Scholars, 1, Peter Lang, Berne, 1994), 1-14

C. ARTICLES AND ESSAYS IN JOURNALS

1. 'The Church and the Child', *The Fraternal* 50 (April 1943), 9-13.
2. 'The New Testament Doctrine of the End', *Evangelical Quarterly* 16 (1944), 202-218.
3. 'The Eschatology of the Fourth Gospel', *Evangelical Quarterly* 18 (1946), 97-108.
4. 'The Second Coming of Christ', *The Fraternal* 61 (July 1946), 6-10.
5. 'The Relation of the Fourth Gospel to the Apocalypse', *Evangelical Quarterly* 18 (1946), 173-186.
6. 'The Two Messiahs in the Testaments of the Twelve Patriarchs', *Journal of Theological Studies* 48 (1947), 1-12.
7. 'Doctrinal Developments in the Apocrypha and Pseudepigrapha', *Evangelical Quarterly* 19 (1947), 178-195.
8. 'Immortality', *Journal of the Transactions of the Victoria Institute* 79 (1947).
9. 'A Conservative Thinks Again about Daniel', *Baptist Quarterly* 12 (1948), 341-346, 366-371.
10. 'Biblical Eschatology: 1. The Interpretation of Prophecy', *Evangelical Quarterly* 20 (1948), 221-229.
11. 'Biblical Eschatology: II. Apocalyptic Literature and the Book of Revelation', *Evangelical Quarterly* 20 (1948), 272-282.
12. 'The Sacraments', *The Fraternal* 70 (October 1948), 3-7.
13. 'The Second Coming in the Book of Revelation', *Evangelical Quarterly* 23 (1951), 40-45.
14. 'A Century of Eschatological Discussion', *Expository Times* 64 (1952–53), 312-316.
15. 'The Rise and Fall of the Little Apocalypse Theory', *Expository Times* 64 (1952–53), 346-349.

16. 'A Minister and His Bible', *The Fraternal* 92 (April 1954), 1-16.

17. 'Important and Influential Foreign Books: Gloege's *Reich Gottes and Kirche*', *Expository Times* 66 (1954–55), 153-155.

18. 'The Church of England and Baptism', *The Fraternal* 99 (January 1956), 7-10.

19. 'Demythologized Eschatology', *Theology Today* 14 (1957), 61-79.

20. 'The Significance of the Second Coming of Christ', *The Fraternal* 103 (January 1957), 6-9.

21. 'Das Reich Gottes and die sittliche Forderung Jesu', *Wort and Tat* 12 (Heft 1: January–February 1958) [in German].

22. 'Gesetz and Geist in die christlichen Lebens-fuhrung (Die Ethik des Apostels Paulus)', *Wort and Tat* 12 (Heft 2: Marz–April 1958) [in German].

23. 'Baptism in the New Testament', *Foundations* 3 (1960), 15-31.

24. 'The Eschatological Discourses of Jesus', *Review and Expositor* 57 (1960), 153-166.

25. 'Nya testamentets dopteologi', *Tro och Liv* 6, (1960), 246-250, 268 [in Swedish].

26. 'Interpretation av Rom. 6:1-11', *Tro och Liv* 1 (1961), 10-21 [in Swedish].

27. 'Ecumenical Encounter in Russia', *The Fraternal* 127 (January 1963), 18-22.

28. 'The Case Against Infant Baptism', *Christianity Today* 9 (1964), 11-14.

29. 'Baptist Interpretation of the Place of the Child in the Church', *Foundations* 8 (1965), 146-160.

30. 'Church and Child in the New Testament', *Baptist Quarterly* 21 (1966), 206-218.

31. 'Holy Spirit, Baptism, and Body of Christ', *Review and Expositor* 63 (1966), 177-185.

32. 'Das Christusbild des Neuen Testaments and unsere Verkündigung', *Wort and Tat* 21 (Heft 5: September–Oktober 1967) [in German].

33. 'I Still Find Infant Baptism Difficult', *Baptist Quarterly* 22 (1967), 225-236.

34. 'Easter 1969', *The Fraternal* 149 (July 1968), 4-7.

35. 'The Second Chapter of Colossians', *Review and Expositor* 70 (1973), 469-479.

36. 'The Contribution of the Book of Revelation to the Christian Belief in Immortality', *Scottish Journal of Theology* 27 (1974), 76-93. (Reprinted in Charles S. Duthie [ed.], *Resurrection and Immortality: Aspects of Twentieth-Century Christian Belief* [Samuel Bagster & Sons: London, 1979], 104-124.)

37. 'New Testament Apocalyptic: A Christological Eschatology', *Review and Expositor* 72 (1975), 317-330.

38. 'The Preparation of the Gospel', *Review and Expositor* 73 (1976), 205-212.

39. 'The Righteousness of God in the History of Israel and the Nations: Romans 9–11', *Review and Expositor* 73 (1976), 437-450.

40. 'Eschatology in the Gospel of Mark', *Southwestern Journal of Theology* 21 (1978), 37-53.

41. 'The Parousia in Mark', *Review and Expositor* 75 (1978), 565-581.

42. 'The Authority and Justification for Believers' Baptism', *Review and Expositor* 77 (1980), 63-70.

43. 'Faith in the New Testament: A Baptist Perspective', *American Baptist Quarterly* 1 (1982), 137-143.

44. 'The Theology of the Child', *American Baptist Quarterly* 1 (1982), 197-202.

45. 'The Interpretation of Daniel 7', *Catholic Biblical Quarterly* 45 (1983), 44-58.

46. 'Second Thoughts on the Composition of Mark 13', *New Testament Studies* 29 (1983), 414-420.

47. 'John 3:3, 5: Baptism, Spirit and the Kingdom', *Expository Times* 97 (March 1986), 167-170.

48. 'Jesus and the Kingdom of God', *Baptist Quarterly* 32 (1987), 141-147.

49. 'The Community of the New Life: John 13–17', *Review and Expositor* 85 (1988), 473-483.

50. 'The Vision on the Mount: The Eschatological Discourse of Mark 13', *Ex Auditu* 6 (1990), 39-52.

51. 'The Resurrection and the Parousia of the Son of Man', *Tyndale Bulletin* 42 (1992), 296-309,

52. 'The Kingdom of God in the Teaching of Jesus', *Journal of the Evangelical Theological Society* 35 (March 1992), 19-30.

53. 'Ten books to rescue from the fire', *Ministry Today* 12 (February 1998), 31-32.

D. PUBLISHED LECTURES, PAMPHLETS, REPORTS AND TRACTS

1. 'The Fact of Hell' (Newport, Isle of Wight, 1943). An address delivered in the Metropolitan Hall, Newport in June 1943.

2. 'Religious History and Eschatology' (Norwood Papers, 1, Battley Brothers, London, 1949).

3. 'Can An Honest Man Be A Christian?' (Victory Tract Club, London, 1950).

4. 'Man Alive After Death and Burial' (Victory Tract Club, London & Croydon, n.d.).

5. 'The Second Coming of Christ' (Norwood Papers, 3, Battley Brothers, London, 1951).

6. 'The News No One Knows' (The Advance Series of Pamphlets, 1, Carey Kingsgate Press, London, 1952).

7. 'A Baptist Interpretation of the Place of the Child in the Church' (Commission on Baptist Doctrine Study Paper, Baptist World Alliance, Washington, DC). Meeting held at Hamburg, Germany, 19–21 August 1964.

8. 'Reflections on the Ecumenical Movement' (Living Issues Booklets, 5, Baptist Union, London, 1965).

9. 'The Servant of God' (The Baptist Missionary sermon delivered at Leeds, Carey Kingsgate Press, London, 1965).

10. 'Renewed for Mission' (Baptist Union Presidential Address delivered in London, 29 April 1968, Baptist Union, London, 1968).

11. 'Evangelizing the Post-Christian Man' (Diamond Jubilee Lecture of the London Baptist Preachers' Association, delivered 21 March 1969 at Bloomsbury Central Baptist Church, London, 1969).

12. 'Worship and the Sacraments' (Second Holdsworth–Grigg Memorial Lecture delivered 6 August 1970 at the Baptist College of Victoria, Whitley College, Melbourne, Australia, 1970).

13. 'The Contribution of the Book of Revelation to the Christian Belief in Immortality', being the 1972 Drew Lecture on Immortality, delivered on 27 October 1972 at the Whitefield Memorial Church, London. Published in *Scottish Journal of Theology* 27 (1974), 76-93, and reprinted in Charles S. Duthie (ed.), *Resurrection and Immortality: Aspects of Twentieth-Century Christian Belief* (Samuel Bagster & Sons: London, 1979), 104-124.

14. 'The Christological Controversy in the Baptist Union' (privately published, 1972).

15. 'The Authority of Scripture' (Commission on Baptist Doctrine Study Paper, Baptist World Alliance, Washington, DC. Meeting held at Stockholm, Sweden, 8–10 July 1975).

16. 'A Response to T.R. Hobbs' paper on "Revelation as Given"' (Commission on Doctrine and Interchurch Co-operation Study Paper, Baptist World Alliance, Washington, DC). Meeting held at Miami Beach, Florida, 11–14 July 1977.

17. *Man and Woman in the Church* (Baptist Union: London, 1983).

E. TRANSLATIONS OF BOOKS
(from German)

1. Kurt Aland, *Did the Early Church Baptize Infants?* (SCM Press: London, 1963).

2. Rudolf Schnackenburg, *Baptism in the Thought of St Paul: A Study of Pauline Theology* (Basil Blackwell Oxford, 1964).

3. Rudolf Bultmann, *The Gospel of John: A Commentary* (edited and supervised with assistance from R.W.N. Hoare and J.K. Riches, Basil Blackwell, Oxford, 1971).

F. TRANSLATIONS OF BOOKS
(into other languages)

1. *Gesichtspunkte zum Taufgespräch* (J.G. Oncken Verlag, Kassel, 1965). German edition of *Baptism Today and Tomorrow*.
2. *Die Evangelien als Predigt* (J.G. Oncken Verlag, Kassel, 1966). German edition of *Preaching the Gospel from the Gospels*.
3. *Dapsyn under debatt* (Norsk Litteraturselskap, Oslo, 1966). Norwegian edition of *Baptism Today and Tomorrow*.
4. *Dopet Idag Och I Morgon* (Westerbergs, Hassleholm, 1967). Swedish edition of *Baptism Today and Tomorrow*.
5. *Wachset in der Gnade und in der Erkenntnis: Die Briefe des Jakobus, Petrus und Judas* (J.G. Oncken Verlag, Kassel, 1968). German edition of *The General Epistles*.
6. *Die Christliche Taufe: Eine Untersuchung über ihr Verständnis in Geschichte und Gegenwart* (J.G. Oncken Verlag, Kassel, 1968; later published by R. Brockhaus Verlag, Wuppertal, 1998). German edition of *Baptism in the New Testament*.
7. *The Coming of God* translated into Korean by Kwang Man Oh and published by Jeshurun.

G. BOOK REVIEWS IN MAJOR THEOLOGICAL JOURNALS

1. E. Bundy, *Jesus and the First Three Gospels: An Introduction to the Synoptic Tradition* (1955), *Journal of Theological Studies* n.s. 7 (1956), 350.

2. W.D. Davies and D. Daube (eds.), *The Background of the New Testament and Its Eschatology: Studies in Honour of C.H. Dodd* (1956), *Journal of Theological Studies* 8 (1957), 153-156.

3. James M. Robinson, *The Problem of History in Mark* (1957), *Journal of Theological Studies* 9 (1958), 126-127.

4. J.A.T. Robinson, *Jesus and His Coming* (1957), *Journal of Theological Studies* 10 (1959), 134-140.

5. Joachim Jeremias, *The Parables of Jesus* (1963), *Journal of Theological Studies* 15 (1964), 359-361.

6. J. Ysebaert, *Greek Baptismal Terminology: Its Origins and Early Development* (1962), *Journal of Theological Studies* 15 (1964), 381-384.

7. Rudolf Schnackenburg, *La Théologie du Nouveau Testament* (1961), *Scottish Journal of Theology* 17 (1964), 240-241.

8. John Calvin, *The Second Epistle of Paul the Apostle to the Corinthians and the Epistles of Timothy, Titus and Philemon* (1964); Rudolf Schnackenburg, *New Testament Theology Today* (1963); and H. Anderson, *Jesus and Christian Origins: A Commentary on Modern Viewpoints* (1964), *Scottish Journal of Theology* 18 (1965), 238-241.

9. Dale Moody, *The Hope of Glory* (1964), *Review and Expositor* 62 (1965), 367-369.

10. D.S. Russell, *The Method and Message of Jewish Apocalyptic: 100 B.C.–A.D. 100* (1964), *Journal of Theological Studies* 18 (1967), 177-179.

11. Mathias Rissi, *Time and History: A Study on the Revelation* (1966), *Scottish Journal of Theology* 20 (1967), 359-360.

12. Raymond E. Brown, Karl P. Donfried and John Reumann (eds.), *Peter in the New Testament* (1973), *Review and Expositor* 71 (1974), 539-540.

13. John Allen Moore (ed.), *Baptist Witness in Catholic Europe* (1973), *Review and Expositor* 71 (1974), 555.

14. Norman Perrin, *A Modern Pilgrimage in New Testament Christology* (1974), *Review and Expositor* 72 (1975), 373-375.

15. Vernard Eller, *The Most Revealing Book of the Bible* (1974), *Review and Expositor* 72 (1975), 373.

16. William F. Farmer, *The Last Twelve Verses of Mark* (1974), *Review and Expositor* 72 (1975), 373-375.

17. Ray Frank Robbins, *The Revelation of Jesus Christ* (1975), *Review and Expositor* 73 (1976), 359.

18. J.P.M. Sweet, *Revelation* (1979), *Interpretation* 34 (1980), 321-322.

H. ARTICLES IN CHRISTIAN PAPERS

1 'The Ascended Lord', *The Life of Faith* (29 May 1946), 396-397.

2. 'After Death—What?', *Young Life: Official Organ of the National Young Life Campaign*, 21.27 (July 1946), 74.

3. 'The Preacher's Motive', *The Christian* (28 January 1949), 3.

4. 'The Christian Commando Campaign', *The Christian* (8 May 1947), 9.

5. 'Jephthah and his Vow: wherein he is an example to us', *The Christian* (17 July 1947), 15.

6. 'Is There a Millennium in the Book of Revelation?', *The Life of Faith* (24 September 1947), 635.

7. 'The Importance of the Millennium in the Book of Revelation', *The Life of Faith* (1 October 1947), 656.

8. 'The Christian Millennium: a lost doctrine', *The Life of Faith* (5 November 1947). 764.

9. 'My Gospel', *The Christian* (13 January 1950), 3.

10. 'Christianity and the Kingdom of Communism', *The Christian* (20 January 1950), 9.

11. 'The Wealth of a Christian', *The Life of Faith* (1 February 1950), 73.

12. 'The Church, the Remnant and the Jew', *The Christian* (17 March 1950), 4.

13. 'The Church as the Body of Christ: what do we mean by it?', *The Christian* (18 May 1951), 4.

14. 'Stephen and the Epistle to the Hebrews: a new suggestion', *The Christian* (13 July 1951), 4.

15. 'Learning to read the Greek New Testament', *The Christian* (30 January 1953), 12.

16. 'The Second Advent and the Coming of the Kingdom: 1. The Second Coming of Christ and the Gospel', *The Christian* (13 February 1953), 4.

17. 'The Second Advent and the Coming of the Kingdom: 2. The Millennium in the New Testament', *The Christian* (20 February 1953), 4.

18. 'The Second Advent and the Coming of the Kingdom: 3. The Millennium in the New Testament, Some Difficulties Considered', *The Christian* (February 27, 1953), 4.

19. 'The Second Advent and the Coming of the Kingdom: 7. The Necessity of the Advent of the Kingdom', *The Christian* (27 March 1953), 4.

20. 'Rudolf Bultmann—Remedy or Disease?', *Baptist Times* (4 February 1954), 8.

21. 'Judgment and Love in the Second Coming', *The Morning Star* (December 1955), 5-7.

22. 'The Second Coming of Christ', *The Morning Star* (September 1956), 9-10.

23. 'The Significance of the Second Coming of Christ', *The Morning Star* (October 1956), 3-5.

24. 'Working Out Salvation: An exposition of Phil 2.12-18', *Baptist Times* (28 March 1957), 6.

25. 'Progress and Pilgrimage: Studies in Phil 3.12-16', *Baptist Times* (9 May 1957), p. 6.

26. 'The Return of our Lord: Various Viewpoints held by Bible Students: How can we live together?', *The Life of Faith* (20 June 1957), 427.

27. 'A Faith to Die for: Studies in the Book of Revelation', *Baptist Times* (1 August 1957), 8.

28. 'A Faith to Die for: Studies in Rev 1', *Baptist Times* (15 August 1957), 8.

29. 'Seven Letters to the Churches: Studies in Rev 2–3', *Baptist Times* (29 August 1957), 8.

30. 'The Glory of God and the Lamb: Studies in Rev 4–5', *Baptist Times* (12 September 1957), 10.

31. 'Judgments Unsealed: Studies in Rev 6.1–8.5', *Baptist Times* (26 September 1957), 10.

32. 'Life beyond Death III: In Jesus and Paul', *Baptist Times* (3 October 1957), 1-2.

33. 'Judgment Proclaimed: Studies in Rev 8.6–11.19', *Baptist Times* (October 10, 1957), 10.

34. 'The Church and the Antichrist: Studies in Rev 12-14', *Baptist Times* (24 October 1957), 10.

35. 'Fall of an Empire: Studies in Rev 17-19', *Baptist Times* (21 November 1957), 10.

36. 'The Kingdom come with Power: Studies in Rev 20.1–22.5', *Baptist Times* (12 December 1957), 11.

37. 'Last Words on the Last Things: Studies in Rev 22.6-11', *Baptist Times* (26 December 1957), 8.

38. 'A Baptist goes to Rome', *Baptist Times* (6 February 1958), 12.

39. 'Gospel of the Kingdom: Studies in the Kingdom Sayings of Jesus—Mark 1.15', *Baptist Times* (13 February 1958), 10.

40. 'The Lord who sets men free: Studies in the Kingdom Sayings of Jesus—Matt 12.28,29', *Baptist Times* (6 March 1958), 11.

41. 'Secret of the Kingdom: Studies in the Kingdom Sayings of Jesus—Mark 4.11,12', *Baptist Times* (27 March 1958), 11.

42. 'The Gospel of the Beatitudes: a study in the Gospel of the Kingdom', *Baptist Times* (17 April 1958), 10.

43. 'The Gospel to the Baptist: a study in Matt 11.2-6', *Baptist Times* (12 June 1958), 11.

44. 'The Kingdom and the Violent: a study of Matt 11.12-13', *Baptist Times* (26 June 1958), 11.

45. 'Baptism Controversy— "The Spirit is There"', *Baptist Times* (10 December 1959), 8.

46. 'Baptism and the Sacramental View', *Baptist Times* (11 Februaary 1960), 9.

47. 'A Baptist Church Dies', *Baptist Times* (1 September 1960), 6.

48. 'The Sin of the Teacher: Jas 3', *Baptist Times* (1 June 1961), 5.

49. 'Is the Church of Rome Christian?', *Baptist Times* (21 June 1962), 9.

50. 'How sad that believers in Christ should do the Devil's work for him!', *The Christian and Christianity Today* (10 February 1967), 12-13.

51. 'Let's stop apologising for the church', *Baptist Times* (2 May 1968), 8-9.

52. 'The Person of Christ: the New Testament Witness to Christ', *Baptist Times* (29 July 1971), 7.

53. 'F.F. Bruce dies at the age of 79', *Baptist Times* 27 September 1990, 13.

I. DENOMINATIONAL PUBLICATIONS

1. G.R. Beasley-Murray served as Chairman for the Advisory Committee for Church Relations which produced the Report *Baptists and Unity* (Baptist Union, London, 1965).

2. Regular contributions to *Spurgeon's College Record*, especially when Tutor (1950–56) and Principal (1958–73).

J. FESTSCHRIFTEN DEDICATED TO G.R. BEASLEY-MURRAY

1. H. Gloer (ed.), *Eschatology and the New Testament: Essays in Honour of George Raymond Beasley-Murray* (Hendrickson, Peabody, Massachusetts, 1988).

Contributions:

Eduard Schweizer: 'The Significance of Eschatology in the Teaching of Jesus'

Ronald E. Clements: 'Apocalyptic, Literacy, and the Canonical Tradition'

James D.G. Dunn: 'Matthew 12:28/Luke 11:20: A Word of Jesus?'

F.F. Bruce: 'Eschatology in Acts'

C.K. Barrett: 'The Gentile Mission as an Eschatological Phenomenon'

Günter Wagner: 'The Future of Israel: Reflections on Romans 9–11'

Ralph P. Martin: 'The Spirit in 2 Corinthians in Light of the "Fellowship of the Holy Spirit"'

I. Howard Marshall: 'Jesus as Lord: The Development of the Concept'

2.	Paul Beasley-Murray (ed.), *Mission to the World: Essays to Celebrate the 50th Anniversary of the Ordination of George Raymond Beasley-Murray to the Christian Ministry* (Baptist Historical Society, Didcot, 1991).

Contributions:

Paul Beasley-Murray: 'Foreword'

J.J. Brown: 'A personal appreciation of George Raymond Beasley-Murray'

Michael K. Nicholls: 'Charles Haddon Spurgeon 1834–1892: Church Planter'

Colin Marchant: 'Urban Mission'

Athol Gill: 'Beyond the Boundaries: Marcan Mission Perspectives for Today's Church'

John E. Colwell: 'Proclamation as Event: Barth's supposed 'universalism' in the context of his mission'

Bruce Milne: 'Even so I send you': an expository and theological reflection on John 20:21'

Nigel G. Wright: 'Mission, the Shape of the Church and Ecumenism'

Derek Winter: 'The Road to Damascus'

238   *Bibliography*

L.J. Kreitzer: 'Bibliography of Writings of
George Raymond Beasley-Murray'

K. BIOGRAPHICAL MATERIAL

1. R. Alan Culpepper, 'George R. Beasley-Murray', in
Timothy George and David S. Dockery (eds.), *Baptist
Theologians* (Broadman Press, Nashville, Tennessee,
1990), 567-587
2. J.J. Brown, 'A personal appreciation of George
Raymond Beasley-Murray', in Paul Beasley-Murray
(ed.), *Mission to the World: Essays to Celebrate the 50th
Anniversary of the Ordination of George Raymond
Beasley-Murray to the Christian Ministry* (Baptist
Historical Society, Didcot, 1991), 9-19.

Index